D0484877

"This is an outstanding reference—an indispensible guide for those providing care for gender-nonconforming youth. Dr. Ehrensaft eloquently presents evidence to support her enlightened and impassioned plea to advocate for the 'true gender self' of all children."

—STEPHEN M. ROSENTHAL, MD, professor of pediatrics, director, Pediatric Endocrine Clinics, University of California, San Francisco

"Courageous and clear, this book tells gender like it is—with real advice for those brave parents who are helping their transgender children to lead the 21st-century world toward an understanding of what it means to be fully human. *Gender Born, Gender Made* is a must-read for anyone who wants to comprehend the function and importance of gender in American culture, and learn how we can break gender's irrational stranglehold on the human spirit."

—JAMISON GREEN, PhD, educator, policy consultant, and author of *Becoming a Visible Man*

"Dr. Ehrensaft uses her own experience and the narratives of her patients to provide a glimpse into the obstacles that children with gender dysphoria and their families face. Their strengths are reflected in their stories. This provocative book will be helpful for parents, teachers, and clinicians working with children along the continuum of gender expression. These are children who, like all children, do not want to adapt to the expectations of others, but wish to be embraced for who they are."

—CYNTHIA J. TELINGATOR, MD, child and adult psychiatrist; faculty member, Cambridge Health Alliance; and assistant professor, Harvard Medical School

"This book provides a creative approach in the evolution of our understanding of gender-nonconforming children, a thoughtful way forward from oppression towards affirmation. There is important information here for all who care about the quality of life for all children and their families."

—CATHERINE TUERK, APRN, cofounder and senior consultant, Gender and Sexual Advocacy and Education Program, Children's National Medical Center

THE EXPERIMENT

BECAUSE EVERY BOOK IS A TEST OF NEW IDEAS

"Dr. Ehrensaft has written a seminal and informative book that fills what has been a gaping abyss in the literature for parents rearing gender-nonconforming children. There have been few resources available for parents with children whose gender expression is notably different from that of their peers, and they are often isolated and frightened . . . This is a book that is informed by scholarly advice, yet reads with a gentle advocacy—it will be read and earmarked. Finally, a book I can hand parents that guides them in this unique and rewarding journey."

—ARLENE LEV, founder of Choices Counseling and Consulting, Albany, New York, and Rainbow Access Initiative

"In *Gender Born, Gender Made*, Dr. Ehrensaft issues a clear and compelling call to parents and professionals in support of children living outside of society's narrow gender expectations. Building on her vast experience working with children, families, and professionals, she beckons all of us to expand our traditional notions of gender, challenging us to create affirming spaces in which children can discover and celebrate their authentic selves. Hers is a model of gender acceptance and inclusion, not only for children pushing the boundaries of gender, but for all children simply wishing to be themselves."

—JOEL BAUM, MS, director of education and training, Gender Spectrum

"Parents need to make decisions now, about the children they have now, and the fact that the science can't keep pace with the culture doesn't diminish that need one iota. *Gender Born, Gender Made* speaks to this reality . . . Ehrensaft's experience as a therapist working with gender-creative children, and her own experience as a parent of a gender-nonconforming child, make this book unique. She's a double expert, both parent and supportive professional, and while we wait for the research to trickle in, for the science to come of age, it is people like her to whom we should listen when it comes to understanding this exquisite mystery of male and female, mind and body, love and identity."

—BEDFORD HOPE, Accepting Dad blog

"Diane Ehrensaft is the patron saint of kids who don't conform to traditional gender norms . . . Her book should be recommended reading for all parents-to-be . . . [and] for all parents and family members even remotely involved in the life of a gender creative child."

—Raising My Rainbow blog

GENDER BORN, GENDER MADE

ALSO BY DIANE EHRENSAFT, PhD

Parenting Together:
Men and Women Sharing the Care of Their Children

Spoiling Childhood: How Well-Meaning Parents Are Giving
Children Too Much—But Not What They Need

Mommies, Daddies, Donors, Surrogates:
Answering Tough Questions and Building Strong Families

WITH TONI VAUGHN HEINEMAN
Building a Home Within:
Meeting the Emotional Needs of Children and Youth
in Foster Care

GENDER BORN, GENDER MADE

Raising Healthy
Gender-Nonconforming Children

DIANE EHRENSAFT, PhD

Foreword by
EDGARDO MENVIELLE, MD, MSHS

THE EXPERIMENT
NEW YORK

To Rebecca Hawley, Jesse Ehrensaft-Hawley, and Satya Hawley—
my teachers

The Experiment, LLC
220 East 23rd Street, Suite 301
New York, NY 10010–4674
www.theexperimentpublishing.com

Grateful acknowledgment is made to Phyllis Rothblatt for permission to reprint lyrics from "I Just Want to Be Me."

The Experiment's books are available at special discounts when purchased in bulk for premiums and sales promotions as well as for fund-raising or educational use. For details, contact us at info@theexperimentpublishing.com.

Many of the designations used by manufacturers and sellers to distinguish their products are claimed as trademarks. Where those designations appear in this book and The Experiment was aware of a trademark claim, the designations have been capitalized.

This book is sold with the understanding that neither the author nor the publisher are engaged in rendering medical or other professional services to individual readers. It is not intended as a substitute for consultation with a health professional. Names and identifying details have been changed to protect the privacy of individuals.

Library of Congress Control Number: 2010934615
ISBN 978-1-61519-060-7
Ebook ISBN 978-1-61519-158-1
Cover design by Alison Forner
Cover photograph by Rick Chapman | Corbis
Author photograph by Jim Hawley
Text design by Pauline Neuwirth, Neuwirth & Associates, Inc.

Manufactured in the United States of America
Distributed by Workman Publishing Company, Inc.
Distributed simultaneously in Canada by Thomas Allen and Son Limited
First published May 2011

10 9 8 7 6

▪ CONTENTS ▪

by Edgardo Menvielle, MD, MSHS

The setting is our parent group in Washington, D.C., in the basement of the church where we meet monthly. The children are playing in an adjacent room while the parents sit in a circle and discuss their latest experiences, and their fears and hopes for their children. A knock on the door is followed by the triumphant entry of two little boys draped in lace, pretending to be two matching brides. Layers of cloth are wrapped around their bodies and heads, making dresses, veils, and trains that keep getting in the way of their small feet. Fancy jewelry complements the over-the-top outfits. "Let's walk down the aisle," one says to the other, and they proceed to march around the circle of parents, taking little steps. They are beaming with joy. The sight is reminiscent of the opening scene of *Ma Vie en Rose*, when the protagonist, Ludovic, descends the stairs in a princess costume and made-up to perfection to meet unsuspecting neighbors for the first time. There is none of Ludovic's gravitas in these boys, only joy. (Ludovic only smiles after the crowd cheers—they take him for his sister; he assumes that the cheers celebrate his glamorous beauty.) Do I see a tinge of the excitement that comes from transgression, the spark of satisfaction that comes from getting away with small, forbidden pleasures? Or is it the joy of cooperative play, in which individual fantasies mesh in perfect creative unison and flawlessly coordinated execution?

When the boys finish circling the parents, they exit the room amid appreciative applause. It is rare that children come to the parents' room; this was a special offering, a proud show of an artistic achievement. The discussion in the parent group resumes. The questions raised by gender nonconformity are complex. The parents grapple with their children's safety and what might lie ahead for them. They raise questions of fairness, freedom of expression, sexuality, individuality, tradition, creativity, continuity versus change, pleasure and renunciation, bullying, and femininity and masculinity in multiple combinations and permutations. Simple answers are elusive.

In the same group meeting, a parent tells us about a children's book that is likely to win a statewide competition in which early elementary school students vote for their favorite book. In the book, the cat character tries to wrest control of the story's narrative from the author. After a struggle, the author puts the cat in a pink tutu. The cat is utterly mortified and gives up. The parent remarks on the delighted response of schoolchildren who are in on the story's joke about social emasculation. She observes that this scene is not generally used as a teachable moment to criticize the devaluation of femininity or to raise awareness of the social opprobrium experienced by males who express it. This, the parent sees, is an example of the uncontested gender indoctrination of children that makes her son vulnerable to his peers' taunting.

Socially sanctioned parenting scripts are ubiquitous and yet often invisible. A potent one is that parents must inculcate proper gender roles in their children at all costs. That was the starting point for the parents in our group, as it is for all parents, but over time the cumulative evidence at home has shown that expectations of strict gender enforcement are neither realistic nor advisable. Knowing that children who deviate from gender mandates are susceptible to social exclusion, these parents must instead learn to support their children as they walk through social minefields, figuring out their own steps.

A person's gender is no more and no less than a creative individual achievement, and yet it can only develop through social exchange. It is informed by biology, culture, society, and the times in which we live. But it's not clear in what proportions these elements contribute, or whether all these ingredients are really necessary. Diane Ehrensaft, PhD, does not advocate the elimination of gender, but a loosening of its mandates, allowing the boundaries to be blurred. She proposes shedding the gender corset to create room to breathe, room to grow. She shows us that gender is different things for different people, and she makes a compelling case for allowing children and adults to play with gender— without the severe punishments often inflicted on those who are making up the rules of the game as they play it. She helps us open our eyes, minds, and hearts so we can see and hear beyond the surface in order to help each child find his or her own truth and flourish.

Let people be and let's support who people are: the proposition is simple, but the road to that goal is fraught with obstacles. *Gender Born, Gender Made* brings to our homes, schools, and clinicians' offices a wealth of ideas and tools that will prove invaluable as we move toward a more empathic, just, and inclusive society.

EDGARDO J. MENVIELLE, MD, MSHS, is the director of the Gender and Sexuality Development Program and of the Gender and Sexuality Advocacy and Education Program in the Psychiatry Department of the Children's National Medical Center in Washington, D.C. He started a national outreach group for parents of gender-variant children in 1998, and later a gender and sexuality development clinic. He is also an associate professor of psychiatry and behavioral sciences at The George Washington University. An internationally recognized authority on childhood and adolescent gender and sexuality, Dr. Menvielle has been quoted in the *New York Times* and *Newsweek*. He lives in Washington, D.C.

Princesses, Priuses, and Penises

"Can't everyone see I'm a girl? I'm a princess with a penis."

▼

"I'm a boy in the front, and a girl in the back.
Kind of a Prius—a hybrid."

▼

"They got it all wrong. I do not want to be a girl.
I just like to dress up."

▼

Above, three young people—a boy, a girl, and a boy, respectively—describes his or her gender-creative journey through childhood in the twenty-first century. Each of them, in his or her own way, does not accept the binary concept of "Boys will be boys, girls will be girls," prescribed by and promoted in our culture. Two of them are questioning whether the gender assigned to them at birth is really who they are. The third is questioning the culture's gender policing of dress-up and cross-gender play. Their queries and explorations are what qualify them as "gender creative." Their travels will not be easy, and that is why I am writing this book—to carve a path toward gender health for all the children and youth who go against the normative gender grain of our culture.

We can never know the exact moment of conception, but when I think about the birth of this book, I always go back to a particular moment in 1980. It was evening, and the fog and the chill had come in over the Berkeley Hills right through the front door of the warm and usually cozy home where my then three-and-a-half-year-old son attended the preschool that was his beloved home away from home. The directors, two wonderful sisters who couldn't have been better at getting the finger on the pulse of all that little people need to grow, along with the then love of my son's life—the clinical psychology graduate student doing an internship at the program—had asked that my husband and I come in for a special meeting. As much as they adored our son and his blissful spirit and creativity, they were worried. "Why?" we asked. Because Jesse repeatedly announced that he wished he were a girl. Therein began a long journey of advocating for our gender-bending little boy. Even in a setting as "free to be you and me" as Berkeley and the San Francisco Bay Area, and even in a preschool as open and progressive as the one he attended, the world was truly not ready to receive a male tutu-wearing porcelain-doll collector who only played with boys who played with girls.

For years I went on to live my life, raising a son and a daughter who both liked dolls and frills, and opening up my clinical practice to children and their families who played outside the binary gender box. I am remembering yet another moment from those times. It is 1984. The doorbell rings. It's Cassie, one of Jesse's close friends from down the block, coming to look for Jesse to play. She's known Jesse since they were two, as they both went to that same preschool that worried about Jesse's possible gender disorder. My mother, who is visiting, runs up to Jesse's room when she sees who's at the door. "Jesse, your friend's here. Hurry, take off the clothes." Now, she wasn't asking him to do a striptease. She was engaged in an urgent intervention—getting Jesse to take off his layers of filmy pink and rose-colored nightgowns before Cassie saw him in them, nightgowns that were actually cast-offs of my mother's, meant not for him but for his older sister's dress-up box. Jesse's grandmother loved him dearly and was only trying to protect him from social humiliation, believing that his drag dress-up routines should remain in the privacy of his home, or maybe his room, kind of like masturbation. Jesse's mother (that would be me) had other ideas—that if Jesse wanted to dress up as an ethereal fairy, that was just fine. So back to Cassie. Hopping up the stairs to the second floor two at a time, in she sailed. Jesse had paid not a whit of attention to his grandmother's storm warning. Cassie trotted over to his bedroom, peeked in, and with neither a flinch nor a minute's hesitation, piped up, "Oh, hi, Jess. Want to play?" And off they went, Jesse in his layers of chiffon, Cassie in her jeans and boy's T-shirt. In those five minutes we had enacted a fine moment of three generations making gender: a grandmother who felt queasy about her grandson's cross-gender expressions and only wanted him to be safe and protected, a mother who was spending hours and hours sorting out how to meet her gender-creative son where he needed to be met, and her son and his little friend who gave it not a second's thought and couldn't see what the big fuss was about. And not one of us could yet know that Jesse would someday grow up to be a gay man seemingly quite content in his male gender identity.

Now, so many years later, it is I who am the grandmother. I watch my granddaughter in her adamant insistence that she will *not* wear a dress. Pink is her least favorite color in the whole world. In contrast to both her uncle and her mother, she rarely has played with a doll. I try to attend all her softball games and marvel at her grace as a natural jock. And I am now old enough and wise enough, I hope, to know that her own journey in finding her unique gender self is a work in progress that will unfold over many years and with all our support, including from her great-grandmother, who is still alive and well and has definitely come around to being a firm advocate of gender-nonconforming children.

Yet it is not my personal stories that I want to showcase in this book, but rather what I as a developmental and clinical psychologist have set out to learn about the biology, about the developmental milestones, about the intricate choreography between nature and nurture, about our social constructs and our social mores that weave together to create such incredibly unique gender options for every child. The particular children I am interested in are those who transgressively and creatively define themselves as outside the traditional binary boxes of boy/girl and are desperately in need of someone to speak on their behalf. It may be four-year-old Seth who likes to wear dresses to school, but ask him anytime and he'll tell you he's a boy. It may be six-year-old SaraJane who used to be Craig until making it clear over and over again that they all got it wrong—"You may think I'm a boy, but I'm not. I don't feel like a girl. I *am* a girl." It may be seven-year-old Maggie who says, "I'm both, a boy in the front and a girl in the back." Some people like to refer to these children as *gender variant,* but *variant* has a somewhat negative connotation of "other than normal," not too far off from *deviant.* Some people like to place these children on a gender spectrum, with the understanding that children can slide along this spectrum from one pole to the other (male/female), allowing for incredible variation along the way. But a spectrum is a very two-dimensional, linear concept, and doesn't give full weight to the myriad possibilities in establishing one's true gender identity. So I would like to refer instead to a *gender web,* in which there are intricate pathways in three dimensions, side to side, up and down. This web will have to take into account any particular child's assigned gender, that which appears on the birth certificate; the child's gender expressions—those feelings, behaviors, activities, and attitudes that communicate to both self and other one's presentation of self as either male, female, or other; and the child's core gender identity—the inner sense of self as male, female, or other.

A large number of children will find a fairly good match between their assigned gender, their core gender identity, and their gender expressions. But a fair number, and it seems a number that is steadily increasing, will not. Those are the children who find themselves in my made-up category of "gender creative," a developmental position in which the child transcends the culture's normative definitions of male/female to creatively interweave a sense of gender that comes neither totally from the inside (the body, the psyche), nor totally from the outside (the culture, others' perceptions of the child's gender), but resides somewhere in between.

In this day and age, raising a gender-creative child is still never an easy matter, despite years of hard effort on the part of feminists, gay and transgender activists, and progressive gender specialists to make room for broadened expressions of gender as a healthy rather than pathological way of being. I've never been shocked, but have nonetheless felt chagrined, as I bear witness to the hard road these families travel, watching their children insist on following the directives of their inner desires and wishes in the face of aspersion from a surrounding culture that attempts to impose prescriptions and proscriptions for "appropriate" gender behavior. Most disturbing to me was coming to realize the harm done to these children if they fell into the wrong hands—the hands of my own profession. As a clinical psychologist, I am bound by the oath that dictates the actions of all medical and mental health professionals: Do No Harm. Yet all around me, physicians, psychiatrists, and child therapists are doing just that—in clinics and private practice consultation rooms where parents are advised to take away their little boys' dolls and pink tights or make their little girls grow out their buzz cuts; mothers and fathers are directed to ignore or punish their children's "inappropriate" gender expressions and pay attention to or reward only the "gender-appropriate" ones; and families are sent home to make sure the gender-nonconforming children are redirected to same-sex friendships and to their same-sex parent as the main or only parent to identify with. In such treatment, considered by its critics to be a form of *reparative* or *conversion* (which with a scrambling of a few letters could be read as "coercion") *therapy*, parents come to learn that until they follow through with this treatment regime that has as its ultimate goal their child's conforming to binary gender norms and accepting his or her assigned gender, their child will be stuck with the stigma of a psychiatric malady—*gender identity disorder*, as clearly laid out in the mental health bible, the *Diagnostic and Statistical Manual of Mental Disorders*.

Yet, I open the January 2009 issue of *Pediatrics* to learn of a large-scale study by Caitlin Ryan and her team of researchers, which found that young adults whose parents supported their gay and lesbian identities showed good mental health outcomes, whereas those youth who were not supported had a higher incidence of poor mental outcomes, including depression; suicidal feelings thoughts, or attempts; sexual acting out; and drug abuse.[1] Holding those findings in mind, I know, from my own experiences and others', that some gender-creative children are undergoing reparative therapies aimed at "setting them binary" (a variation on "setting them straight"), and they become listless or agitated, long for their taken-away favorite toys and clothes, and even literally go hiding in closets to continue playing with the verboten toys or wearing the forbidden clothes. And I think to myself, "We have no more time to spare."

I had first thought that before embarking on this book it would be best to wait until we had more large-scale scientific outcome studies such as Caitlin Ryan's group, now targeted not at gay and lesbian young adults but at gender-nonconforming children and youth. But I felt a pressing urgency to speak out with a call for action right now. More and more children are coming forward and expressing themselves in gender-nonconforming ways at a moment when such children continue to be harmed by outmoded or misguided practices that treat their gender creativity as disease rather than health, and do everything possible to ward off budding homosexuality or transgender identity. Although harmful, these practices still dominate the field and are reflected in the continuing reliance on gender identity disorder as a valid assessment of children who go against the grain of gender norms. As a licensed mental health professional, I have tried to take my oath very seriously and I see doing no harm not only as my individual but also my collective responsibility to children and their families. I feel I can no longer wait to share what I've learned from listening to my young patients and from having the opportunity to join with their families in helping their children grow healthy and strong as gender-creative children—some transgender, some gender fluid, some of whom we don't yet know where they will land. So I write this book, perhaps prematurely, understanding that I have so much more to learn—most important, from the children and their parents—and that we and my like-minded colleagues are just beginning to embark on a long project of reexamining what it means to be a gender-healthy boy, girl, or other in the twenty-first century.

Those who either practice or advocate reparative therapies will argue that we already have sufficient scientific evidence to demonstrate that it would be best for children to accept the gender assigned to them at birth, and that treatment by both professionals and parents that is designed to curb children's cross-gender identifications demonstrates good results, including allowing the children to fit into society and protecting those children from potential ostracism and rejection. This would include the clinical research of Drs. Kenneth Zucker and Susan Bradley in Toronto and Dr. Richard Green at UCLA. Others, like myself, question whether those results, in which children learn to accept who others want them to be, are read through a biased lens, do not have adequate long-term outcome studies, are based on a selected population of children, and lack a comparison study measuring the outcomes for gender-nonconforming children whose parents refused, sometimes even fled from, such treatment for their children. In other words, we challenge whether those studies tell the whole or real truth about children's gender health.

As part of that challenge, I would like to offer a new lens, one that casts gender nonconformity in a positive light, in order not to squelch but to facilitate it. It is also a lens that can see clearly the vibrant polyglot of gender-creative children. Looking through this lens, we see children who declare to us, sometimes at a very early age, that the gender they are is not the one they were assigned at birth. We locate gender-fluid children who slide along a gender spectrum or weave their own intricate individual patterns along the gender web. In both past and present days, we have known the gender-fluid child as the "androgynous" child or the "tomboy," or, in more pejorative terms, the "sissy boy." We zoom in on "Gender Priuses." I am borrowing this from a term coined by Maggie, a seven-year-old gender-nonconforming child I saw for a single consultation. You will recognize her from the opening quotes of this introduction. Maggie wore only boys' clothes, including boys' underpants ("Girls' ones give me wedgies") and walked through my office door looking like any other gender-normative boy in my practice. But then Maggie swirled around and flaunted a long, blond, meticulously coifed braid cascading down his/her back. Then we have my own coined term, Gender Tauruses. Rather than being a bull on the bottom and a man on the top, Gender Tauruses are children who are aware of their genitalia and the gender assignations of those organs, but know that the rest of their torso can speak a different story. So said one assigned-male four-year-old child, Lex—again, in our very first meeting: "You see, I'm a girl on the top and a boy on the bottom." Just as a footnote, in the following meeting, our second session, Lex announced to me, "Now I'm all girl." I wondered with Lex whatever happened to the bottom half, the boy half. Lex looked me straight in the eye, and explained, with great aplomb, "Oh, it just walked off, so now I'm all girl. You can call me Lexi." We may also encounter protogay children, boys and girls who are on their way to declaring their gay identity and first explore and express their nonheterosexual selves through playing at the gender margins in early and middle childhood. Many, but

CHILDREN AND YOUTH
BEYOND THE GENDER BINARY

Transgender Children: Children who declare, sometimes at a very early age, that the gender they are is not the one they were assigned at birth, but the opposite one.

Gender-Nonconforming Children: Children who do not abide by the prescribed gender norms of their culture.

Gender-Fluid Children: Children who defy the norms of binary gender and either slide along a gender spectrum or weave their own intricate individual patterns along the gender web.

Gender Hybrids: Children who experience themselves as a combination of girl/boy:

> **Type 1: Gender Prius:** A half-and-half (boy/girl) gender
> **Type 2: Gender Taurus:** Girl (boy) on top, boy (girl) on the bottom

Gender Smoothies: Children and youth who take all aspects of gender, mix them up, and come up with a blended sense of gender that is "me."

Gender-Queer Youth: Children and youth who reject binary gender categories altogether and focus on establishing their own unique gender identity, neither male nor female.

Protogay Children: Children who play along the margins of gender in the context of their journey toward a gay identity.

Prototransgender Youth: Youth who first declare themselves as gay or lesbian and then discover, often in late adolescence or early adulthood, that they are actually transgender, and had used sexual identity as a stepping-stone toward their transgender true gender self.

not all, gay men will indeed report a childhood history of going against the norms of "appropriate" gender behavior as children but ultimately growing to embrace the gender assigned to them at birth as they embraced others of that same gender as the objects of their desire. We have the queer youth of today who like to keep people guessing and wonder why we have to categorize by gender at all. And then we have, as one teenaged patient of mine described him/herself: Gender Smoothies—"Just take every part of gender and mix it up and you have me." All of these children and youth qualify as "gender creative," if that is defined, as I explained earlier, as living in a space that is neither dictated by the inside nor the outside but resides somewhere in between. All of these children bring together a rich and varied palette of the possibilities of gender uniqueness rather than the old-fashioned strict Dick and Jane gender dichotomy.

In the spirit of creating this new lens, I would like to devote *Gender Born, Gender Made* to helping families and professionals untangle gender and learn to identify each child's unique gender web as they listen to the children and help them be the most authentic people they can be in their gender identity and expression. The princess with a penis is very different from the girl-boy Prius who is very different from the dress-up boy who is different from the Gender Smoothie. If we are not able to make these distinctions and if we lump all the gender-creative children together, we may simply create new ill-fitting boxes of gender-nonconforming children and unwittingly promote unhealthy if not dire outcomes for everyone who deserves to be recognized as his or her unique gender self.

The two-spirits, or third or fourth genders, of Native American culture do not live as either boys or girls, men or women, but somewhere in between, having the spirit of both the male and female within them. They have often been healers, artists, mediators, and leaders, recognized among their people for their flexibility and expanded perspectives. They signify the postmodern concept of gender fluidity, except they go back to premodern times. The two-spirits show up early in childhood—"It's natural. They were born that way. It is their nature." In the words of Osh-Tisch, a third-gender member of the Crow tribe, "That is my road. . . . I have done it ever since I remember because I wanted to do it."[2] Since it was in the child's nature, Native American parents knew not to try to change the child. Instead, they were to allow the child to either cross genders or live as both.

This is exactly the model that informs my work with gender-nonconforming children and their families. The difference is that, unlike Native American tribal culture, we do not live in a society that supports our two-spirited children. Instead, we want to classify them as male or female, based purely on the sex assigned to them at birth. Like the white man who decimated the Indian nations and in the process either murdered or forced the third- and fourth-gender individuals to live in accordance with binary gender norms, there are those today who would wish to see gender-nonconforming people totally eradicated. There are mental health professionals whose aim is to make gender-nonconforming children gender normative—that is, to force them to accept the gender associated with their genitals rather than with what their mind and heart tell them.

The model of ensuring children's healthy growth that I will present in this book does not have that aim. Instead, it follows the child's lead and goes where the child takes us. It assumes that the child most likely comes to us with his or her gender creativity intact, rather than being shaped after birth by hapless parents who have some gender-skewed agenda or are incapable of setting appropriate limits with their children and providing proper gender guidance. My greatest hope is that this model will prove reparative of the harm heretofore and currently done to gender-nonconforming children by our dominant culture. In presenting this model to you, I also hope it will serve as a tribute to all of the parents who have turned to community and professional organizations and individuals that honor and foster their child's unique gender self, understanding that it is located somewhere within a beautifully spun web rather than within one of two stark boxes. Such parents recognize, accept, and affirm their children, rather than trying to bend their twigs or break their spirit. Unfortunately, they, like the Native American elders who accept and embrace two-spirit or third- and fourth-gender members amid their communities, are not looked at kindly by the outside world—in particular, by members of professions that work with children and youth. My son Jesse's preschool directors who were worried about Jesse's "gender dysphoria" were not pleased that we were not. Drs. Ken Zucker and Susan Bradley, in their book *Gender Identity Disorder and Psychosexual Problems in Children and Adolescents*, found troubling the decision of two parents *not* to have their son, Ben, "treated" at the Child and Adolescent Gender Identity Clinic in Toronto, as it was clear to them that treatment with a set goal of helping Ben be happier with being a boy was absolutely warranted. They assured readers:

> Although it is important to be aware of parental ambivalence about the assessment process, such ambivalence is not necessarily an indication that parents will reject a recommendation for treatment when it is warranted. We have had experience with a number of other parents who chose to pursue therapy, despite the intense anxiety activated by the assessment process.[3]

In the face of such confusion, disapproval, and outright opposition, it is a challenging, confusing, and brave journey that parents embark on when gender-creative children appear on the family scene. I often wonder what happened to Ben; but in the meantime, if his parents might possibly be reading this book, I would like to thank them for having the wisdom, at least a decade and a half ago, which so easily came to our Native American elders but is so grossly denied or misapprehended when a North American family takes their child in their arms and flees from those who would potentially harm that child in the name of mental health. Rather than being blamed, which is the wont of my profession when it comes to parents, Ben's father and mother should be applauded for their protective actions in the name of their son.

OUR JOURNEY TOGETHER

This book will explore the developmental unfolding, the psychological experiences, the needed supports, the relationship between the child and the family, and the social milieu of the gender-creative child, with recommendations of steps to be taken to ensure not just the health of this child, but the health of each and every one of our children. Obviously, nonconformity can only exist in relation to conformity, so in that way the gender-nonconforming child is closely tied to the gender-conforming child. As long as gender continues to be a defining feature of identity in our culture, every single one of our sons and daughters, whether conforming or not, will need to spin his or her unique gender web.

Before I give you a short preview, I would like to take a moment to remind you that we are talking not about sexuality, but about gender. The two are certainly intertwined but are often confused for each other. Our sexuality and our sexual identity have to do with many things, but at their center is the object of desire—do we desire people who are the same or opposite gender as us, people of any gender, people of fluidly defined gender, people who are transgender, people of no declared gender? Our gender identity and expression, on the other hand, have to do with how we incorporate our own culture's definitions about being male or female with our own internal preferences, desires, and recognition of who we are as a male, a female, a third gender, a fourth gender, and so on. As we reach adulthood, we can think of it this way: Our sexual identity has to do with who we get into bed *with*; our gender identity has to do with who we get into bed *as*. A transgender individual can be gay or straight. A gay person can be gender conforming or gender nonconforming. And so forth. I hope that this differentiation between gender and sexual identity will serve as a helpful compass to hold in hand as we unfold and follow the map of the gender-creative child's journey through childhood.

The first two chapters will pick up on the hard journey ahead, looking at the culture of transphobia and our cultural assumptions about gender and gender development that will have to be unlearned to make room for the gender-creative child and family. I will then turn to the concept of the *true gender self,* which is the core of gender identity, to be differentiated from the *false gender self*—the accommodations a child makes to either please or fit in with the surrounding culture and which can sometimes shield the true gender self. The true gender self is presented as the antidote to gender identity disorder, a concept of pathology that thwarts rather than fertilizes the growth of the true gender self. We will be exploring the answer to the question, "Where does gender nonconformity come from and where does it go?" To that end, we will put the concept of gender creativity in developmental perspective, in order to understand that these are children who are blessed with the ability to hold on to the concept that we all had one time in our lives that we were free to be anything we wanted—boy, girl, maybe both. We will zero in on the complexities of raising a gender-creative child who "just comes to us" that way, and follow the trajectory of the child who shapes the parent as the parent in turn shapes the child, looking at the joys but also the conflicts and anxieties experienced by such children, their parents, and their siblings.

One particular complexity is that a child is a moving target and gender development is a lifelong process—so parents and professionals alike will have to train themselves both to listen carefully to the child and to live comfortably in a state of not knowing exactly where the child is ultimately headed, a task so challenging that it warrants a chapter in itself. We will consider the dangers when parents cannot listen and wait, and instead feel compelled to either bend a child's gender twig or catapult their child into a clearly defined gender category that might not be his or her true one, sometimes under the auspices of a mental health professional's advice. This will lead to a discussion of the particular challenges of puberty and adolescence for both the child and the parents of a gender-creative child, including the decision, with the help of enlightened professionals, to use puberty-delaying hormone blockers or for a youth to be administered cross-hormone therapy or even sex reassignment surgery in his or her adolescent years, circling back to the concept of the true gender self. We will get a lively profile of the protogay child, the gender-fluid child, and the transgender child, to provide a window into that vibrant polyglot of the cohort of gender-creative children. Finally, I will present the model of relational true gender self therapy to give us an idea of the ways in which a therapy office can provide a haven for the gender-nonconforming child to thrive and grow, in contrast to a hell in which their dollhouses are boarded up and their budding creativity squelched.

Throughout all the chapters, we will have to constantly hold in mind that to raise a gender-healthy child takes an entire village. It will take parents, it will take mental health and health professionals, it will take schools, it will take community educators and advocates, it will take lawmakers and judges, it will take the highest echelons of our government to make sure these children and their families can truly make a go of it. So let us begin with some realities about the village.

CHAPTER ONE

Relearning Gender

If my son, God forbid, if my son put on a pair of high heels, I would probably hit him with one of my shoes. I would throw a shoe at him. Because, you know what? Boys don't wear high heels. And in my house, they definitely don't wear high heels. . . . You got a boy saying, "I wanna wear dresses." I'm going to look at him and go, "You know what? You're a little idiot! You little dumbass! Look, you are a boy! Boys don't wear dresses."

—ARNIE STATES, KRXQ RADIO HOST, MAY 28, 2009

▼

They are freaks. They are abnormal. Not because they're girls trapped in boys' bodies but because they have a mental disorder that needs to be somehow gotten out of them.

—ROB WILLIAMS, KRXQ RADIO HOST, MAY 28, 2009

▼

only wish that these were the ignorant remarks of two men whistling in the wind. Unfortunately, they were broadcast over the airwaves and memorialized in an Internet recording for any and all around the world to hear. Ironically, just as I sat down to write this chapter, I received an e-mail with a call to action, citing these two radio announcers' comments and asking people to send a letter of protest to the head of the radio station, which I immediately did. (Footnote: As a result of a collective public outcry—mine and others—the show was temporarily taken off the air.) But the fact that these vitriolic and bigoted words were not only said publicly but broadcast globally to the masses is a clear reminder of the road of thorns that is still before us as we struggle to substitute a bed of roses for our gender-creative children.

It is not just the transphobic comments of misinformed rabble-rousers that ring in our ears. Dr. Phil, the renowned psychologist of media fame, has echoed these negative sentiments, albeit in milder, kinder tones. I am referring to a televised program on gender confusion that aired in January 2009. In no uncertain terms and with firm authority, Dr. Phil told a mother of a five-year-old, gender-fluid, Barbie-loving, dress-coveting little boy: "Direct your son in an unconfusing way. Don't buy him Barbie dolls or girls' clothes. You don't want to do things that seem to support the confusion at this stage of the game. . . . Take the girl things away, and buy him boy toys." I watched in fascination as Dr. Phil touted his wares without a grain of humility, and I questioned the extent of his training as a child gender specialist. I said to myself: "Okay, Dr. Phil. Do you have a son? Do you have a 'gender-traditional' son—a 'boy's boy'? Let's say you do. Imagine him at age five. Imagine that his favorite toy was his G.I. Joe army tank and his favorite outfit was his Incredible Hulk T-shirt, baseball jacket, and camouflage pants, finished off with Spiderman shoes. Imagine one day you go into his room and announce—'Okay, buddy, all the tanks have to go, and the trucks and the cars, too. They're just not appropriate—they're making you too macho. From now on, Barbie dolls. And the T-shirt, we're trading it in for a pink My Little Mermaid rhinestone-studded tunic with sparkles.' You wonder why he's sobbing as you pack away all his favorite boy things, but you reassure him, 'Don't worry. You'll get over it. We know what's best for you.' Now let's go one step further. Imagine it was you who was that five-year-old G.I. Joe boy. How would you have felt?"

In such exercises of imagination I hope we can begin to grasp the oppressive culture that bears down on our gender-creative children when their parents, under the tutelage of self-declared experts, are instructed to take away their favorite toys, favorite clothes, and favorite colors, and then to help their children grin and bear it. As long as popular media continues to run the gamut from horrible, incendiary remarks to misinformed professional advice, the parents of gender-creative children will have to confront and transcend a consistent, damning message: "Your child is sick." And the stakes are high as long as we do not pull out the stops to replace that message with a new and correct one: "Your child is healthy."

ONGOING PREJUDICE

In the first years of the new millennium, as I began speaking publicly on the topic of gender-nonconforming children and their parents, I wrote the following as the introduction to one of my talks:

> At age fourteen, Eddie Araujo of Newark, California, had come out and began living as a young woman. On October 3, 2002, Eddie, now seventeen and now also known as Gwen, was strangled and beaten to death by three young men after appearing at a party in women's clothing.[4] His death is being considered a hate crime. On October 19, 2002, *The San Francisco Chronicle* reported this statement from his mother, thirty-eight-year-old Sylvia Guerrero: "His tombstone will say Gwen. This kid was a great kid, and he suffered so much. He's my Gwen, and he's beautiful. I just wish I could have saved him from this."[5] I would like to dedicate my talk today to Eddie Araujo and his mother, Sylvia Guerrero, in memory of a boy who died for having the courage to go against the grain and in tribute to a mother who supported him in his journey. I am sharing my thoughts with you today as my small contribution to averting further tragedies such as this. For until we enlighten ourselves

about both the experience of growing up against the grain of prescribed gender norms and the challenges for the parents of those children, and until we then inform our actions accordingly, there are more children who will be beaten.

With a heavy heart, I realized some years later that my words rang hollow in the halls of recent history. More children have been beaten, and killed. By 2008, the picture of a fifteen-year-old boy, Larry King, had made the front page or cover of almost every major U.S. newspaper and news magazine, not because he was a spelling bee champion or child prodigy, but because he had been murdered by a classmate. Larry was in junior high school in Oxnard, California. With the support of the group home in which he was then living, Larry came out publicly as gay. He began wearing makeup, jewelry, and high-heeled boots to school. He expressed interest in another boy at the school. This made the other boy feel uncomfortable, so uncomfortable that he brought a gun to school and shot Larry in the head as he sat in his computer class. A few days later, Larry died. Had he lived, he might have explored further whether he was gay or transgender, or maybe he might have spun some other unique gender web. Tragically, Larry will never get that chance.

To be gender nonconforming is to risk being killed, but on a daily basis it more likely means being harassed, confused, and misunderstood in the community or maltreated by mental health professionals who traditionally have wanted to pathologize and fix, rather than explore and support, the gender-creative children who come to them. There is no doubt that these children are among the ranks of minority individuals in our society who must anticipate bigotry and antipathy from those who either do not understand, are ill-informed, govern their thinking with myth rather than reality, or may, from their own insecurities and internalized prejudices that can go back to their earliest childhood, project hatred onto those who are so different from themselves. At the same time, gender-creative children diverge from almost all other minority children in that they have an additional mark against them: They may face aspersion from their very own family, loved ones who are supposed to be their protectors. Unlike black parents, for example, who do their best to instill racial pride in and watch the backs of their children as they attempt to negotiate a racist world, some parents of gender-bending or gay children may feel distressed or disgusted by their own offspring and wonder why they are being punished with such "perversion." By adolescence, these youth may find themselves thrown out on the streets by their own family—poor, homeless, and socially orphaned. Or they themselves may have fled from the family, foster care, or group home where they have been harassed and bullied because of their gender presentation. Presumably, if you are reading this book, you are not among those rejecting people, but we can still assume that your child or any gender-nonconforming child you know or are working with has a caregiver, grandparent, aunt, uncle, maybe even a sibling who cannot accept his or her gender presentation. So not only the harm outside the family but the harm in the very inside of the family needs tending.

The good news in all of this is that neither culture, family, nor individuals are static, so we are not talking about immovable forces but works in progress on every front when we pose the question, What will it take to pave the road to healthy development for all gender-bending children?

The first thing it will take is to unlearn what we have been taught about gender and its development.

WHAT DID YOU LEARN IN SCHOOL TODAY?

I recall a moment from my graduate school career at the University of Michigan in the late 1960s. We were studying gender development. Before us was a grainy black-and-white film of children in white lace dresses flitting through the grass. The children were all little boys, presumably forced by their parents, particularly their overly enmeshed mothers, to become pathologically and perversely feminized, the extreme of the "sissy boy." We were taught that these boys needed help, and their mothers, a good talking to—accompanied by intensive psychoanalysis. With some room for titillation, it was nonetheless impressed upon us that we were looking at a very serious childhood disorder.

Now let's fast-forward to 2009. I am participating in a panel titled "Lesbian, Gay, Transgender Youth: Family Approaches," at the American Psychiatric Association's annual convention. I am seated, facing the audience, straining my neck to see the PowerPoint presentation of one of my copresenters. There I see photographs from the most recent annual weekend family get-together of the Outreach Program for Children with Gender Variant Behaviors and Their Families. The children on-screen are participating in a fashion show. It is no longer the era of boys in white lace dresses. These children are decked out in high-heeled boots, glitter, boas, jewelry, wigs, makeup, and more. It is hard to tell any of the children's assigned gender at birth. My copresenters are not talking pathology; they are teaching the audience about the joy and delight that ensued when these gender-creative children found a safe haven in which to truly express themselves. I sat there smiling, honored to be invited to share panel time with Catherine Tuerk and Edgardo Menvielle, the founders of the outreach program. These pictures spoke a thousand words. I was deeply moved by the aliveness on the faces of the children looking into the camera. Actually, as I think back, those children running across the lawn some half century earlier on that grainy movie screen looked no less pleased with themselves. It was we, the audience, who were instructed to be disturbed.

There is much I had to unlearn to get from my graduate program to my place on the podium at that convention, where I spoke on the importance of the gender-nonconforming child's finding his or her authentic gender self and on the role of the parent in either supporting or impeding that journey. The depth of my reprogramming to reach an enlightened point B from that rigid point A is reflected in the words of Stephanie Brill and Rachel Pepper, authors of *The Transgender Child*:

> Today, gender can no longer really be considered a two-option category. That form of thinking is outdated. It can be compared to trying to view the world in distinct racial categories without an understanding that an ever-growing percentage of the population is beautifully multi-ethnic. Gender is very similar. Most of us were taught, and most firmly adhere to, the concept that there are only two distinct categories of gender, male and female.[6]

Most developmental psychologists, mental health professionals, and medical providers of my and earlier generations were taught even more than that during our training. We learned that the two distinct categories of gender were the bellwether of normality—if you clearly placed yourself in one or the other box, based on the gender stamped on your birth certificate, you were normal. Otherwise, you were an aberration. So, to fully give children today the space for gender creativity, there is much complex unlearning and relearning to do—about development, psychology, and health.

Those of us who are professionals in the field will have to unlearn our theories of gender development that taught us that, by age five or six, healthy children are totally secure in their gender identity, based on the sex assigned to them at birth, and will also be set in their (hetero) sexual orientation. Whether we were trained in psychoanalytic, behavioral, cognitive, or developmental psychology, the overarching theme was the same. At birth, all children were assigned a sex, male or female, based on what the doctor saw between their legs. A few babies had the misfortune of being born with ambiguous genitalia, and these children would need to be "fixed" and assigned a singular gender, male or female, as soon as possible. The urgency stemmed from the belief that after the first two years of life, it would be hard, if not impossible, to change an intersex (known then as hermaphrodite) child's, or for that matter any child's, "core gender identity," which was defined as the sense of self being either male or female, based on sex assignment at birth, which in turn is based on genitalia and X and Y chromosomes. This identity— "I am boy" or "I am girl"—appeared to be firmly established and immutable by the time a child was eighteen to twenty-four months, facilitated or actually established by the treatment of the child as male or female by those caring for or relating to the child. Whereas toddlers may have little understanding of what it *means* to be male or female and no comprehension that this is a permanent status in life based on having either a male or female body, they nonetheless are now able to declare their gender—to themselves and to the world.

After children establish their core gender identity, they enter their preschool years, when they will be socialized in the ways of male and female that are normative in their culture. This is when they start their education in what it means to be male and female, known in my training years as *sex role socialization*. Learning to take on the accoutrements of boy or girl is dependent on the presence of both older males and older females who will be role models and reinforcers of "gender-appropriate" behaviors and will also serve as emotional objects of identification in which children will want to be just like their same-sex parent or caregiver. The gender notion is that likes will attract likes in terms of how to be, and that opposites will attract opposites in terms of whom to be with. So boys will become men who love women, and girls will become women who love men. Particularly in the psychoanalytic account, this is no easy accomplishment but follows a turbulent preschool period, known as the Oedipal stage, in which girls fall in love with their father and imagine having a baby with him, boys worry about losing their penis and facing retaliation from their father for falling in love and attempting to steal away their father's wife, and little girls have to give up on having a penis and settle for having a baby.

In a variation on that theme, boys have to mourn that they will never be able to have babies themselves and girls will grow to feel sorry for boys who have no aperture to their insides but are all closed up and barren. But the central theme remains the same: By the time boys and girls enter grade school, it will be clear that all children are either male or female and that there are no backsies on that; they will know how to behave as that male or female; and they will accept that someday they will find a wife or husband and have a fulfilled heterosexual life with their own marriage and babies, as modeled on their mom and dad's.

This unfolding drama is predicated on a model of men, women, and babies as the universal family type, which we know no longer to be true, and posits that all children have three developmental gender tasks: (1) establishing a core gender identity as either male or female (by two years of age); (2) learning what it means to be male or female and learning that it is a permanent fixture of who they are (known as *gender permanence* and set as an accomplishment of the preschool years); and (3) establishing their sexual orientation and object of sexual desire.

In this model, if a five- or six-year-old boy is still unclear about whether he is male or female, if a seven-year-old girl asserts that her real name is Samuel and she's always been a boy, if a four-year-old's love affair with a same-sex parent never fades and mutates into persistent same-sex crushes and "effeminate" behavior in the fourth grade, you've got trouble on your hands. Something went awry in the establishment of core gender identity, the sex role socialization, or the emotional drama of the Oedipal stage, or perhaps all three. As a result, any one of these children will be assessed as *gender dysphoric, gender inappropriate, gender confused, gender disorganized* (because he or she is devoid of gender permanence), or *inverted* (a euphemism for homosexuality) in his or her psychosexual development. As a result of what? Typically, the confusion, instability, pathology, malevolence, or neglect of—who else but the parents.

This is what I was originally taught during my academic gender education and original clinical training. If you will notice, I have provided not one citation; I did this on purpose as an exercise to see exactly what I remember from my training years, kind of like a post-test. I will leave with you the puzzle of matching each idea with an author or theorist.

Contrast this picture of the life and classification of a gender-nonconforming child with a more modern, open-minded appraisal. Recently, Marian and Sam came to me for couples therapy, but in the course of our work I learned that their son, Andy, then age four, insisted on wearing dresses, barrettes, and girls' leggings. Nothing pleased him more than having someone on the street mistake him for a girl. Nothing infuriated him more than having his parents correct a confused onlooker, providing what they felt was an honest reply, "Well, actually, Andy is a boy." One day, in a fit of anger, he burst out, "If they ask, just tell them I'm a chipmunk." Andy tucked his penis between his legs and longed for the day when he would no longer have one. He also was prone to ultra-crabby moods or downtrodden moments of despair. As his fifth birthday drew near, Andy began wailing that he was not a boy, he was a girl, and would everyone just let him be who he was. His parents listened, thought, and consulted. By the time he was ready to enroll in kindergarten, they decided to allow Andy to transition to Andi and enroll in his new school as a girl. Following that decision, Andi's agitation and unhappiness subsided and she became a happy kindergarten girl. Andi's greater ease as an affirmed girl has remained consistent up to the present, which marks the end of her second grade year. Sam and Marian's description of Andi's psychological transformation is identical to accounts from parents all around the country, as reported to Gender Spectrum, a national organization that provides education and training to create and support gender-sensitive environments: "When they [parents] allow their children and teens to express themselves in the ways that are most natural to them, to live in accordance with their true gender identity, the improvement is amazing. Depressed, anxious, hostile, or withdrawn children become visibly happier. A greater sense of inner peace appears in them."[7] We could wonder whether these accounts are merely testimonials through the rose-tinted lenses of parents who only want to see the best both in their children and in their parental decisions to allow their children their affirmed gender self-expression, except that the parent reports match outside observations on the part of child care providers, teachers, therapists, and health professionals alike.

Now, how was my original gender training going to help me understand Andi? Andy was not about to accept gender permanence, if that was to be based purely on XY chromosomes and genitalia. Andy did not go along with the sex role training that would tell him that dresses and barrettes are for girls, of which he was not one. In his preschool years, Andy seemed far more identified with his mother than with his father in terms of who he wanted to style himself after, and was persistent that the gender confusion was not his, but everyone else's, at least everybody who insisted he was a boy when he knew he was a girl. By measures taught to me in my original training, Andi's gender development was way off track—as Andy, he lacked core gender identity, his sex role socialization led to inappropriate gender behaviors, and he was identifying with his opposite-sex rather than like-sex parent. Yet by teachers' and parents' report, there were no signs of trouble, and Andi was reported to be a happy, creative child, well liked and sought out by her peers, many of whom knew she was born a boy but was now an affirmed girl. And the main difference that I could see between Andi and the little boys romping in their dresses a half-century ago is that Andi had the firm support of her family, her school, her community, and her family's therapist, whereas way back when, those little boys did not, except perhaps from their parents, who were then pathologized for just that.

THREE STRIKES FOR MY LEARNING

My teachers are now such gender-nonconforming children as Andi, who declare their gender identity to be what they know it to be from the inside, rather than what their genitalia and social norms say from the outside. Each and every one of them has challenged me to unlearn what I learned originally, because learning is of no value if it does not test out in the real world. These children have clearly taught me that when it comes to understanding gender development, my early learning has miserably failed in that department.

Let's start with the notions of *core gender identity* (acceptance and acknowledgement of the gender assigned at birth) and *gender permanence*. A growing number of very young children do not settle in to the gender assigned to them at birth, and persist in insisting that the world has it wrong—they are not the gender on their birth certificate. According to my old theories, these children should be developmentally delayed and cognitively confused, if not emotionally distraught. Yet, allowed to be "gender impermanent" by living fully as either the opposite gender or as some unique gender blend, these children seem happier and more at one with themselves once allowed to express themselves, rather than confused, tormented, or disorganized. Strike one for my earlier training.

Now let's add *sex role socialization*. The linchpin of sex role socialization is the parents—it is they who are responsible for first firming up their children's core gender identity by teaching them the ropes of what it means to be a boy or a girl in the culture in which they live. Although it is recognized that the content of those sex role norms will vary from culture to culture, what is held as universal is the parents' and the surrounding community's responsibility to train the children to fit in harmoniously within the society in which they are growing up, which is assumed to be a society based on binary gender categories.

So what about children like Andi, who as young as toddler age indicate that their core gender identity does not match the one assigned to them at birth and balk at conforming to the norms that dictate "appropriate" gender behavior? Where does that come from? Are their parents bad "trainers"?

I am going to let the parents of these children themselves be the spokespeople on this one. Some of them addressed me directly. Others reported their observations elsewhere:

When he was two, he was always in my jewelry, my purses, always in the closet for my shoes, wanting to dress like me. . . . I don't think anyone encouraged it.[8]

I am the mum to an almost-four-year-old boy with some very strong and persistent gender variant behaviours. Since he was old enough to talk—around sixteen months—he has let us know that he prefers "girl" things. For example, he dresses exclusively in girl clothes (at home, at day care, etc.).

Even before her son turned two, [his mother] noticed that he wasn't like other boys. When she took him shopping, he would go gaga at sparkly dresses. He would toss his baby blanket around his head like a wig and prance on the balls of his feet.[9]

I remember it was Lyla's second birthday. We bought her such a beautiful little dress. She just tore it off and started screaming. She only calmed down when we brought out her favorite overalls. Even when she was just learning to walk, she threw away the baby dolls and grabbed her brother's trucks. Her older sister isn't anything like this. She's as fem as you will ever find—she makes the Little Mermaid look butchy. We have no idea how this all happened. Lyla just seemed to come to us that way. Her sister didn't.

I'll stop there, but I hope you get the drift. The gender non-conformity just seems to show up, even as early as the end of the children's first year of life. Their parents are often as perplexed as anyone else. They have heard the theories that gender-bending stuff comes from parents' [mis]handling of their children, but will swear to you that they treated their gender-nonconforming child just like their other children, did nothing to encourage the nonconformity, and in fact sometimes tried unsuccessfully to squelch it or to bend their child toward more appropriate gender expression.

Studies have shown that children have been known to insist on a change in gender or become gender-confused after a trauma or major disruption in their attachments. For example, a three-year-old boy survived a serious car accident that his mother did not. Afterward, he started insisting he was a girl. Before that, he never indicated any gender-nonconforming behavior. Now, to reclaim his dead mother, he became her.[10] There is no doubt that children like this little boy did not just roll into the world as gender non-conforming, like those in parents' reports of their children who "just show up" that way, but were responding to intense emotional issues in or outside the family through their expression of gender. Another obvious example of what I will call "reactive gender dys-phoria" is how a young girl who has been molested may go on to create an emotional equation that if she becomes a boy, no one will bother her anymore. Children with reactive gender dysphoria do present themselves, and it is our responsibility to first get to the root of the emotional problems causing them to express their gender in the ways they do, and then to untangle those underlying psychological knots so the children can evolve into their authentic gender, based not on trauma but desire. Yet I would argue that these children represent only a tiny minority of gender-nonconforming children. And often the strongest indicator of their "minority" sta-tus is that they did not gradually become that way but changed their gender expression, at times suddenly and radically, subsequent to a trauma or emotionally distressing experience.

We might also discover in other instances that in subtle or not-so-subtle ways, the parents forced cross-gender behavior on their child, either unconsciously or consciously, from the earliest months of life, as when a parent has wished so hard for a girl but, with great disappointment, ends up with a boy. But there is little evidence to support the presence of such direct or insidious parental coaxing or coercion toward gender nonconformity in most children who display that trait.

In fact, the vast majority of gender-nonconforming children are like the ones described by their parents earlier: those who just seem to be evolving that way, with little influence from the outside.

Another force behind my rethinking gender identification concerns my own experience with my two children. I entered motherhood as a feminist determined to break down sex role stereotypes and afford my children a wide range of toys and options—my girl would have trucks, my boy would have dolls. My first child was a girl. Trained by my years in the day care field, I made sure to intersperse "girl" toys and "boy" toys on her play shelves. So next to her crawling, feeding baby doll was her bright yellow dump truck, standing tall next to her patent leather purse. As the years went by, the dump truck collected dust while the doll and the purse grew tattered with daily use. Then one day, when Rebecca was almost four—she had a baby brother. The day I brought Jesse home from the hospital, I noticed Rebecca scurrying back and forth between her bedroom and her new baby brother's room, her little arms stacked with things on the way there, empty on the way back. The transported objects consisted of just about every one of her "boy" toys—the dusty dump truck, little cars, a foam baseball, and so forth. I asked her what was happening. She looked up at me with earnest eyes and explained, "Well, I never played with them, so I thought maybe he would." More years went by. The hand-me-down toys now found themselves interspersed with the dolls and tea sets in Jesse's room, once again never touched. One day, when he was about two, he pulled out the dump truck. I watched, intrigued. He then went to find a little blanket and swiftly transformed the dump truck into a cradle for his newest little stuffed animal. And that is the only use any of those "boy" toys ever had in our house.

Like most children, both Jesse and Rebecca knew who they were from early on, Rebecca in her affirmed "fem" identity and Jesse in his affirmed "girlyboy" identity. Except for making room for it, I do not think my husband or I had any more influence over Jesse's gender-nonconforming childhood than we did over his eventual gay identity. And as much as I tried to steer her away from traditionally "fem" accoutrements of girlhood, Rebecca remained stalwart in her very feminine presentation, even insisting on dressing up in a long dress, Mary Jane shoes, and her famous patent leather purse for a trip to the Berkeley garbage dump. And, rightfully so, she will never forgive me for sewing her an elegant, streamlined, "practical princess" costume rather than a sparkly gown replete with frills, rhinestones, and a hooped skirt for Halloween in her kindergarten year. Rebecca began and remained a wonderful girls' girl in so many ways, despite my misguided feminist attempts to bend her toward androgyny. So I will definitely join the ranks of the parents above who repeatedly give the same report: "My child just showed up that way." Strike two for my original gender training, regarding sex role socialization.

And then there is *gender and sexual identity*. According to the gender-development model from my training years, a heterosexual male or female will go through the grade school years consolidated in a firm gender identity, fully accepting that someday, but not now, a true love of the opposite sex will come along, and that prediction will come to pass in neat, binary order. However, life tells us otherwise. If you walk down Castro Street in San Francisco, you will see a rainbow of people—a Clark Gable look-alike holding hands with a John Wayne double; a man with a female gender presentation buying a present for his new boyfriend; an affirmed female who used to be a male and has maintained her love of men, but this time as a woman; a wife who is adjusting to her marriage to an affirmed female who used to be male but is now a woman who will stay married to her wife, but this time in a lesbian relationship. Gender and sexual orientation may go together like a horse and carriage, but they are two very separate lines of development. It does not work to lump them together, as I had been taught to do in my original training, whereby a healthy boy knows and accepts that he is a boy, has learned and internalized what it means to be a boy, and is crystal clear about his prospects for love and marriage with a female; and a healthy girl knows and accepts that she is a girl, has learned and internalized what it is to be a girl, and is crystal clear about her prospects for love and marriage with a male. Yet, boys walk into my office who are clear about their male gender identity but can say by age twelve that they are gay—they will never love or desire women, only men. According to my old training, they flunk healthy gender development because they got derailed from liking girls. Another boy walks in wearing makeup and high heels. He dreams of taking hormones to make him more girl. As the weeks go on, he affirms that he is a girl. He becomes a she, a she who wants to marry a man. She will have flunked basic healthy gender development because of her gender dysphoria and cross-gender identification. But in her transgender self, she will have fulfilled the requirements of heterosexual orientation—as a female, she desires men.

Sexuality is not gender, and gender is not sexuality. Both come in all shapes and sizes, and weave together in a myriad of different tapestries. There is increasing evidence that one does not become homosexual from nurture alone, and the more salient variable seems to be nature. Scientific research suggests we may even locate homosexuality in the brain or in the chromosomal matrix.[11] More recently, there has been similar discussion about gender: that the core of our gender identity lies not between our legs but between our ears—in the physiology of our brains and in the working of our minds as we internally mediate what gender means to us and who we feel ourselves to be. I am referring here not to what gender means in terms of social norms and expectations but rather how we in our own mind integrate knowledge of our genitalia or chromosomes with our sense of ourselves as male, female, or other. In the 1970s, I made presentations around the country saying that girls could play football and do math, and boys could sew and cook. I never knew that forty years later I'd be going around the country saying that girls could have a penis and boys could have a vagina. That evolution in thinking has emerged from unlearning what I had learned. Biology is not destiny when it comes to the gonads we are born with and the gender we become. Gender is not dictated by our chromosomes, hormone receptors, or genitalia but by our own internal sense of self, a self that will be influenced by biology, by rearing, and by culture. That self may grow to love men, women, both, or other. Strike three for a training model that dictated that by grade school, children will be unchangingly clear about their gender identity based on the sex on their birth certificate, and will be set in the sexual orientation that correlates with that gender identity—boys will like girls, girls will like boys.

UNLEARNING WHAT WE HAVE LEARNED

So what happens after you strike out? Does the other team come up to bat? Is the game over? In this case, three strikes is a call for a new gender model. In this new model, core gender identity is not the physical one assigned at birth; it is the psychological core sense of self as male, female, or other that may or may not match the box checked on the birth certificate. Recent theories that preempt my early training model look to neurology and the brain to explain how both matches and mismatches can occur. To stay for a moment in a binary gender formulation, there is some evidence that the "female" brain is different from the "male" brain. Some boys are born with a penis and testes, which matches their boy brain and their XY chromosomes. Some girls are born with a vagina and ovaries, which matches their girl brain and their XX chromosomes. Some boys are born with a penis and testes, but with a girl brain. Some girls are born with a vagina and ovaries, but with a boy brain. These latter may feel like a girl trapped in a boy's body or a boy trapped in a girl's body. And some children have a combination of chromosomes other than XX or XY, such as XXY, which can lead to yet other combinations of brain and genital development.

How do we get a boy brain or a girl brain? On the basis of our hormone receptors. It is determined by how we absorb the hormones that come to us as we float around in our mother's (or gestational carrier's) uterus. It may also have to do with the surges of hormones that come our way as we gestate. Sometime in the first trimester, the male fetus begins producing sex hormones that bathe his brain in testosterone for the rest of his gestation, producing the boy brain. Girls whose mother had high levels of testosterone in pregnancy have been found to more likely prefer playing with trucks than with dolls. A heavy dose of testosterone creates "tomboys." A heavy dose of estrogen or progesterone may be correlated with "girlyboys."[12] At its extreme, these hormonal surges may be correlated with a girl brain in a boy's body or a boy brain in a girl's body.

If we think about it, a child's gender journey launched at birth is based on (1) genetic gender: chromosomal inheritance, be it XX, XY, or other; (2) physical gender: primary and secondary sexual characteristics—penis and testicles, or a vagina, ovaries, and uterus; and (3) "brain gender," or functional structures of the brain along gender lines. In the large majority of children, there will be a match among chromosomes, genitalia, and brain signals, but in others there will not be. To date we have no accurate statistics regarding who will comprise this latter group, but estimated numbers are 1 percent or less of the population. Members of the nonmatching group are no more abnormal than are left-handed people (of which I am one), who are less than 10 percent of the population but perfectly healthy and well functioning (until they have to use a right-handed can opener). And if we throw out the binary norms of gender altogether, we are left with an intriguing polyglot of factors—the chromosomes, the brain, the hormones, the body, and the psyche—an exciting multiplicity of combinations and permutations that weave together an individual child's gender web.

Yet all of this leaves out the environment. What is to replace the sex-role socialization paradigm when it comes to making meaning of gender? Who or what will shape a child's gender presentation? Now we are faced with a more complicated dialectic: Gender seems stamped in the brain somewhere; or gender is a fluid process over the life span. Gender is born, yet gender is also made. Gender is an interweaving of nature and nurture. Gender as nature is no starker than in the parents' reports that their gender-nonconforming child "just came to me that way." Gender as nurture in no more evident than in the reported experience of adults who live as one gender for many years and then affirm another gender, finding themselves incorporating the gender expressions they learned over the course of their earlier life with the new gender expressions they are learning in their present life as an adult of the opposite gender. The operative word here is *learn*. There could be no full expression of gender without a culture to teach us how to express it and to communicate to us what it thinks gender to mean, known as the *acculturation process*. And, as I said earlier, that teaching may vary remarkably from one culture to another. The proudly worn manly kilt in Scotland is the scandalous sissy-boy skirt in America. Not only do gender mores differ from country to country, but even within one country, gender norms do not stay static over time. When I was growing up in Chicago in the 1950s and early 1960s, girls in public school were required to wear skirts or dresses—no pants allowed, even in the freezing winters. That would be unheard of today in the United States. Yet despite variations across time or across localities, every one of us is acculturated within a social system that will inform us about the prevailing "ways" of gender, whether we conform to those ways or not.

But in the new paradigm of gender's being an intricate choreography of nature and nurture, it is not just the role of the parents to teach the children but that of the children to teach the parents—about their internal sense of self as girls, as boys, as others, from what their mind and the organ between their ears tells them. Rather than serving as a strong role model and guiding light, as in the original sex role socialization model, the new role of the parents is to oversee the delicate dance and evolving transactions between constitution and environment as they help their children find an authentic gender identity and expression that will in the best of all possible worlds be a good fit for their sons or daughters.

No longer will there be only one healthy gender outcome. No longer will there be a fixed process that is all wrapped up by age six. Many children will go through a fluid process that extends well beyond their fifth or sixth year. Some children will know by age three that their affirmed gender is not the one on their birth certificate. Others will live for several years as the gender assigned to them at birth, only to discover later that they really don't identify with that gender and are much more the other. Some children may be so fluid that they will experiment for a while with one gender and then another, signifying not that they are gender chaotic or confused but that they are trying out different gender expressions or identities for size. The key premise is that gender identity formation does not end at a point in time but is a fluid process that might extend over the course of a boy or girl's childhood or even into adulthood.

What about unhealthy gender? I know that some people will say, "Your early training, which you are now discarding, taught you to recognize when gender development gets off course. So are you now saying that anything goes?" Of course not. There are many things that can go wrong as a child embarks on the journey to discover his or her gender identity and expression.

This then leads to the question, "Then is there such a thing as a gender identity disorder?" I am going to save the lengthier answer to this question for a later chapter. But for the time being I'd like to point out that the majority of young children who have been diagnosed with a gender identity disorder—which is defined as a strong and persistent cross-gender identification and persistent discomfort with their sex or sense of inappropriateness in the gender role of that sex—are simply children who did not conform to the developmental model for the "healthy" boy or girl promoted in my earlier training, the model I had to unlearn. If that developmental model is invalid, then it cannot rightly be used as a measure of disorder, can it? If we do use it, we end up labeling all children who go against the grain of binary gender norms as disordered—a serious mistake causing harm to many children.

So when is a child's gender disordered? A child may live in a swirl of inner chaos and disorganization, never being able to stably locate him- or herself on some gender spectrum. A child may be stuck so rigidly within a binary gender box that he or she becomes a robotic stereotype of the "macho" boy or the "super-fem" girl. A child might want to dispense with gender altogether as a threatening poltergeist. For example, Natalie came to me in "gender distress." She was no longer a child; she had just had her nineteenth birthday. Natalie insisted that she was transgender and began attending transgender support groups with an eye toward sex reassignment surgery. She had been hospitalized in high school for suicidal depression. Her suicidal state mirrored the sad situation of so many transgender youth, particularly if their gender dysphoria remains hidden and unacknowledged or if their gender expression leads to harassment and rejection. Before attending the support group, Natalie had been hanging out in Internet chat rooms for transgender youth for some time. However, she did not feel or wish to become male. Her greatest desire was to get rid of her breasts and sew up her vagina. She did not want a penis; she did not want testosterone. She just wanted to rid herself of any genitalia and secondary sexual characteristics, so she could become gender neutered. However, her therapist had her doubts. Feeling out of her league, not having had any training as a gender specialist, the therapist referred Natalie to me for the purpose of assessing her gender issues. It was my impression that Natalie's gender and sexual development had been seriously derailed, maybe secondary to another psychiatric disorder, perhaps post-traumatic stress disorder, or maybe primary to her horror about gender and its related sexual components. Natalie is not transgender but rather antigender. This is a young woman whose gender is disordered, and Natalie will need help from her therapist to work through her distress that is expressed through the lens of gender. However, I must stress that most children's gender nonconformity is *not* rooted in psychological disorder, and should not be viewed or treated as such.

In our new gender development model that encompasses gender creativity, we will be challenged to differentiate disordered gender from nonconforming gender, providing kind and empathic care from a trained mental health professional for the former and simply making room for support and acceptance of the latter. As we do this, some have asked, "How come it seems like so many more children are showing up these days at younger and younger ages who are transgender or gender nonconforming?" This is a question raised by many, as they puzzle over what to make of the Barbara Walters specials and Dr. Phil interviews that put the spotlight on transgender little children as a phenomenon that apparently seems to be pouring out of the woodwork. Is it because we have simply lifted the lid on cultural proscriptions that heretofore forced all of these children underground, thereby freeing up the gender-creative children to come forth? Is it our seriously questioning our society's binary notions of gender for people of any age, and our modern-day expanded options for both males and females based not on gender policing but on individual desire? Or are there really more such children today—not just because of social permission, but also as a result of in utero hormonal influences, especially fertility drugs and reproductive technology manipulations of gametes and embryos; environmental chemical infusions that are affecting the hormonal balance of estrogens and androgens in all our children; or some other not yet uncovered variable? If transgender rights are the new terrain for political struggle following on the heels of the civil rights movement, feminism, and gay pride, should we also be asking whether parents, support organizations, and mental health professionals like myself may actually be encouraging these behaviors and jumping to conclusions that appear politically correct rather than psychologically sound? I wish I could give you a definitive answer to the question of, "Why now?" but suffice it to say that I believe we are witnessing a sea change in our cultural sensibilities about gender and that the growing incidence is most likely a product of all of these factors. I would like to believe that we are actually following children's lead to afford them a full and good life, instead of enforcing or reinforcing gender creativity as our own political agenda.

TO WHAT END OUR NEW LEARNING?

When it comes to the treatment and socialization of gender-creative children, we will need to reteach ourselves: Our main job as adults is to listen and respond, rather than guide, enforce, or force.

Professionals in the field will have to unlearn our theories of gender development. We will need to replace those teachings with an understanding that there is more than one healthy gender outcome and that many children will go through a fluid process that extends well beyond their fifth or sixth year; in other words, that gender-identity formation does not end at a point in time but might extend over the course of a boy or girl's childhood or even into adulthood.

Parents will have to unlearn the idea that it is our role to keep our children on the straight and narrow gender path prescribed by society (no pun intended). And we will need to remember that acting on what we know may not be taken kindly by those who don't know. Let me close this chapter by returning to Dr. Phil. In one of his programs on gender, "Little Boy Lost" (January 13, 2009), a mother of a gender-nonconforming child sits listening to the opinions of two mental health experts who posit that parents are responsible for their child's gender "choices" and that there is something wrong with parents who allow a child to transition from male to female. This mother had just one thing to say in response: "Oh, my God, you guys are nuts." If we are going to listen to the children, we are going to have to learn to listen to the parents as well. When a mother is so emotionally triggered that she yells at a so-called expert, we have to ask, "Is she unhinged or she is screaming for her child's life?" With that question in mind, I would now like to look at the experience of the parents of a gender-creative child.

CHAPTER TWO

The Family's Path Is Covered with Roses and Thorns

I am the mum to an almost 4-year-old boy with some very strong and persistent gender-variant behaviors. Since he was old enough to talk— around 16 months—he has let us know that he prefers "girl" things. . . . My husband and I support him no matter what, whichever gender he is. . . . [We] are looking for parenting resources so we will be better equipped to help our child become whoever he is, and to make sure we have the tools to ensure he remains a happy and self-confident child (and adult). . . . We are not having much luck however. . . . Everything I've read and everyone I've talked to points me in the direction of Ken Zucker. I've read a lot about him, and I will not subject my child to his therapies. They go against everything I believe in as a parent and a human being.

—MOTHER OF A GENDER-CREATIVE CHILD

▼

I n 2008 I was featured, along with Dr. Ken Zucker, on an NPR *All Things Considered* program, "Two Families Grapple with Sons' Gender Preferences." To quote Alix Spiegel, producer of the show, "NPR talks with two psychologists who take radically different approaches to the issue—one whose treatment aims to help kids feel comfortable with their biological sex, and the other whose approach is to allow the children to live as the gender with which they most closely identify at the time."[13]

Ever since appearing on that show, I receive a continual flow of e-mails like the one from this woman. The mothers and fathers contacting me are desperate to do right by their children and find mental health supports that will help rather than harm their children. They will search all over the country and cross national borders to find that help. Parents and other family members are such a critical factor in the growth and development of all children, but especially of those who go against the gender grain, that I decided to devote an entire chapter to unlearning what we have learned about daddies, mommies, and gender, so as to transcend blame and introduce support for parents facilitating their children's true gender self.

BLAMING THE PARENT

When I was in graduate school, Robert Stoller was considered the guru of gender studies, particularly regarding "gender-aberrant" children. When it came to "marked femininity" in boys, Stoller formed a simple hypothesis: "In boys, in the absence of special biologic circumstances (for example, certain chromosomal disorders), the more mother and the less father, the more femininity."[14] According to this philosophy, a mother will err in being blissfully merged with her son, holding him within an encapsulated bubble of femininity and mutual infatuation, where no men need apply; whereas the child's father, chosen by his wife for his passivity and general wimpiness, will fail miserably in popping the sissy bubble that a mother has constructed around herself and her son. Instead, he will withdraw, both physically and emotionally, leaving the child with no adult male figure to escape to. I could continue, but suffice it to say that, according to Stoller, if a boy is a sissy or a girl an inveterate tomboy, look no further than to the mother, and secondarily to the father, to blame for their child's transgression from "healthy" gender development.

In recent history, the fields of psychology and psychiatry have left no stone unturned in their feeding frenzy to find something to blame parents for. We have had the icebox mother responsible for her child's autism, the schizophrenogenic parents responsible for their child's mental illness, the deadbeat father responsible for his child's poor academic performance. When it comes to blaming someone for gender-bending children, the experts easily join with the community surrounding them in pointing their finger at parents. Internalized homophobia and transphobia are no more apparent than in the anxiety that gets stirred up in the public at large when a child transgresses culturally prescribed norms of male and female. That anxiety, when placed in the hands of mental health professionals and psychological researchers and theorists, transforms into a lethal weapon, with the target of the attack being the parents who are either making, encouraging, allowing, or forcing their children to act in these "odd" ways. So I would say that mental health experts scrutinizing sex role socialization have typically skewered any parent who does not abide by the social rules of making boys be boys and girls be girls.

Were this assignment of blame simply part of the archaic training of a young developmental psychologist forty years ago, we could let it go as obsolete history. But bear with me as I offer you an extensive quote from Ken Zucker and Susan Bradley's 1995 book, *Gender Identity Disorder and Psychosexual Problems in Children and Adolescents,* describing the mother of a little boy, Jeremiah, who liked girl things:

> Jeremiah's mother had profound ambivalence about his cross-gender identification in the sense that she was quite unsure whether it was a problem, and she strongly reinforced his feminine behaviours (buying him female dolls, allowing him to

cross-dress, etc.). In contrast, Jeremiah's father was very worried about his gender identity development, commenting, for example, that it was inappropriate to allow him to wear dresses on the street. During an intake telephone interview, Jeremiah's mother said that she would leave her partner [in a common-law marriage; both are Jeremiah's birth parents] if he continued questioning her about Jeremiah's cross-gender behavior. She indicated forcefully that it would not bother her in the least if Jeremiah developed a homosexual orientation. Asked how she would feel if he were to seek sex reassignment, she answered this was fine with her as long as he was happy.[15]

I have never met Jeremiah nor his mother or father, but all three sound recognizable to me, emblematic of the many families who show up in my office with a gender-creative child. Were Jeremiah brought to me, my inclination would be to explore further with his parents the meaning of the boy's gender-nonconforming actions and feelings for each of them, asking each to reflect on their ideas about where these behaviors came from and how much control they really think they might have over their son's gender preferences and expressions. I would have empathy for both mother and father but would also feel a clinical and ethical obligation to advocate for the gender-creative boy unfolding before our eyes. Zucker and Bradley see it differently: "It was our clinical opinion that Jeremiah's mother had a great deal of anxiety regarding men and masculinity, and that it was probably very difficult for her to tolerate any signs of masculinity in Jeremiah."[16] The mother is pathologized for trying to honor her son's true gender self, which the authors view as forcing him to remain within a sphere of femininity. Jeremiah's father, who may be homophobic or transphobic, is instead normalized for standing up and fighting for the masculinity of his son. The mother's threat to leave the father is seen as man-hating, rather than child-protective.

In fairness to Zucker and Bradley, they do make attempts to both modernize and extend Dr. Stoller's earlier hypothesis:

"One could hypothesise two pure subgroups of boys with gender identity disorder [Stoller's feminized boys]. In one subgroup the familial dynamics pertain largely to maternal unavailability (e.g., due to depression), whereas in the other subgroup the familial dynamics pertain largely to maternal hostility and anger that revolve around masculinity-femininity issues."[17] So mothers of gender-nonconforming sons can now be blamed from all different directions—they are depressed or checked out, or are angry due to being gender-conflicted themselves.

My point: The socialization model that promotes gender conformity as normality and vilifies parents who defy this model when they support their "gender-transgressive" children is alive and well. Fortunately, the traditional model is being challenged vociferously by me and other twenty-first-century gender specialists who recognize the dangers of the culturally biased lens and the lack of reliability and validity in the claim that parents, particularly mothers, are the ones responsible for making their children "gender abnormal."

For example, several studies have examined the levels of psychopathology in the mothers of children who have received a diagnosis of *gender identity disorder—childhood* (GID). Such factors as overprotectiveness, marital discord, lack of enjoyment in the child, and prior contact with mental health professionals have been identified as potential "risk" factors for a child's GID. In other words, if mothers are overprotective, don't get along with their husband, are finding the relationship with their child fraught, or have sought out the services of a mental health professional in the past, their gender-nonconforming children may be more vulnerable to being labeled with this diagnosis. Both the shaky validity and cultural bias in such findings are evident as we ask the following chicken-and-egg questions: Could not all of these risk factors be *side effects* for the parents rather than the *cause* of their children's gender nonconformity? Why wouldn't mothers be protective of their children, if fearing for their safety in the face of teasing, harassment, bullying, or physical violence at the hands of peers and even adult community members? Would it not make sense that marital discord would ensue if parents, as in Jeremiah's family, are in strong disagreement about a very sensitive issue within the family—the best way to handle their gender-nonconforming child? If the parents are either worried for the children's safety or do not feel that their gender habits are normal, couldn't it render their enjoyment of their children difficult? And what about prior contact with a mental health professional? The implication is that such mothers have had mental health problems of their own, but could it not also be possible that they have gone in search of emotional support in the challenging task of raising gender-nonconforming children, a search that in the face of a pathologizing diagnosis of GID may have caused both psychological distress and more harm than good?

Parents indeed play a critical role in teaching, shepherding, and shaping their children's gender journey—but not as the villains who twist potentially "normal" children into gender perverts. Mothers and fathers like Jeremiah's deserve better than being cast as the perpetrators of a so-called disorder and criticized for unwittingly or intentionally inflicting an aberration on their children. To unlearn what many of us were taught and to counteract that prejudice, we will have to rethink what role parents *do* play in ensuring the gender health of their children. Edgardo Menvielle, codirector of the Gender and Sexuality Advocacy and Education Program (previously known as the Outreach Program for Children with Gender-Variant Behaviors and Their Families), absolves parents of that blame: "Parents can model and otherwise teach respect for and appreciation of the other gender and the values of gender equality and fairness and many other values and principles, but parents probably have little or no influence on the child's core feelings that define him or her as gender typical or gender variant. Such core feelings appear immutable."[18] A far cry from the long-standing model for diagnosis that pathologizes both the parents and children.

CHANGING TIMES?

Catherine Tuerk is the codirector, alongside Edgardo Menvielle, of the above-named outreach program. In 2003, she reported to a journalist her experience thirty years earlier with her gender-variant son (who grew up to be gay). In the journalist's words:

> She felt afraid that he might become gay or transsexual and that she might have done something to cause his "problem." Mental health professionals told her that her son could be "fixed," so she and her husband put him through years of psychotherapy to make him more "masculine." After he came out at age twenty, Tuerk "realized that everything I had been told by professionals was wrong or harmful to him and our family."[19]

For many years after he came out, Catherine's son estranged himself from his parents. To assuage her own guilt and right a wrong done to her own child and thousands of others, Catherine went on to found the support group for gender-nonconforming children and their families in Washington, D.C.

Catherine, her husband, and their son were victims of their time. Had it been thirty years later, when she could have had access to her own support group or to another program such as Gender Spectrum in the San Francisco Bay Area, her entire family might have avoided years of contortion and estrangement. But even in these changing times, parents who attempt to facilitate rather than block their children's true gender expressions may face aspersion, pathological diagnostic labeling, or dire legal consequences—specifically, having their children taken away from them, as happened to the parents of Aurora in Ohio.

In the summer of 2000, the Lipscombs, of Westerville, Ohio, a suburb outside Columbus, finally allowed their six-year-old son, Zachary, to transition to being female, after four years of his persistence in gender nonconformity. He was Zachary by day, Aurora by night throughout his kindergarten year, then announced to his neighbors the following summer, "I am a girl." With the help of a Cleveland support group for transgendered people, the Lipscombs hired an attorney, legally changed Zachary's name to Rori, and enrolled Rori in first grade, the next school year, as a girl. Hearing the news, an anonymous tipster contacted the local children's service agency, who took swift action to remove Rori from her home and place her in foster care—a request that was granted by the court magistrate, who cited "reasonable grounds to believe that the child is suffering from illness . . . and is not receiving proper care."[20]

This isolated case in a small town in Ohio has set a precedent for other parents throughout the country to either worry or feel hog-tied in their attempts to support their gender-creative children, particularly if there are postdivorce custody issues. I had been working with Bobby and Bobby's mother, Marguerite, since Bobby confided to her that he really wished God had made him a girl and that he could go back into Mommy's tummy and come out female. After attending the Gender Spectrum annual family conference in Seattle, where for the first time Bobby had the opportunity to present as a girl and declared it as the happiest time in his/her life, Marguerite began to explore the possibility of moving to a new community with more progressive schools, where Bobby could enroll as a girl. Knowing that Marguerite was divorced from Bobby's father and that there was no love lost between them, I suggested that she consult an attorney or gender advocate before proceeding, even though she presently had primary legal and physical custody of Bobby. In the meantime, Bobby's father, Jack, caught a whiff of Marguerite's plan to allow Bobby to transition to female, and had this to say: "What are you talking about? I refuse to allow you to do this to my son. He's just a little kid. He doesn't know what he wants. If I had known I would have a child who ended up like this, I never would have had a child with you." He followed this with a clearly stated threat to take Marguerite to court if she dared to go forward with her plan, where he would petition for sole custody and request that Bobby be removed from his ex-wife's care. Marguerite had followed my advice and consulted an attorney. The lawyer delivered the sobering news that Bobby's father might have a strong leg to stand on in court, precisely because of the legal precedent set by the case of Aurora and because of the continuing bias in the courts against parents who support rather than curb their gender-nonconforming children. So with heavy heart, Marguerite reported to Bobby that Dad didn't agree that Bobby could be a "young lady" and that for the time being, he could be a boy who likes girl things. There is, of course, another lesson embedded in this story, and that is the importance of protecting gender-nonconforming children from cross fire between disagreeing parents regarding their best interests. But for now, I share this story simply to emphasize that the times, they are a-changing—but not as quickly as we would like, leaving parents in a conundrum: How do they help their children grow, while keeping them safe and dodging the bullets aimed at *them* as parents who go against the gender grain?

Optimistically, I am witnessing a shake-up in the mental health community as training sessions, workshops, and conferences are proliferating all over this country and around the world, demanding that we reevaluate the binary system of gender, throw out the idea that gender nonconformity is a disorder, and establish new guidelines for facilitating the healthy development of gender-creative children. But when I was asked by the NPR interviewer Alix Spiegel which approach dominated in the United States, mine or Ken Zucker's, Spiegel summarized my response, which I might add I answered without a nanosecond's thought, as follows: "In terms of which of these therapies is more prevalent in the U.S., Diane Ehrensaft says there's absolutely no doubt in her mind: Zucker's."[21] This doesn't mean I believe his is the right way to respond to these children. Unfortunately, we are still waiting for that time when I might respond to an interviewer, "Which approach dominates? Oh, mine, of course." I do believe this will come to pass, just as feminism has created radical changes in the equality between the sexes, and gay and transgender organizations both in our nation's capitol and state by state are working day and night to ensure civil rights for all gay, lesbian, and transgender people. But until that time comes, both legal statutes and the dominant trend in the mental health community, which remains diametrically opposed to the gender acceptance approach espoused by me and others, will leave parents submerged in a sea of questions and doubts. To quote Hanna Rosin, whose moving piece, "A Boy's Life," appeared in the November 2008 issue of *The Atlantic*:

> Doubts may plague parents. Should they let their child express themselves as the opposite gender? Can they accept the new "normalcy" approach? Are the children really happy if they are allowed to transition or express themselves as their inner identity tells them? How will that play in small town America? What does it mean to defy the advice of the psychiatric experts, who tell them to get their child to accept the gender they were assigned at birth?[22]

How could doubts *not* plague parents in the face of (1) the standing existence of a diagnosis (gender identity disorder) that says that their children are mentally ill[23]; (2) the prevalent attitude of mental health professionals that children should accept the gender given to them at birth; and (3) the specific messages these mothers and fathers get—from experts, from their own parents and other family members, from teachers, from strangers on the street—that they are to blame for the dire consequences that will befall their children if they cave in to their children's demands to be free to be themselves?

There is no limit to the opposition that parents may face every day when they let their boys be girls, their girls be boys, their hybrids be hybrids, and their gender-fluid children be gender fluid. Not every mother will be as clear as the mom we met at the beginning of this chapter, who wrote, "[We] are looking for parenting resources so we will be better equipped to help our child become whoever he is, and to make sure we have the tools to ensure he remains a happy and self-confident child (and adult)." Never having met this woman in person, I cannot know if she has always been that clear, which leads me to my next point: As the times do change, so do parents when it comes to understanding their gender-nonconforming children.

ON BECOMING A GENDER-SENSITIVE PARENT

The story is all too common of a child harassed, abused, or disowned by family members for being other than gender normal, as a result of parental or even sibling behaviors driven by fear, anxiety, or hatred. It is a disturbing story. But there is also another troubling story: Many who have written about the psychological experiences of the child who defies gender norms assume that the parents resist and object to the child's gender defiance. Dr. Susannah Moore, who wrote a compelling doctoral dissertation entitled "Diagnosis for a Straight Planet: A Critique of Gender Identity Disorder for Children and Adolescents in the DSM IV," describes the expected reactions of parents to their child's gender nonconformity: "Like the protagonist in the French film *Ma Vie en Rose* . . . a boy may in fact feel most comfortable and least distressed when wearing a dress and making clothes for his Barbie doll; yet, when he is his happiest his parents are most distressed and his peer group least tolerant."[24] But not all parents are like this. We have a strong cohort of sensitized mothers and fathers who have developed into or came onto to the scene as parents dedicated to facilitating the healthy growth of their gender-creative children. How do they do that? Who are they?

Some of them are very strongly influenced by the feminist wave that began in the late 1960s. Some are gay or lesbian parents who have been sensitized to gender issues by their own experiences growing up and living against the grain, and some are just "plain old folks" from small towns or big cities all over the country who love their children enough to devote themselves to doing not necessarily what comes naturally, but what will be in their children's best interests. From any one of these parents we can learn something: what parents can do to facilitate and what parents can do to obstruct their child's authentic gender self.

One of the most important lessons I learned in my training as a developmental psychologist is that the child shapes the parent just as the parent shapes the child, somewhat in round-robin fashion.[25] We have already talked about children who present their true gender self without having been molded by their parents. According to PFLAG, families of gay, lesbian, bisexual, and transgender persons may all experience the same stages of denial, anger, and grief, along with safety concerns and confusion, when a family member comes out.[26] Yet in families with very small children who transgress cultural norms of gender, the children do not *come out* to us; rather, they *come to* us, not all at once but in an evolving journey—they just *are*. We know that gender is always a fine choreography between the child and the people who care for him or her, people who in turn will be influenced by their own culture's definitions of male and female. Yet the number of small children who simply present themselves to us as gender-creative little people very early in their lives remind us that these small children may have been born to be free, if we consider freedom to be liberation from the constricting social norms of gender. But born to be free doesn't necessarily mean destined to be free. Because once these children are born, their parents will then respond positively, negatively, with ambivalence or confusion, and perhaps with inconsistency over time. As so eloquently expressed by Paul, one such confused father faced with a three-year-old son who insisted on princess dresses over baseball bats from the time he was two: "It was really hard for me to be with him. I just wanted to play ball, not go to the ball." Depending on how Paul actually responds to his princess-identified toddler, he will in turn shape how his son feels about his gendered self, whether he will feel permission versus proscription in dancing at the ball rather than batting on the ball field.

The other important lesson I learned is that no system or organism is static. Babies grow and change, parents grow and change, families grow and change, whole communities grow and change, either as a result of developmental thrusts, life experiences, or direct interventions. These processes of transformation are never a point in time but may unfold over many years of family life. They also are not straight lines but complicated tapestries woven from the warp of the individual and the weft of the environment. The transphobic or homophobic parent of today may be the PFLAG parent of tomorrow. Marlene Shyer raised a gender-nonconforming son in the 1960s and '70s, a boy who came out as gay in his college years. When Christopher was in kindergarten, Marlene went to the teacher, saying she was afraid that he might grow up to be a homosexual, based on his cross-sex interests and aversion to rough-and-tumble play. Throughout his childhood, she took Christopher to several professionals. One administered a full-day battery of tests with the following feedback: "'This test is perfectly conclusive. It's just as I suspected: it indicates without any doubt that your son is perfectly normal, and will grow up to be totally heterosexual." Marlene describes her response at that time: "I sailed, wafted, skipped, whistled and sang my way out of that office." Years later, looking back, she, like Catherine Tuerk, laments her lack of support for her protogay son and the pain she caused him: "I suppose like many people of my generation, I deserve to have my brain washed out with soap, but it's a long evolutionary process and I'm still learning." Indeed, her attitude toward her son has done a 180-degree turn: "I see my son as the special bequest the gods had up their sleeves for me, a gift so generous I sometimes think I don't deserve my luck. It is not that I'm privileged to have a child who is gay; I am privileged to have a gay son who is Chris."[27]

When Felicia was three, she used to throw her dresses into the garbage. Her mother would pull them out and punish her. When it was time to get dressed for a birthday party, Felicia would beg to wear her football jersey. Her father would send her right back in her room, to pick out an appropriate party dress. Both of Felicia's parents felt it their responsibility to teach their child the appropriate behavior for a little girl. They also lived in a conservative community and attended a church that underlined the importance of preparing boys and girls for their gender-divided adult roles as breadwinner and homemaker, respectively. As Felicia moved through grade school, she drew more and more withdrawn and lackluster. Fortunately, she met up with a teacher in fifth grade who "got" Felicia, because the teacher was just like her—a gender-fluid woman who had had to fight to get her own gender creativity acknowledged. Similar to Marlene, Felicia's parents, with the help of Felicia's teacher, changed over time, evolving into accepting parents who could celebrate rather than condemn Felicia's unique gender-nonconforming self.

Several years ago, parents would appear in my office crying that their child might be gay. These days I more likely hear, "It's just fine if he's gay, but I just couldn't deal with his being transgender." Marlene Shyer's own evolution out of homophobia and toward affirmation of her gay son occurred over these same years, driven not just by the changing times that witnessed the elimination of homosexuality as a disorder in the *Diagnostic and Statistical Manual* and the increasing cultural acceptance of gay people, but also by her deep personal bonds with her son. Now, as with Felicia's parents, I am beginning to see that same transformation occurring for twenty-first-century parents of transgender and gender-nonconforming children, with transphobia as the next social weed that needs to be uprooted.

What about transphobia or genderism—the negative attitudes, beliefs, and behaviors regarding people who violate the culturally prescribed binary norms for males and female? How transphobia or genderism may affect any one of us depends on the religious and social milieu in which we ourselves grew up and the milieu in which our children are growing. But let's tie it in directly to becoming a parent. The family is paramount as the primal and primary place where children first develop a sense of self as boy, girl, or other. Far before your baby ever knows what a boy or girl is, you, the parent, will hold that information in mind as you take care of a baby who was announced at birth to be a boy or a girl.[28] But what happens if for months or years you've built a relationship with your child as a boy or a girl, and then you hear from that child, "Guess what? You got it all wrong. I'm not the gender you think I am." Brandon tells you he's actually a girl. Sarah tells you her real name is Samuel, that Sarah has left and gone fishing. Alexandra tells you she's a girl-boy. Jason tells you he's a boy-girl. Now we have a bit of a situation. Suppose you feel queasy about transgender or gender-transgressive people. But you are by now madly in love with your baby, who may not be such a little baby anymore. Right there lies a potential collision between transphobia and baby love, presenting a profound experience of cognitive dissonance for many a parent: "Transgender people are sick or deviant and to be despised or feared" versus "I love my baby who now may be one of those people." How is this resolved? Can you make room for your gender-nonconforming child to follow his or her own gender path, or will you feel a need to guide your child toward conformity with those social norms for boys/girls in the world in which your child is growing?

A child who goes against the gender grain can be born into any home, in any place. But what happens after birth is unique to each child and each family. We might wonder, "Why do some families allow their child to grow toward his or her own light and others do everything in their power to bend their child's twig?"

There are so many possibilities for the metabolism of transphobia or genderism in a family where boys will be girls or girls will be boys: Here's where I like to play with the seven T words: Transgender, Transgression, Transphobia, Trauma, Transcendence, Tranformation, Transition. For the purposes of alliteration, I am using *transgender* in its broadest definition, which is any child who strays from the traditional binary male-female gender model. Strung together in an extraordinarily long sentence, the seven T's read like this: The *transgender* child who *transgresses* social gender norms may face *transphobia* and *trauma* within the family while helping the family's *transcendence* of that transphobia by providing moms, dads, brothers and sisters with *transformative* experiences as the child *transitions* from the gender assigned at birth and/or the expectations for that gender to his or her authentic and affirmed gender identity. If transformation trumps transphobia, the child stands a good chance of emerging with a positive gender identity. If, on the other hand, transphobia and trauma run transformation into the ground, the child may be left with a bruised and battered psyche, a contorted self, and even a wish not to be around anymore. Obviously, the parents are the key players in this drama, but siblings, grandparents, extended family, and caretakers will play their part as well. Focusing specifically on the parents and translated into simpler English, parents can either listen and respond respectfully to what their child is telling them about his or her gender, or they can feel compelled to lead and direct their child to where they think he or she should be, which may go totally against that child's grain.

THE INGREDIENTS OF TRANSFORMATION

Some time ago, I did an exercise with myself in preparation for a community talk on raising a gender-healthy child. I listed all the things children have to do to figure out their gender, and all the things a parent has to do to help those children get there. Here is what I came up with. As long as we live in a gendered society, children have to:

1. Become aware of the gender their parents think them to be

2. Later, learn how that gender label is related to their body (boys have a penis, girls have a vagina, men can grow a beard, women have breasts, and so forth)

3. Take in what their culture says about what it *means* to be male or female and how males and females are supposed to act, and how their parents feel about that

4. Measure that information against information from their own brain and feelings about how they experience themselves as boy, girl, or other and how they want to express that

5. Put together their thoughts, their feelings, and their body into a cohesive and authentic gender identity, one that can involve many, many variations but also a sense of coherence and unity

6. Find a way to fit themselves into the world that they live in.

Now comes the list for parents. As long as we live in a gendered society, to help their children accomplish their six gender tasks, parents will need to:

1. Provide the children with a consistent gender label (be it male, female, male-female [in the case of an intersexed child], or a more recently coined term, *ze,* which is inclusive of both *she* and *he,* just as *Ms.* was introduced to include both *Mrs.* and *Miss*)[29]

2. Acknowledge the children's desires and recognize when children tell them that whatever gender assigned

at birth or expectations the family or society has for gender expression don't fit

3. Allow children's identifications to unfold with parents of all genders
4. Model expressions of gender
5. Respond to the children's gender expressions
6. Stay attuned to the unfolding over time of the children's authentic gender expressions and identity
7. Represent their own values and beliefs about gender to the children, while being open to reevaluating and shifting those very values and beliefs in accordance with the children's needs and the changing times
8. Provide some open creative space where parents and children together or children on their own can fantasize and play with all different possibilities of gender
9. Over the course of time, provide the children with updated information about the "gendered" society in which they live: what to expect from it and how to meet up with it
10. Accept the children's evolving gender identity and advocate for the children's acceptance in the larger culture.

As is the case in almost every arena of family life, the parents end up with many more tasks than the children—in the case of gender, a ratio of 5:3, to be exact.

Sometimes, if you have a child who comes to you in full gender nonconformity, you may feel a need to sweep your own feelings under the rug—they're embarrassingly negative, they will be toxic to your child, they are politically incorrect, the new gender specialists won't understand and will be critical of you. So you put on a happy face and leap forward with an attitude that it's all going to be fine. But you don't feel fine inside and you keep getting stuck or tripping over tasks five through eight on your parent list—responding positively to your child, staying attuned, tweaking your own gender values, providing creative space for expression and experimentation. Denying or disavowing your uneasy feelings is not the making of a truly transformative experience. To really meet your child honestly and wholly, it will take rolling up your sleeves and facing the good, the bad, and the ugly within yourself, rather than just assuming that *you* are fine and that the totality of the bad and the ugly is "out there" in the unfriendly world. Just as our children will be strongly affected by how we respond to them, so, too, were we strongly affected by our parents who were in turn strongly affected by their parents. Recall back in the introduction—my son in his grandmother's nightgowns and her sounds of alarm. Although in the moment I stalwartly supported my son's life as a preschool drag queen, I still had to negotiate the messages from my own childhood and my training as a psychologist that boys just don't do that and, if they do, there's something indeed wrong, and who wants to be a sissy? Those are the kinds of ghosts from the nursery that will need tending if we are to truly support our children's authentic gender development.

What makes it easy, what makes it hard to embark on the process of confronting your own anxieties about your gender-creative child's presentation? What makes some parents surrender to either coercive or manipulative measures in an attempt to legislate their children's gender outcomes, whereas others do not? There are some obvious answers, which concern the open versus close-mindedness of the surrounding community, the religious or philosophical beliefs deeply embedded within us, the availability of family and personal support, and the level of anxiety we might have about our children's safety in a world unfriendly to gender-nonconforming children. But there is also a set of deeply personal psychological characteristics and ways of being with other people that will affect how each parent negotiates their ten gender tasks, particularly when he or she has a child who is not abiding by the gender norms of the parent's culture.

Your most vital tool in accomplishing the ten gender tasks is your personal success in working through and feeling comfortable in your own gender authenticity, whatever that may be. Add to that the capacity to stay steady when the going gets rough, not letting yourself get bowled over by anxiety or head for the hills when you see conflict coming your way, either from within yourself or between yourself and someone else. Then there is the capacity to de-center. That means taking the focus off yourself; seeing your child as a separate person; reflecting and organizing around his or her needs, rather than your own. Throw in a final ingredient—bonds of love to your child so stalwart that they transcend all other adversities that come your way in your relationship with your child. These characteristics are the ingredients of the ideal recipe for overcoming whatever transphobic or queasy reactions might reside within you, giving you a good chance to become a parent who will both meet your child where he or she is and stand as an advocate for your child in the outside world, where needed. Indeed, if your child announces that she is not the gender you thought she was or doesn't want to be the kind of boy you had hoped he would be, you may very well have to confront a period of loss and mourning for the child you thought you would have but didn't. Although this process may be a necessary and painful one, it should never be mistaken for unremitting transphobia. See it as an organic, evolving, and inevitable segment in the journey with your child.

Paul was the father who lamented his son Jonathan's going to the ball rather than playing ball. He spent the first four years of the boy's life angry at his wife, Francine. He blamed her for cradling their child in a blissful mother-son bubble that he believed shut him out and contributed to Jonathan's wanting to be just like Mom and nothing like a boy. Unconsciously, he had bought into Robert Stoller's hypothesis about "feminine" boys and their mothers. Jonathan, for his part, was acutely aware that his father wasn't happy with him, and imagined his daddy as a big monster who could explode at any time. In reality, Paul was actually a sensitive, gentle man, working in a female-dominated occupation, early childhood education, and maybe even fitting the profile of one of Stoller's "wimpy" fathers. He was actually pretty comfortable in his own gendered self, and in every other way able to hold himself steady with his child and accommodate to his child's needs. Paul agonized over his estranged relationship with his little boy. He also came to realize that no matter what he did to model male behavior and reach out to little Jonathan to do "guy" things, Jonathan wasn't changing; he still wanted to be a princess. Paul began to get it—either he was going to have to accept Jonathan for who he was, or remain forever alienated from his son. He hadn't even begun to imagine the harm he might do to Jonathan if he didn't come around to accepting him as he was. Paul and Francine sought professional help from a child psychiatrist. Paul had the fortitude to examine his own anxieties about having a son who liked to wear gowns. He stopped blaming Francine for the child he was coming to realize was not her creation but Jonathan's own. He is now prepared to go wherever Jonathan might lead him as his son develops. Referring back to the seven T's, Paul's experience with Jonathan has indeed been transformative, for both of them.

What happens when the basic psychological tools aren't in place, when parents may not be as secure in their own gendered selves, or experience their children as an extension of themselves, or respond to their child's differing from themselves as deep narcissistic wounds, or find themselves unable to accept the gender-nonconformity of their children? Such parents may find themselves resorting to psychological defenses to assuage their anxiety. They might even feel disdain, disgust, or despair toward the child they thought they loved but now can't because of the loud alarm signals from the side of the cognitive dissonance that says, "Those people [i.e., now my own child] are sick people, maybe even immoral." There may be a tendency to scapegoat that child.

If we think back to our adolescence, we can remember how one person might be chosen as the outcast, the one who didn't conform to the rules of the group or the norms of the day. During those times in our growing years, there was not a lot of tolerance for difference, either inside ourselves or in the people around us. We were all searching for who we were, and being different was frequently not acceptable. Finding our identity could be a nerve-racking thing, and sometimes in a frenzy to be accepted and to rid ourselves of the things that felt "yucky," we stuck the "yuck" outside ourselves, coming together as a group to find an unsuspecting nonconforming peer, throw him or her out of the group, and batter that person with intolerance.[30] That is the very dynamic that can befall parents who, along with other family members who become active participants in the rejecting group, find themselves disavowing their child in a storm of transphobic fear and anger. There is no room for nonconformity, and woefully, parental love can find itself transformed into hate in the face of their child's not fitting into the gender norms, no matter what they do to try to stuff the child into one or the other binary gender box. It often looks as if the sticking point is strong religious or moral beliefs about gender, but if you search a little deeper, you just might find that such parents have never really mastered the identity struggles of adolescence. These parents may continue to fall prey to the tendency to find a scapegoat to soothe their own anxieties, particular if there are residual anxieties about their own gender or sexual identity. That is, you might find that these parents are struggling with their own unresolved feelings about being a "real" man or a "real" woman. Those who are still stuck in adolescence may have a hard time moving on to meet the challenging demands of parenthood, which involves making room for a children who is "not-me" without condemning or casting that child out for making the parents anxious. Parents who are not up to the task might end up scapegoating their own children.

Sometimes Shannon's a she, sometimes a he. His mother is trying her best to accept Shannon. Yet she sent him to a therapeutic boarding school where the staff set a goal of teaching him how to be a real man, starting with shaving his long locks into a buzz cut. Shannon's mother has a live-in boyfriend who episodically screams at Shannon, calling him a fag and telling him he is disgusting to look at in his eye makeup, leggings, and short shorts. If the boyfriend had his way, he would throw Shannon out. Shannon is already fifteen; although the die may be somewhat cast of his family's not accepting him for his "trany" self, we can still hope that both his mom and her live-in boyfriend do some work to explore the ghosts from their own past that are causing them to deliver mixed messages and damning accusations. But right now, transphobia appears to be the driving force in this family's attitude toward their gender-transgressive son.

Let us go back to the warning that it never serves a good end to sweep uncomfortable gender-queasy feelings under the rug. What happens if you do? On the surface, it can look like family life is harmonious and your child's gender creativity is honored and accepted. From all outward appearances, you appear to have completely purged yourself of any ghosts in the nursery, any transphobic remnants, and you fully embrace your gender-creative child. Yet, upon closer examination, we discover what is known in my field as a *flight into health*, a manic flurry of actions and feelings that serve to reassure both the world and yourself that everything about you and your child is "just fine, thank you."

Maxine is a seventeen-year-old transgender teen growing up in the Midwest. She was catapulted into coming out to her mother because puberty was closing in, sealing the then Max's fate as a boy. In early childhood, Max had displayed cross-gender interests in toys and activities. His parents responded by punishing him, sometimes physically. By middle childhood, Max buried his cross-gender identity underground—until the trauma of puberty hit him and it abruptly resurfaced. Miraculously, both Max's mom and dad were suddenly on board, providing family support for the now Maxine to fully live her life as a girl, including taking her to get hormone blockers and then cross-sex hormones. They allowed their family to be featured in a local newspaper article about transgender youth, thrusting them into the position of poster family in the transgender community. Subsequent to Max's transition to Maxine, Maxine herself does not identify as transgender. She hates the term and insists she has always been a girl, that others just didn't know it. She does not like to be around transgender people—she finds them stylized and over the top in gestures, dress, and behavior. Her parents, her mother in particular, appear to have displayed no mourning whatsoever for the son they had lost and instead seemed gleeful about the daughter they now gained. Maxine's parents also do not see that Maxine has any more psychological issues to deal with—to them, Maxine has completed all the transitioning steps, and life is just fine now that she is her affirmed gender. Yet her therapist sees Maxine struggling mightily to find her bearings and acculturate to the high school world of girls. Unlike Paul and Francine, Maxine's parents are not true-blue "transcendent." Instead, it looks as if they have attempted to transport themselves, skipping over the period of anxiety, mourning, and worry, and calling forth the psychological tools of denial, distortion, and delusion to get a speedy delivery into a new life. I applaud Maxine's parents in their support of Max's journey toward Maxine and their acceptance of their child's affirmed gender identity, but I think they may have to back up and do some more work in exploring their feelings, anxieties, and conflicts that began a long time ago when they hit their boy for playing with dolls.

Jonathan's, Shannon's, and Maxine's parents are each actively engaged in the ten tasks of raising a gender-healthy child. There are both successes and failures in their attempts. For all of them, the final goal will be to affirm their child. Here's where I come in— as a mental health professional. Disquieting feelings, bolstered by the transphobia that runs through our culture and into our own bloodstream, can get in the way of meeting our gender-nonconforming children where they need to be met. Yet those same feelings that can run into the family can also be bled out of the family. Not every family will need such "blood-letting," but a sensitive and trained psychotherapist—someone who has gone through self-reflection about his or her gender steadiness and unlearned previous misinformation about gender development—can be at the ready to provide therapeutic space for parents and for their gender-creative children, so that internalized transphobia can be transcended and trauma or tragedy averted. My colleagues and I offer help to parents who are in the process of affirming their child's authentic gender self and also make room for them to safely work on deeply embedded negative attitudes and reactions that, if left untouched, stand to damage the parent-child bonds or actually damage the child. And as parents and professionals alike open up our minds and hearts to do this work, our best allies and teachers will be the children themselves.

ODE TO GRANDPARENTS

Before I close this chapter on parents, I would like to take a moment to acknowledge grandparents, who can be the second-strongest allies in the work to help gender-creative children find their authentic identity. So many times I have heard parents complain about the heat they get from their own parents for allowing their child to act in these strange ways and not just standing up to the job of teaching their children that boys need to be boys and girls need to be girls, as everybody always did in the old days. We see this played out painfully in the story of Bridget, as reported by Hanna Rosin in "A Boy's Life":

> Brandon became Bridget. They were visiting Bridget's grandmother and step-grandfather. Bridget found a pair of high heel shoes and went outside in them. His step-grandfather yelled, "Get those damned shoes off!" Bridget responded, "Make me." The step-grandfather then turned to Bridget's mother and said, "You're ruining his fucking life." This was said loud enough for Bridget to hear.[31]

No parent would ever want to expose their child to this kind of familial condemnation from their own parent or stepparent. But on the other side of the coin is the flow of e-mails and calls I get from grandparents who want my advice on how best to help their grandchildren be healthy and happy as gender non-conformers. Now, some of those grandparents are young enough to be products of the 1960s, the sexual revolution, and the then feminist challenge to traditional sex stereotyping. But others are older and/or from small-town America, and it is not their acculturation but their wisdom of age and their advantage of not being their grandchild's parents that allows them to have an outside eye on the situation. Grandparents are one generation removed from the narcissistic investment of raising a good-enough child and freed from the pressures their own grown children may face when their little son skips out of a store caressing his new sparkly tutu or their daughter takes fate in her own hands and shaves her long curly locks into a buzz cut, and they overhear comments like, "What kind of parent would let a child do that?" With such freedom, grandparents may be the first to be able to embrace their little grandchild for who he or she actually is.

The grandparent as "facilitator" could be no more eloquently and movingly portrayed than in the movie *Ma Vie en Rose*. Ludovic has described himself as a girl-boy. He dreams of growing up to be a girl and getting married to a boy. He has a media idol, a Barbie-like cartoon princess. His maternal grandmother has come to visit. She happens upon him in the living room as he, with a faraway look, dances by himself in imitation of his beloved princess as his idol dances across the TV screen. The grandmother stops in the doorway, and looks momentarily bemused. Then, with a twinkle and a smile, she joins Ludovic in his lyric "fairy" dance. Ludovic and his grandmother bond in their gender reverie. Ludovic appears utterly blissful in the glow of his grandmother's silent, playful acceptance of his gender-creative self. If a parent can either obstruct or facilitate a child's forward journey toward gender authenticity, so, too, can a grandparent, and Ludovic's grandmother is the quintessence of a positive, facilitating force.

I'm recalling a real-life story from my own clinical practice. The circumstances of my meeting seven-year-old Malcolm had nothing to do with his gender identity. His mother had lost custody of him as a result of neglect and he was now being cared for by his paternal grandmother. Mom had been working to put her life back together and now wanted her son back, and Grandma argued that Malcolm's mother was still using drugs and living an unstable life, and that Malcolm should remain with her. I was asked by the court to evaluate Malcolm's bonds with both his grandmother and his mother. The family was African American and lived in a fairly rough part of the city. Both Mom and Grandma clearly loved this little boy dearly, but each saw him in a very different light. When Malcolm was brought to his session with me by his grandmother, he shyly pulled out a miniature Barbie doll from his pocket and began playing with it at my desk. It was his favorite toy and he tried to bring it everywhere—except to his mother's house, where it was forbidden. While Grandma totally supported his Barbie play and his desire to wrap himself in boas and beads to run out to play, Mom was adamantly opposed and thought his "effeminate" behaviors would turn him into a freak. Grandma explained to me that Malcolm was like that for as long as she could remember, and she sure wasn't going to stop it "if that's the way he be." For completely separate reasons, having to do with the reliability of the grandmother and the psychological fragility of the mom at that time, I made a recommendation to the court that Malcolm remain with his grandmother and continue visits with his mother. But I was also comforted to know that he would receive the gender support he needed under his grandmother's loving care. It is just that kind of grandparental care which I do not want to overlook in discussing how parents may facilitate their child's authentic gender self.

ABOVE ALL, IT TAKES COURAGE

Even the strongest, most stalwart parent among us could crumble under the vitriolic condemnation, "You're ruining his fucking life," especially if it comes from your own mother or father. You can be as conscientious as you might like about the ten gender tasks. You can seek out mental health counseling to deal with the demons within you that may get in the way of affirming your gender-creative child. You can read all the books about how to do it and go to all the workshops sharing ideas about how it actually unfolds. But more than anything else, the trump card in your back pocket will be courage. It takes courage to let your little girl swim in bathing trunks and no top because she's on her way to being a boy. It takes courage to let your little boy not only sign up for a ballet class but show up in a tutu under the shocked and disapproving gaze of the other parents. It takes courage to survive the shock that might run through you as you confront the hard road your child may face in going against the gender grain. With that said, I'd like to finish with a story.

I was invited to give a community presentation to parents titled "What's a Boy? What's a Girl?: Raising Gender Healthy Children." In the course of the presentation, I mentioned that puberty can often be a time of crisis for transgender children, including suicidal feelings in the face of the horror that their body is betraying them by sprouting facial hair or breast buds. Suddenly, I noticed a flurry of activity on the left side of the room. Teachers from the school sponsoring the event were running to get tissues for a mother from their school, who had burst into quiet sobs. She was the mother of a daughter who was about to go into puberty. She came to the talk because she wondered if her daughter might be transgender and how she might help her. When she heard about the dire feelings and maybe even the risk to her life that might befall her daughter as the girl's body began to change, she just broke down. I put down my notes, turned off the PowerPoint, and stopped so we as a parent–teacher–mental health community could offer her a place to express her fears and receive support from the people in the room. I remembered the words of Stephanie Brill and Rachel Pepper in *The Transgender Child*: "We are aware that the world is not as safe as we all hope it could be for transgender, gender-variant, and gender-nonconforming teens."[32] No one could be more aware of that than the parent whose child is entering it. It is the courage to stand by your child that is at the crux of the parental path, the crux that will surround the children with roses rather than thorns as we help our children find their true gender self among their own thorns and roses, which is the topic to which I would now like to turn.

CHAPTER THREE

True Gender Self, False Gender Self, Gender Creativity

I always felt when I looked into the mirror
There was someone looking back from there
Somewhere beyond where I could see
Awaited the one who is the real me

—LAUREN RENEE HOTCHKISS, "THE GIRL BEYOND THE GLASS"[33]

▼

L
auren Hotchkiss is a transgender woman. The "real me" was her "girl me." It seems to be part of the human spirit to want to find who we really are and to claim that discovery as the sturdy pole that runs through our core and buffers us against the vagaries of life. Right now, it also seems universal that our gender identity is a key component of the "real me." I would like to dub that key component *the true gender self*—a person's stable internal sense of him- or herself as either male, female, or other, a sense that may or may not match the gender label assigned to that person at birth or even earlier.

Before I go on to talk about the beauty of the concept of the true gender self in providing our children with a healthy gender journey, let me say a few more things about myself. I have been trained and work as a psychoanalytic psychologist. I truly believe in the power of the unconscious, the use of psychological defenses to help us adapt to life's challenges and tame the passions or urges that pulse within us, the existence of a world of relationships that we create within us both as a result of and in preparation for our intimate ties with others, the unfolding of psychosexual and psychosocial stages, and the emergence of an internal censorship system (the superego) that serves as either our guiding light or our internal prison. I'm aware that this admission comes close to a "coming out" moment. Most people equate psychoanalysis with coercion, constriction, and pathologizing when it comes to gender-nonconforming children. A little boy is brought to the wise psychoanalyst by his distraught mother. Whenever they go to visit the mom's sister, the little boy sneaks into his cousin's bedroom, hides one of her Barbies under his shirt, and then stuffs it in his backpack, spiriting it home so he can run to his room and cradle Barbie in his arms, pretending that *he* is the high-heeled, bikini'd beauty at the beach. He sobs uncontrollably when his mother says he has to return the doll to his cousin and that it's not right to steal, and no he can't have his own Barbie because Daddy says that's for girls. He can't wait until he grows up and turns into a girl and buys his own Barbies. "Oh, my," says the wise therapist. "Something must have gone awry here. The Oedipal phase got twisted upside down and now your little boy wants to be you instead of his daddy, as it should be." "But he's always been that way, wise therapist, as long as I can remember," says the mom, now growing increasingly anxious. "Well, of course," says the wise therapist. "From the day he was born, maybe even before, you were sending him messages through the unconscious pipeline that you need him to be the little girl you wished you had had, like your sister has. From what you've told me, it seems you always hated your brother. I don't think you like your husband much, either. And you're always criticizing him for trying to steer your little boy toward sports, when that's exactly the right thing to do. But no matter, we can fix that. You, dear mother, must go into your own psychoanalysis to deal with your unresolved Oedipal conflicts and your repudiation of men. And your dear little son, poor soul, will come to me five times a week so that I can interpret his own tangled-up Oedipal complex, analyze his castration anxieties, and fortify his true masculine self. It will take time, money, and emotional sweat, as his gender dysphoria is a fairly serious disorder, but if we nip it in the bud, we should be able to get him to become the boy he was meant to be."

This, of course, is a caricature of the therapeutic enterprise, but regretfully not so far from the truth for many a psychoanalytic clinician. Yet that is not me. So how could I label myself psychoanalytic and have anything helpful or healthy to offer to gender-nonconforming children and their parents? As in most fields today, psychoanalysis is not monolithic. There are reformists, dissidents, and troublemakers among us. When it comes to reformulating our psychoanalytic understanding of gender development and gender health, I count myself as one of those challengers. Yes, I adhere to the principles of an unconscious life. I recognize the psychological defenses we develop to negotiate our inner conflicts and manage the outside world. I embrace the value of insight and have seen the value of bringing the unconscious to the light of day to untangle knots in development and build a sturdy self that can successfully traverse the demands of life. Yet I think our psychoanalytic forefathers and foremothers, products of their own times, completely missed the boat in proposing a theory of gender development for all people. This so-called universal theory does not hold up empirically and has proved to do significant harm when applied to people, both young and old, who transgress the binary norms of male/female or the defined standard of heterosexuality.

Ironic, then, that I found my gender bearings with the help of one of those very elders. I have been deeply influenced by the thinking and writing of D. W. Winnicott, a British pediatrician and psychoanalyst. During his lifetime he never specifically wrote about gender nonconformity, but he did spend much time developing and then applying three major psychological concepts: the true self, the false self, and individual creativity. Unbeknownst to him, in creating these concepts he has left a tremendous gift to the transgender and gender diverse community, because when I extend the concepts to the gender-healthy development of children, all the pieces suddenly fall into place in answer to the two key questions, "What is gender health?" and "How can we support our gender-nonconforming children?" True self, false self, individual creativity—I have taken the liberty to borrow all three concepts to create my own categories of the true gender self, the false gender self, and gender creativity. When I think about it, these concepts, along with the children themselves, have proved to be instrumental in guiding me toward opening the doors for gender-nonconforming children to feel the freedom to express who they really are rather than who the culture expects them to be. Not only that, these concepts have given me the tools to fight back against the practices of my colleagues who put all their efforts into sending children back into their assigned gender boxes.

MY BORROWED CONCEPTS: TRUE SELF, FALSE SELF, INDIVIDUAL CREATIVITY

The *true self* is the kernel of individuality and personality that is there from birth. For each of us, it is what is real and authentic inside us. Have you known a newborn baby who popped out screaming and kicking and ready for the next new adventure, tracking every move in the room? You may have been witnessing the very beginning of that child's true self. Or have you known a newborn who quietly slid out, cried a little, looked around, and then went dreamy? That would have been that second baby's quite different true self beginning to emerge.

The *false self* is the layer that we build around the true self to protect it from harm and to conform to the expectations of the environment. It may be the congenial face we put on at work that accommodates to our workplace requirements, the very face that we finally get to take off when we get home, kick up our heels, and let down our hair. Or it may be the face we put on to our parents or to our church or synagogue to protect us from their wrath if they were to know who we really are.

Individual creativity is what makes the true self get launched and stay afloat. It's about being spontaneous, being authentic, feeling real. It's not the kind of creativity you learn in preschool when you first play with finger paints. You don't even have to know how to draw a straight line to have it, because it's an impulse inside you that starts the day you're born. But you can't construct it by yourself. You need an environment—hopefully one filled with people who can match who you are and follow your lead, rather than imposing their own ideas about who they want you to be and breaking your spirit in the process. Individual creativity is simply your building a personal world for yourself—half from the inside, half from the outside—that, well, just feels like the quintessential you. Everyone has this creativity, and each person's is different, like fingerprints. It is the opposite of compliance. In compliance, you recognize that there's a world out there that you will have to fit into. In creativity, you have your own lens to look out into that world and you take liberties to define what that vision means personally to you.

Why should we care about individual creativity? In Dr. Winnicott's own words: "We find either that individuals live creatively and feel that life is worth living or else that they cannot live creatively and are doubtful about the value of living."[34] The creative impulse is alive in all of us, comes to the fore in everyday life, and can become deeply buried yet never disappears.

The people in our lives can either make or break our creative selves. In the beginning of our lives, those people will be our parents. The goal of life is to allow our true self and individuality to blossom. The danger is when the false self takes over and suffocates the true self. In the most extreme case, we might want to stop living completely rather than let the false self continue to beat the true self into submission, which in turn suffocates the creative self. Now let's see how the three concepts—true self, false self, individual creativity—translate for our children who challenge the traditional binary categories of gender, whatever creative gender identities and expressions they themselves come up with to define themselves.

CREATIVE CONCEPT #1: TRUE GENDER SELF

Alex was six when he first came to see me. He had thrown a fit because his school chorus was having its winter concert and all the boys were to wear black pants and white shirts; all the girls, black skirts and white blouses. It wasn't the first tantrum he had thrown. Why couldn't he wear a skirt like all the girls? And why couldn't he go to school with barrettes in his hair? And why couldn't pink be his favorite color ever? His parents weren't quite sure how to help him and found him impossible to deal with at home. In every one of our first sessions together, Alex would look at me slyly and announce, "I have a secret and you will never, never, never know what it is." And so it went, until one day, several weeks later, with no pressure at all from me, Alex heaved a big sigh and announced, "Oh, all right, all right. I'll tell you the secret, since you want to know so much. I wish I was a girl." In fact, this had been the secret that had never been a secret from the first day I met Alex, as he told me in every other way without putting it into words that this was his wish—in his drawings, in his puppet shows, in his pretend stories, in the clothes he chose to wear to therapy. All Alex was trying to both hide and reveal was his true gender self—a boy who felt on the cusp of boy and girl.

Like the true self, the true gender self begins as the kernel of gender identity that is there from birth, residing within us in a web of chromosomes, gonads, hormones, hormone receptors, genitalia, and secondary sex characteristics, but most important, in our brain and mind. Once we are born, the true gender self is most definitely shaped and channeled through our experiences in life, but its center always remains our own personal possession, driven from within rather than without. Even in the face of imposed proscriptions or repudiation, we strive to both establish and claim rights to it, which will include both our gender identity and our gender expression, and which, although stable, may still shift over the course of our life.

We define *gender expression* as those behaviors, actions, and choices we make to present ourselves as male, female, or some conglomeration, or even negation of gender categories altogether. What's most important to remember is that the true gender self does not necessarily match gender expression. A transgender female adult reflects back on high school: "I never dressed in women's clothes at school and usually I became alienated from my friends who did this. They caught a lot of heat. But I was different. For me, it wasn't the way I *looked or dressed*, it was the way I *felt*. It's who I *was*, it's how I identified at that particular time inside."[35] Inner feelings, not outer accoutrements, are the cornerstone of the true gender self, which sounds strikingly similar, if not identical, to *core gender identity*.

Surprisingly, it was no less than a court of law that brought to my attention the meaning of the true gender self. In the millennial year 2000 came the Massachusetts case of *Doe v. Yunits*: A transgender female student won a lawsuit against her school district, which had mandated that she dress in a "masculine" way. The court ruled that this young woman had a constitutional right to dress and express herself in accordance with her deeply rooted female identity, which reflected her "quintessence." The presiding judge truly understood the concept of the true gender self—the very essence of oneself, not based on how others label one but on who one asserts oneself to be. Would that others could learn from this sage judge.

Now let's plug the notion of the true gender self into the idea of a child's affirmed versus assigned gender. Your gender assignment is done by others. It is the label you get on your birth certificate, based on the determination of the adults looking at you and then translated into everyday understanding of who you are—first by your parents, and then by others. Your gender affirmation, on the other hand, is done by you. It is yours for the asking to affirm who you are as a boy, a girl, a boy-girl, and so forth. The prerequisite to gender affirmation is having a mind of your own. The majority of children growing up today have a fairly easy road in affirming their gender—the one assigned to them at birth is in sync with who their mind tells them they are. But for a minority of children, the road to the true gender self may be a much rockier one—because the assigned and affirmed gender are not in sync.

When I was born, I was celebrated as the first girl cousin among a slew of boys in a close-knit extended family. As I grew, there were occasional moments when I wanted to pass as a boy so I could be like my brothers and all my male cousins, but at my core I knew I was a girl, felt in sync with being a girl, and seamlessly embraced my true gender self—a female self. But now let's compare my experience with Lily's. As she recalled as an adult, at her seventh birthday party, her mother reminded her to make a wish before she blew out the candles. She blurted out her wish: "My wish is to grow a penis before my next birthday!"[36] Lily's assigned gender just was not working for her. Her wish for a penis transformed later into her affirmation as a male, and her birthday wish was merely an early expression of the true gender self—a male self. Lily's gender journey was harder than mine. She watched her relatives gawk in shock as she revealed her seven-year-old birthday wish. She had to affirm a gender identity that defied preset cultural and familial expectations, in asserting to everyone around her, "Who you think I am is not in sync with who I experience myself to be." Unlike me, she didn't just want to pass as a boy; she *was* a boy.

That was her true gender self, one that she had to wait until adulthood to live out.

As I think about Lily, I think about the debate in the field of transgender health concerning the appropriate language to use when referring to people who repudiate their assigned gender and affirm for themselves another gender identity, maybe as early as their seventh birthday, maybe as late as their fiftieth. Some argue that using the term *transgender* inappropriately privileges assigned gender over affirmed gender, implying that a child has had to cross over from their original "real" gender to a new, assumed one, rather than acknowledging that the person had an authentic gender all along that was other than the assigned gender and just needed time to affirm it. We could say that using the term *true gender self* would bypass this problem, leaving room for any combination of assigned and affirmed gender identity. Yet for the time being, I myself will also stick with *transgender*—not to privilege assigned over affirmed gender, but to acknowledge in this moment of history the group of children (and adults) who are given a gender label at birth and then must reeducate their family and others through their own true gender self-expressions that the correct label and identity is other than the original one.

Max was a boy in England struggling to let his true gender self be seen and known. He was an assigned female at birth, but at age thirteen was now sure that he was male and was living as a boy. An excerpt of a family therapy session with Max and his mother gives us a glimpse into the true gender self in motion. Max chastises his mother for referring to Max as a "she." He tells his mom she does it all the time and it hurts. He launches the same complaint against his therapist. The therapist tries to defend the elders' persistent use of the female pronoun, using an analogy: "I think it is a difficult issue to tackle because it's a bit similar to an English boy, born in England, brought up in England, about 15, 16, who emigrates to France and then goes around and says to everybody that I'm French. That I want to be considered French. While his accent will show that he is not French." Max interrupts and challenges the therapist, explaining that this fictitious English boy just wants to be French, even though he isn't, but for Max it is not a matter of wanting to be male, he *is* male. Having no working model of the true gender self, the therapist doesn't budge from the "English boy" line of thinking. "But that is one of the problems because, of course, what your body says is different from what you feel inside you are. Like in this person, what he would like to be is French and this is different from . . . his accent." Max persists, asserting that his gender identity has nothing to do with *wanting* to be a boy and it has nothing to do with his assigned gender being his "real" self. Finally, a second therapist in attendance at the session steps in and asks Max: "You are a boy?" Max's response: "Yes."[37] There is a concrete reality that Max was born with a body that was assigned to the female gender and that he lived the first years of his life as a girl, an experience that cannot be denied. But that should not be equated with his affirmed gender identity being anything but real and quintessential. If the world insists on calling him a she, then they will be negating, rather than acknowledging, his true gender self, at great expense to his well-being. Perhaps if the first therapist had access to the concept of the true gender self, Max would have been relieved of the burden of being forced to defend, both to parents and professionals, not who he wanted to be, but who he actually was.

I liken the first therapist's English boy argument to Dr. Zucker's defense of his therapeutic approach of helping young children to accept their assigned gender, when they are attempting to affirm another. He asks, if a young black child came in and wanted to be white, would you help that child transform to a white identity or would you help that child accept his or her black identity? But if we hold to the concept of the true gender self, equating the black child who wants to be white, or the English school child who wants to be French, with Max's affirmation that he is male, is like comparing apples and oranges. The apple is the transgender child who from birth onward has carried the seed and then a blossoming fruit of a true gender self—Max doesn't want to be a boy, he *is* a boy. He is not defying his body self, the one defined by his female genitalia or his gonads. He is simply explaining that another part of his body—his mind and brain, maybe also his hormones and hormone receptors—tells him otherwise. The orange is the situation of children who wish to be something they are not—an English boy wishing he were French, a black child wishing he were white. Such wishes, if fulfilled, would be based on false rather than true selves. According to my model, Max is expressing his true self, whereas these other two children are not.

Another example of the true gender self in action is the calming of the storm that often follows in the wake of a family allowing their child to transition from assigned to affirmed gender. Patrick came to see me amid a whirlwind of tantrums and destructive behaviors, tearing apart his room and everything else in sight when he was feeling distraught. He was almost five. At night, he could not settle himself down to sleep. Instead, he would sit in bed for hours wailing, "Why did God make a mistake and give me a penis? I don't want one. When's my 'bagina' going to grow? Will someone please help me?" Patrick's parents did not know what to do about Patrick's anger and despair. They had sought out a counselor, who advised them to help Patrick embrace his boyhood. It was okay for him to play with dolls and dress up, the counselor explained, as long as Patrick understood that he was always going to be a boy. Why shouldn't boys get to dress up, put on nail polish, have tea parties, and so forth? Why should it just have to be for girls? The parents tried this strategy, but Patrick wasn't appeased. "No," he cried. "I know that boys can play with dolls. My teacher read us *William's Doll*. I don't want to *play* with my American Girl doll. I want to *be* her." His angry and frustrated behaviors only escalated. I was the "second opinion" for Patrick. After several meetings, it seemed clear to me that Patrick was not a gender-fluid child; he was not a gender hybrid. He was a transgender child. His affirmed gender was clearly female. Like many other transgender children, he did not say he wished he were a girl, he asserted that he *was* a girl. His parents made a decision to allow Patrick to transition to Patti, and they enrolled Patti in kindergarten that coming fall as a little girl. The tantrums receded. No more destructive behaviors. Patti could sleep at night. She was a popular, creative, and curious kindergarten girl. Once allowed to live in accordance with her true gender self, the cloak of despair dropped and in its place bloomed a life that felt real and vibrant to her.

In 2008, Dr. Phil hosted two programs on "gender-confused" children. The misnomer of the show was itself an indication of his disbelief in the capacity of children like Patti to know, rather than be confused about, their true gender. The show became a lightning rod for impassioned responses from the public. Here's one:

> "These children are not 'confused,' they are being themselves. It's simple . . . honestly! It's the greater American cultures and people who think they have all the answers who are confused. The concept of gender is very dependent on our socialization. There are some cultures, specifically Native American cultures that not only recognize, but revere more than 2 genders. . . . I argue that being transgender, transsexual, and of other so-called divergent sexualities, are not the result of mental disorder. It's simply self!"[38]

"It's simply self" and it is we, not the children, who are confused. And as I said that same year in my interview for the NPR *All Things Considered* program on transgender children, if you listen carefully, the children will tell you who they are. Not only will the children tell you, but their little friends will have a lot easier time hearing it than do we programmed and confused adults. In speaking about the greater ease of very young children accepting that a boy can turn into a girl or a girl into a boy, Dr. Nick Gordon, a physician in San Francisco who works with transgender youth, explained it like this: "If you believe a frog can turn into a prince, then a girl can turn into a boy."[39] In their whimsical ways, small children can be less literal than we are, and they understand transition and transformation, not based on the dictations of the body apparent, but on the powers of the mind and the imagination. Regretfully, we lose this capacity as we move on to later childhood and adulthood. If only we can reclaim this capacity, we need not fear losing sight of our sanity. We stand to gain greater insight into the deep meaning of the true gender self, which, like the frog claiming his true status as prince, allows the child to go through whatever transformations it takes to get *back* to the self that the child knows him- or herself to be—the true gender self.

For a child, the true gender self is like a young plant reaching toward the sun—even in the face of perpetual clouds. Reflecting back on childhood experiences, a transgender woman shares her life as a boy: "I didn't even fit in on the playground. I didn't care for those little dominance games the boys played. Nor did I like basketball or baseball or football or running fast or being better or stronger or smarter. I just wanted out of everything. I just wanted freedom. I didn't know at the time exactly how to put it in words, but I knew that I just wanted to be me, not something that society and biology wanted to be me, not something that society and biology wanted to program me to be."[40] In the time when this woman was a child, there were few places to find sunlight to nurture the true gender self. So a youth might withdraw into a shell of loneliness and isolation. Today a child has much more access to that nurturing sunlight, through the Internet, support groups, public education, scientific research about the gender brain, and changing norms of gender. But what happens if the clouds still keep blocking the sun?

CREATIVE CONCEPT #2: THE FALSE GENDER SELF

Ma Vie en Rose is one of my all-time favorite movies. The main character, Ludovic, describes himself as a girl-boy. He is in search of his second X chromosome. He plays the bride to his boyfriend's groom. He decks himself in gowns, jewels, high heels, and makeup. When he is not distraught about being kept from being a girl-boy, he is animated and exuberant. His parents are in constant turmoil, trying to understand how to help their gender-nonconforming child. At one point, after he has acted out one too many times, they decide to bring him to a therapist. In one of the most compelling scenes in the movie (at least for me as a psychologist), the therapist is in animated conversation with the parents about "fixing" Ludovic, while in the foreground Ludovic sits listlessly on the floor, lethargically and dispassionately pushing a toy train back and forth. He sees the writing on the wall. They're going to make a real boy out of him. He'll have to go through the motions. He'll have to squelch his true gender self and replace it with a false one.

The false gender self is the face a child puts on for the world, based on what the world expects from that child and what the child then takes in as either "appropriate" or adaptive gender behavior. Any child can develop a false gender self. When I was in high school, girls weren't supposed to be good at math. But I was. I took advanced-placement calculus. I was the only girl in the class. I didn't want everyone to know, because it might be an aspersion on my "feminine" self—translated to, no one would ever ask me out on a date. So I came up with a strategy. Instead of walking into the classroom, I backed into it. Then anyone who passed by in the hall would just capture a snapshot of me walking *out* of the regular algebra class from the period before, rather than entering the next boys-only chamber of college-level math. That was me putting on a false gender self—a girl who liked ballet and French, not a math geek who would never get a date. This many years later, I'm embarrassed to admit this put-on act, but I wasn't even that conscious of it at the time—I was just trying to survive the gender constrictions of a tight-laced early 1960s suburban high school where I didn't totally fit in.

Yet my false gender self experience was so much less painful than the one that must be endured by so many children who experience a far more extreme discrepancy between the gender prescriptions and proscriptions that unfold from what is stated on their birth certificate and who they know themselves to be as a girl, a boy, a girl-boy, and so forth. The gender-nonconforming and particularly the transgender child may need to wrap a blanket over the true gender self not just to ensure getting a date someday but to ensure literally surviving in a world that might not be ready to embrace the whole of that child for who he or she is.

Mildred Brown, an expert working with transgender adults, reported that "[t]he overwhelming majority of my patients—approximately 85%—recognized their gender dysphoria by the time they started grade school. They all report that their grade school years were a torturous experience as they struggled with the constant burden of trying to live up to the expectations of their family and society about the gender role they were *supposed* to play."[41] The false gender self is the construction each of those patients attempted to contrive, either consciously or unconsciously, to live up to those expectations. It is living life as both a chameleon and a pleaser, with an aim to hide the truth of who you really are—which is a gender-creative little person. Or, to mix metaphors, it is like a turtle and its shell—the shell is the cover that protects the turtle inside, just as the false gender self is the protective covering that shields the true gender self from harm. The difference is that the turtle's shell is a part of the turtle's core essence, whereas the false self is exactly what's indicated in its wording—an artifice.

To switch metaphors one more time, let's go back to the false gender self as a blanket over the true self. We all know that blankets can either keep us warm or, in the worst of circumstances, suffocate us. The false self is Joshua dressed in prep clothes for school and hiding his nail polish and makeup in a metal box under his bed for middle-of-the-night makeovers, a box that is kept locked so his parents won't find out the truth about who he is and throw him out. If he never gets a chance to unlock and take out his metal box for all to see, his true self may die on the vine, or he may want to die himself because he'll never have a chance to be his true gender self. So the false gender self is a protective layer, but also a binding blanket that can smother.

But why should the true gender self be subject to harm? Simply because the world isn't ready for it. Here's an example of its lack of readiness, an excerpt from a request from Jan Hoffman, a reporter from *The New York Times*, for an interview with me in preparation for her article, "Can a Boy Wear a Skirt to School?": "We've noticed a few cases, recently, in which high school students got into some kind of trouble for dressing in a manner that violated gender-specific dress codes, or, because of what they wore (there are a few cross-dressers as examples), the school decided they were disruptive and had to leave."[42] Perhaps the school administrators were unaware of the ruling in the *Doe v. Yunits* case that youth have a right to wear what they want to school in accordance with their authentic gender identity, or perhaps, because of their own values, they simply chose not to abide by that ruling. I've never had any personal contact with these particular students reprimanded for their gender behavior, but let us just assume for the moment that they are simply expressing their true gender selves and discovering that it doesn't play in Peoria. They can choose to hold their own and continue to be upstarts and get sent away from school, or they can succumb to the demands of their school to conform to social expectations and come to school each day with a false gender self-adaptation, to avoid suspension or even expulsion. If they are college bound, they might just trade in their true gender self-expression for a false gender facade to maintain a clean school record. And if they are emotionally susceptible to the messages from the authorities who are supposed to be their educational and moral guides, they might also internalize that indeed there must be something bad about their true gender self if it is subject to public aspersion and punishment.

For many gender-nonconforming children, such internalized negative self-images can start way before high school, as soon as the children are old enough to have a mind able to fathom what the world around them thinks and how that world reacts to children's gender transgressions. These little minds are still very dependent on the adults who tend to them, and the children may not yet be old enough to understand that it is not they but the world that is wrong. To add insult to injury, when their peers start taunting them or telling them they are weird, the message that there is something wrong with them is pounded in even deeper. So the children may squirrel away their true gender selves and establish a self-protective coating to meet up with the world that just isn't ready yet. That would be the false gender self. Sometimes they're not even consciously aware that they're doing this. In their youthful innocence and vulnerability, if they don't cover themselves up and continue to promote their true gender self in the absence of any social supports, they might just end up hating themselves:

> "I [a gender-nonconforming child] wasn't liked for who I was. I would walk out in the street and express myself in the only way I knew how, with a very childlike innocence. Just being alive seemed to be enough to draw taunts. It was obvious that something about me was so strange that the other kids found me repulsive. I didn't know what they were seeing, but whatever it was, it was me, and they weren't liking me. And so I ended up not liking me."[43]

There is a debate among gender specialists as to whether it is best to support a child expressing his or her true gender self and put pressure on the social world to work through their trans-phobia and support that child, or to teach a child about the unfair world and ask that child to put on a false gender self in situations where the world is not ready to embrace the true one. My response is, "It depends." If we go back to the turtle and its shell, I am reminded of a Malvina Reynolds song I used to play for my kids that taught them that you can't make a turtle come out. You can't make the true gender self come out if the result would be it's getting smashed. If we are to promote gender health for all our children, the goal is not only for the true gender self to "come out," but also for the harm to be removed that required a false gender self in the first place. That means demanding that the world change to be more accepting and understanding. In the meantime, a false gender self is a necessary coating for many a gender-nonconforming child in a community that may at present be so rabidly hostile to these children's true gender selves that their very physical safety is at stake if it "comes out." The important thing in that situation is that the false gender self be a strategy in the children's conscious control in response to a world that is not yet ready, a strategy accompanied by the supportive voices of the people in the children's most intimate world who are indeed ready. The alternative is an inner negotiation, most decidedly outside conscious awareness, that soon gets linked to a deflated feeling of self-hatred for that authentic and hidden true gender self, in the absence of any supportive voices reminding the children that it is the unfair world, not them, that is at fault.

When gender-nonconforming children have to adopt false gender self strategies, it may force them to grow up faster than if they didn't have to. Like black children who must confront racism, or Jewish children who confront anti-Semitism, or children in gay and lesbian families who confront homophobia at a young age, young gender-nonconforming children may learn prematurely that the world is a gender-unfair place that may strike out against them. If they receive that hard lesson, they may find themselves trading the innocence of early childhood for vigilance and the precocious realization that life is full of real dangers, not just make-believe monsters under the bed or goblins in the closet. If all goes well, that realization comes with a sophistication and wisdom about watching your back, defending your pride, and rising above adversity. But such resilience building also comes with a foreshortening of that golden age when you were, relatively, freer to express yourself. Instead, your efforts are directed at donning a false gender self to hide the real you from the dangers that lurk, whether they take the form of the school director, the kids on the playground, or your own family.

Maddy was a four-year-old who was happy as a clam dressing in boys' clothes, making a pretend penis that she stuffed in her pants, and more times than not being mistaken for a boy. Everybody at her small, homey preschool seemed okay with this. But then she got to grade school, a large public school. Here, despite all her parents' efforts to work with the school to create an accepting environment, Maddy was mercilessly teased for being weird and different. Soon she started hiding the make-believe penis under the bed, asked for girls' clothes, and with time let her hair grow out into a "girls'" cut. But the moment she got home, she ran to get her old boy clothes, constructed a row of penises out of surgical gloves, and chose one to place in her pants. By age six, Maddy had learned self-protectively to present to the world as a little girl, albeit a feisty, athletic one, at an age when she just should have been able, like all the other kids, to continue to freely and unselfconsciously unfold her true gender self without aspersion from the outside world.

In their watchfulness, gender-nonconforming children, over the course of their childhood, may make their own personal choices to keep their true gender selves under wraps. Daniel identified with the female in him from the time he was three years old. Even earlier than that, he would put on his mother's high heels and wrap dish towels around his head to make long hair. When he was four, he told his little girlfriend to please refer to him by a girl's name. He announced to the world that he wanted to be a girl, and chose My Little Pony as his favorite toy, spending time combing the pony's long mane and tail. When he played house with his friends, he was the mother. He kept this up until the fifth grade. And then his female self faded away, or shall we say Daniel hid it away, and he learned to stop talking about wanting to be a girl.[44] Daniel may have been gender fluid, or a hybrid, or perhaps protogay, rather than a transgender child, but by age ten, wanting to pass muster in the prepubertal schoolyard dominated by strict gender-divided activities and friendships, he tamped down his gender-bending self and constructed for himself a new image of the gender-conforming boy.

The false gender self is adaptive when children have conscious control over it and call it forth as a form of expedient gender expression, as Daniel did. That doesn't mean that it doesn't come with price tags of feeling inauthentic, like a play actor, or somewhat lifeless. Yet the false gender self that is consciously called forth is far less dangerous or destructive than the one that children have no control over, either because of oppressive gender policing by the outside world or because of the children's own unconscious working of the mind that causes them to totally split off the true gender self from awareness. Under guard by the false gender self, there it sits locked inside, festering and wanting to come out, but with no way to get out. To protect against that tragedy, we have gender creativity to save the day.

CREATIVE CONCEPT #3: GENDER CREATIVITY

When Catherine was a preschooler she only wore dresses, and frilly ones at that. But then she entered kindergarten and discovered that she wasn't like all the other girls in her new upper-middle-class suburban grade school. They liked to play with dolls; she wanted to dig in the mud. They never got in trouble; she was always getting sent to the principal's office for not listening or getting too rambunctious. It seemed to her that when the boys did the same thing, the teacher just ignored it. She began to discover that she didn't at all resemble the girls in the storybooks whom she had tried to emulate. Instead, she was more of a Gender Smoothie, a blend of boy and girl. Suddenly, her dresses seemed liked going in drag. She buried them in the back of her closet and insisted that her mom take her to the boys' department and buy her boys' clothes. She asked for a really short haircut. She never said she was a boy, but she loved it when people mistook her for one. This persisted through kindergarten and first grade, and after the end of first grade she refused to go swimming at her summer camp because she would have had to go into the girls' dressing room, and that just didn't feel right. By second grade, something shifted again. Catherine began to realize that she didn't have to turn into a boy to play in the mud. She found another girl like her. She announced to her mom, "So maybe I'm a girl after all. But not the kind everyone wants me to be. And it's no fair that when girls make noise, they get sent to the office, but when boys make noise, the teacher just smiles." With that, she let go of her earlier theory that the only way to avoid so many trips to the principal's office was to become a boy. Instead, she started listening to the teacher and reining in her behavior. She let her hair grow out and even asked her babysitter to put it in a French braid. But no dresses, only boy clothes. And she still got a kick out of people mistaking her for a boy. Catherine is engaged in gender creativity, spinning her own unique gender web over time, and making alterations to her idiosyncratic true gender self. As she does this, she challenges all around her to rethink their gender categories.

Each of us uniquely crafts our gender self based on core feelings about ourselves and our chosen expressions of that self. This is called gender creativity. Gender creativity is eight-year-old Vanessa's soberly stating her presence in a pink cape, sparkly crown, and dashing gilded sword. Winnicott talked about the creative impulse of life. In the creative impulse of gender, little children are drawn to make something of gender that is not based just on the inside (the children's body, the children's thoughts and feelings), not just on the outside (the family, the culture), but a weaving together of the two, with the children in charge of the thread that spins the web. Every single child's gender creativity will be unique. Every child will depend on a supportive environment to allow his or her gender creativity to unfold. Every child will suffer if an intrusive environment grabs the thread from the child to spin its own web around that child. Every parent will have the task of figuring out the web their particular child is weaving, which may take many years and go through many changes over time. For some children it will be a straightforward, simple process. For others, it will be ever so complicated and nonlinear.

Gender creativity comes to save the day by working actively to circumvent the false gender self as well as privately keep the true gender self alive when it is not safe to let it come out. A little boy learns that he is not allowed to wear his favorite red velvet dress to school, only in the sanctity of his bedroom at home. He doesn't like that, but he learns to accept it. Except that when he's sitting as his desk at school, he daydreams. He imagines himself gliding through the classroom door in his beautiful dress. His hair is long and golden and all the girls gather around to admire him. But actually, it's not him. Now he's a she—Genevieve, what a perfect and beautiful name. He may have missed the math lesson, but in his musings he has let his gender creativity reign, asserting in fantasy the girl he knows himself to be deep inside.

In the book *True Selves,* the authors capture the essence of gender creativity for transgender children who remain locked in their assigned gender: "They dream about magically and mysteriously becoming their 'true selves.' After all, their parents read them fairy tales about frogs that turn into princes, ugly ducklings that wondrously emerge as beautiful swans, and 'good little children' who end up living happily ever after. Even though older children recognize these as fables, most transgendered kids still like to believe that transformation does lie within the realm of possibility."[45]

When seven-year-old Lily had fantasies of her penis showing up by her eighth birthday, Lily was not being delusional. She was engaging in gender creativity. When Peter hid in his closet at his father's house and, with his sister's help, put on his secret stash of girl clothes, an act strictly forbidden by his father, he was not just being defiant. He was engaging in gender creativity, nurturing the hidden true gender self through fantasy and role play. If Peter gets caught, he will definitely be punished by his father. This makes Peter frustrated and angry, and sometimes anxious that his cross-gender identifications are really not okay. But it won't make him stop going back into the closet to play and it won't make him start liking his buzz cut, khaki pants, and polo shirt any better. The (literally) closeted girl self is the product of his gender creativity in action, a compelling impulse that will do whatever it can to bring sunlight to Peter's true gender self, even in the face of his father's wrath.

Many parents of gender-nonconforming children come to me because their children are nearly impossible to handle. Little girls throw colossal tantrums when they have to wear dresses. They grab scissors and cut off their long silky hair, self-made hairdressers for their own boy haircuts. Boys steal their sisters' barrettes and butterfly clips, and have a fit when their sisters demand them back:

> Bernice remembers how frustrated she used to get every time her mother tried to dress her in frilly clothes or put ribbons in her long, curly hair. She wanted nothing to do with anything even remotely feminine. She wanted to wear jeans and T-shirts like the "other guys.". . . Whenever her mom insisted that she wear a dress, young Bernice would usually come home with it "accidentally" ripped or stained. Once Bernice even

took scissors to her long hair and hacked it off because it was so incongruous with the boy she knew she was.[46]

These oppositional behaviors are evidence of gender creativity's insistence on the recognition of the true self. Trying to suppress or forbid the gender-creative impulse is typically fruitless. If the children get caught, they might just try to be more creatively careful next time, generating the "underground" true self while reinforcing the embattlement between the imposed false gender self and the environment that demands it.

On the other hand, if we give a child free rein for his or her gender creativity, the noise level may suddenly drop and the war seems over. The boy who is finally allowed to wear his red velvet dress to school or the transgender child who is finally given the green light to reenroll the next school year as the gender that child knows herself to be may quickly dispense with the outburst or temper tantrums or outcries of protest that only persisted as long as the children were blocked from engaging with their gender creativity. That would be Patrick when permitted to become Patti.

So what about the choreography between gender creativity, the true gender self, and the false gender self? The goal for our children is to let their true gender self blossom, with all its creativity and individuality. The danger for our children is when the outside world, including us, imposes on them expectations about how their gender should look, feel, and act. It's dangerous because the children feel coerced, isolated, sad, and unreal. If we stomp on children's gender creativity, we bruise their true gender self, force it underground, and make the false gender self work double time to keep those children afloat.

When children's gender creativity is squashed, that can become burdensome enough to be labeled a childhood trauma. The children live in a constant state of fear or anxiety. Their authentic gender self is unacceptable to everybody, or at least so it seems to them. They might be punished or even physically attacked if they openly express it. Because of the unrelenting stress, they might grow depressed, or angry, or unable to think or concentrate on their schoolwork. As they get older, they might get so desperate about the trauma that won't go away that they will take desperate measures—maybe hurt themselves before anyone else hurts them first, maybe try to deactivate the chronic pain by overriding it with drugs, alcohol, or sexual escapades, or even try to stop their life because they can see no end to this duplicity in their lifetime and they can't bear it anymore.

That is the dark side to the dance between gender creativity, true gender self, and false gender self. But what about the bright side? If children feel that the people around them are really listening carefully and know how to help them let their true gender self emerge, even in the face of outside social constraints, those children will feel excited and alive. Even if they have to call forth a false gender self in certain situations, that will just be superficial rather than the bane of their existence. As they grow, they will not be exempt from realizing and negotiating an "unfair" world out there, but it will be the very strength and confidence in their true gender self that will carry them through. I'm recalling a story that Alex's parents told me about a Passover Seder, some years after he revealed his secret to me—that he wanted to be a girl. At his large public school, he was still restricted in what clothes his parents felt it was safe for him to wear. But in the sanctity of his supportive extended family, Alex was allowed full expression of his gender fluid self. He chose to wear a purple satin shirt to the family Seder. He beamed as he stood up to read the four questions, which is the part of the Seder reserved for the youngest *male* in attendance. Later, he recalled the Seder as one of the happiest moments of that year. There were no limits to Alex's gender creativity, and he only became obstreperous when he watched that creativity thrown into captivity. But when it was freed up, so was Alex.

There's just one problem with all of this. If it is true that the initial kernel of the gender true self is there from birth and that overwhelmingly our gender-nonconforming children just come to us that way, rather than being shaped by us, where really is the creativity in all this? It just *is*. Especially if your child is transgender—if she is like this in the earliest years of life and then sets you straight that you've got it wrong, the birth certificate has it wrong, and that her affirmed gender is opposite to the one on the birth certificate. She was born that way; it is not an applied construct. Does the term *gender identity creativity* suggest that your transgender child just made up her identity, rather than simply coming into the world with it? Not at all. The creative part is putting together the wardrobe of her true gender self, both literally and metaphorically. The creative part is deciding how she wants to express her gender self, and also extends to designing cloaks for the true gender self, in the form of the false gender self, if the true one is in need of protection.

GENDER IDENTITY CREATIVITY AS A REPLACEMENT FOR GENDER IDENTITY DISORDER

There is much controversy in the field of mental health as to whether gender identity disorder (GID) is a legitimate diagnosis, particularly for children. Listen to the description of the diagnosis:

> Gender Identity Disorder is a strong and persistent cross-gender identification (not merely a desire for any perceived cultural advantages of being the other sex) and persistent discomfort with a person's sex or sense of inappropriateness of the gender role of that sex, and is a disturbance that causes clinically significant distress or impairment in social, occupational, or other important areas of functioning.[47]

Doesn't this sound remarkably like the true gender self trying to come out in the face of social disapproval that leads a person to trauma, distress, and even breakdown? As long as this diagnosis remains on the books, gender-nonconforming and transgender children will be mistaken for young ones with a disease, rather than little people trying to find their true gender selves, which is really quite a healthy endeavor.

So my and others' recommendation, which at the writing of this book is seriously being considered, is to throw out the GID diagnosis, just as we once did with homosexuality. Particularly when it comes to children, this diagnosis has proved to be dangerous: It pathologizes what is normal and puts our gender-nonconforming children in harm's way if they land in the hands of the wrong mental health professional who will attempt to "cure" their so-called disease. I know that for adolescents and adults, the GID diagnosis has been a necessary label for them to obtain insurance reimbursement and medical services for hormone treatments and sex reassignment surgeries. But the *Diagnostic and Statistical Manual* has a section for V codes, which are "problems of life" categories. So why not create a V code of *gender dysphoria*: feeling unhappy or distressed with the gender you are living in? Why couldn't we change this from a "disease" to simply a "diagnosis," one that would ensure that transgender youth and adults are afforded the medical treatments needed to fortify their true gender selves?

In the meantime, I would like to make a proposal that we replace *gender identity disorder* with a radically different label— *gender identity creativity* (GIC). Its definition: Each child's (or adult's) constellation of a gender self that weaves together body, brain, mind, and environment to come up with "the gender that is me," a diagnosis based on difference rather than disease. Circling right back to my concepts lifted from D. W. Winnicott, I leave you here with an invitation to adopt GIC as our new cornerstone of gender health—an integrated and cohesive sense that being male, female, or other is based not on anatomy but on a mental discovery of one's true gender self, whose original kernel is already there at birth.

CHAPTER FOUR

The Gender-Creative Parent

When I listened to the NPR program ["Two Families Grapple with Sons' Gender Preferences"], I just cried and cried with happiness and a newfound level of awareness that these young children were being treated appropriately and in a dignified manner. I also wept for the strength of their parents and the difficult process and decisions that they have to go through. I was so young when I went through [being a transgender child], I really never noticed how difficult it must have been for my own parents. . . . [I]t was back in 1966, the world was a very different place back then, still, my parents had the grace and wisdom to move forward and do what they recognized was right. I was so fortunate on so many levels, but it was the guidance of my parents and the strength and courage they had that made my life possible. I can't begin to imagine how difficult it must have been for them, and they never showed a moment of anything other than love and hope for my life.

—LETTER FROM A TRANSGENDER WOMAN

▼

The guidance of her parents and their strength and courage. What if this woman's parents had not offered her love and hope and held to their conviction to do what was right, which was to allow their child to be who she really was, rather than make a "man" out of her? Her tears would more likely have been of sorrow and despair rather than happiness and joy, and failure rather than good fortune might have been her overriding experience in life. Luck was with her in that she was born into a family with gender-creative parents.

What is a gender-creative parent? Let's go back to the definition of gender creativity: the artistry we use to weave together a unique and authentic gender self, based on core feelings and chosen gender expressions. Now let's tweak that definition to apply it to the parents, who have the task of facilitating their child's true gender self. Recall that this self does not emerge in isolation. In the beginning, children can hope that their parents will water their budding shoots rather than bend their twig, to mirror for them what's real for the children, rather than imposing a gender portrait painted by the parents and then policed by the outside world. So how do parents do that? By being creative themselves. Rather than simply abiding by the culture's prescriptions and proscriptions and by the gender listed on their children's birth certificate, parents of gender-nonconforming children may have to jump the social tracks and navigate without them. They must find a way to allow their children's gender creativity to blossom by calling on their own flexibility, honesty, and willingness to play outside the gender boxes. They will have to figure out how to balance the blossoming of their children's true gender self with the natural parental urge, if not obligation, to keep those children as safe as possible in a potentially gender-unfriendly world. They may have to make choices that irk their own extended family, and/or violate the religious or moral practices of the family from which they came. They may have to march into schools, educate their children's pediatrician, or even argue in court for the rights of their children. When parents do any of these things, they are engaging in parental gender creativity.

As soon as anyone becomes a parent, they will hit the ground running to find that balance between allowing their children's essence to unfold while simultaneously protecting them from harm. If you are in the position of calling on your own gender creativity to foster the healthy growth of your gender-nonconforming child, this tension between authenticity and safety can become the most precarious balancing act you will ever have to perform. Actually, the most vital part of your creativity may be in finding ways to walk that tightrope.

You may need to do this balancing act in the midst of completely contradictory advice as to what will make your child a gender-healthy individual. I personally advocate that listening to children and paying attention to what they are telling you about their authentic gender self is the cornerstone of helping them grow healthy and strong. The opposite school of thinking asks you to take a guiding hand to help your child accept his or her assigned gender, and to do that as soon as possible, because if you wait until adolescence it may be "too late." Regretfully, the school of thinking that guides you toward "repair" and acceptance of assigned gender remains the dominant force in the field of mental health. Optimistically, the voice of those of us in the field who have put out a call to stop doing harm to gender-nonconforming and transgender children by trying to convert them, and instead to support the children's authentic gender selves, is gaining ground. But in the meantime, what are you to do amid this mental health controversy and debate, when you are already trying to walk a tightrope? If the experts can't even figure out the right path, how will you?

Here's how I hope I can help with that. Up until recently, and certainly even now, you might have been blamed for all you have done to create a so-called gender identity disorder in your child. I want to turn the tables on that, to address instead not only your struggles but, more important, your victories in facilitating gender identity creativity in your child, by yourself being gender creative in engaging with that child. Becoming gender creative will take your focus off those cultural prescriptions for raising a child that are based on fixed and sometimes rigid binary gender categories, and allow you to discover the best, and perhaps unique, ways to respond to and support whatever form your child's true gender self may take. You will be courageously counteracting rather than invoking and perpetuating the society's gender standards for who that child is supposed to become, ensuring not only the gender health but also the emotional and psychological health of your child.

PARENTS SPEAK

When I sat down to write this chapter, I realized that for me this was absolutely the most important and emotionally laden piece of the book, because I tried so hard to be gender creative, myself. I found myself flooded with memories—such as the time in the late 1970s when I was sitting on our front steps on a beautiful summer day as our daughter pushed our son in the front yard tree swing, our son in pink leotard, tutu, and ballet shoes. It all came alive again—my discomfort as I registered the curious, questioning, surprised, if not alarmed looks on the faces of the people strolling by. The arc of their vision swung from him to me, and their wordless expression spoke clearly: "What's this little boy doing in a tutu and why would you let him?" No doubt it is my own experiences like this that have activated me, but the parents who have come to my office or contacted me by phone over all these years are the ones who have truly inspired me and taught me what I hope to pass on in the pages of this chapter.

I have been particularly moved by the outpouring of e-mails and phone calls I have received from all over the country and beyond, after participating in the National Public Radio program "Two Families Grapple with Sons' Gender Preferences." Many people have asked me if I got any death threats after it aired, threats from people who would accuse me of being a sinner or a dangerous force tearing apart the very fabric of our "gender normal" society. *Au contraire.* I received no such threats, and instead was showered with one moving testimonial after another from parents recounting their own journeys with their gender-nonconforming or transgender children.

As a tribute to these parents, I'd like to share a few of their stories to showcase parental gender creativity in action. In preface, let me say a little more about the two sets of parents who told their stories in the NPR piece. The first was a family with whom I had worked, who allowed their child, Jona (female spelling), to transition from male to female upon entering grade school, after two years of Jonah's (male spelling) begging for dresses and insisting that he was actually a she. The parents, Pam and Joel, reported Jona's joy and excitement after being given the green light to live in her affirmed female gender. In Pam's words, "I thought she was going to hyperventilate and faint because [she] was so incredibly happy. . . . Before then, or since then, I don't think I have seen her so out-of-her-mind happy as that drive to Target that day to pick out her dress."[48] My message to Jona's parents and to the listening audience was pretty much, "If you truly listen, the children will tell you who they are. It is not for us to dictate, but instead it is for us, parents and professionals, to give them the space to establish their authentic gender." The second family's five-year-old son, Bradley, received a gash on his head when two ten-year-old boys pushed him down on the playground for playing with Barbie dolls and then called him a girl. Fearing for his physical safety and emotional well-being, the parents sought out professional advice from Dr. Ken Zucker. He instructed the parents to remove Bradley's "girl" toys, encourage him to find male playmates, and try to extinguish his identifications with female characters and female gender expressions, especially Polly Pockets and the color pink. Carol, Bradley's mom, expressed her own misgivings and Bradley's distress after they implemented those recommendations: "He was much more emotional. . . . He could be very clingy. He didn't want to go to school anymore. Just the smallest thing could, you know, send him into a major crying fit. And . . . he seemed to feel really heavy and really emotional." Stripping him of all his beloved toys seemed to be a central wound, particularly when visiting extended family where those toys were in evidence. Carol continues: "It's really hard for him. He'll disappear and close a door, and we'll find him playing with dolls and Polly Pockets and . . . the stuff that he's drawn to."[49]

Not just the NPR piece itself, with its compelling account of these two families, but the ongoing flow of responses from parents over several months, both to the radio interview and to other news articles in which I have been featured, taught me so much about the daily struggles that come with gender-restrictive parenting, as well as the trials and the joys of gender-creative parenting. From the many responses, I have chosen three e-mails that most poignantly represent parents' "seeking"—seeking, that is, to find ways to support their children to be themselves. To preserve confidentiality, I have changed identifying information, but what remains unchanged is the commitment of each one of these parents to their child and their search for parental gender creativity.

SUBJECT: *Seeking advice about my (possibly transgendered) 3-year-old*

Hello,

I am looking for advice about my three-year-old daughter, Emily, who insists she is a boy. Emily consistently states that she is a boy, and that she has a penis. When we go to the playground and someone asks her name, she tells people her name is Oliver (her best friend is a boy named Oliver), and that she is a boy. She prefers boys' clothes, especially button-down shirts and shorts. When we go to Oliver's house to play, she asks his mom if she can borrow some clothes, which she then hoards and wears repeatedly, until they absolutely must be washed. I finally broke down and bought her some more boy clothes so she could wear something clean. She also lately has been wanting to wear a tie. First she used a pretend tie, made of a scrap of fabric, and now my partner has let her wear one of his ties. She says she wants one her size. She also corrects our pronouns—when we refer to her as "she" or a possession as "hers," she says "no, he" or "say 'his' 'cause I'm a boy." I could go on and on with examples of Emily's behaviors and comments along these lines. She is very active, but her play is not exclusively stereotypically boy-style play. She does play with dolls and in her play kitchen and is very nurturing to her new baby sister (who she says is also a boy), but she also likes to pretend she is a policeman.

I recently listened to the NPR piece on transgendered children which featured you. I definitely agreed with your approach rather than that of the doctor in Toronto, although I am experiencing pressure from my family to see someone to talk her out of this phase. I'm trying to find out if this might be a phase, but I am prepared for the possibility that it might not be. I'm wondering what to do and how to approach this situation. I'm also looking for a referral to a professional who deals with these issues, or possibly to make an appointment with you. We are considering moving to another part of the country where we could afford a better lifestyle; however, if this is not a phase, I think I would want to try to remain in the more tolerant New England university town we live in.

Thank you in advance for any guidance you can provide in this matter.

Andrea

SUBJECT: *Our 6-year-old daughter tells us she is a boy*

Hi Dr. Ehrensaft,

We are a family in the Kansas City area and have a six-year-old daughter who has been telling us that she is a boy since she was 2 years and 8 months old. I read an article that compared your treatment to a Dr. Zucker in Canada and feel that you would be a perfect fit for our family to help us handle this situation in the best possible way.

I am not sure if you would be willing to work with us via phone or even Skype. We are a bit desperate to work with someone who has experience in this area and have not found a therapist in Kansas City who has extensive experience in this area. If you are not interested in working with us long distance perhaps you know of someone who would?

I would very much like to talk with you and would be willing to "pay" a fee for at least a phone conversation to learn if you can help us or at least point us in the right direction? Also, we have not been able to connect with another family in our area who is facing a similar situation. . . . [W]e feel very alone right now.

We adore our daughter—she has the most wonderful spirit. We are so unsure of every step and decision we make and could really use a professional who could give us some direction or confirmation of what we are currently doing.

Thanks so much for taking the time to read this email. . . . [H]ope to hear from you soon.

Janice

SUBJECT: *My Son Danny*

Hi Dr. Ehrensaft,

My name is Marilyn and I found you through the New York Times article "Can a Boy Wear a Skirt to School"?

My son Danny is 16 years old and is Transgender. I have known since he was born (hormones I guess can't really explain, but I knew) that he was very special.

Through the years we have mentioned things to each other, (i.e. when he was walking with a Barbie doll at 3 and people would stare or make inappropriate remarks) he would say to me, "I am different huh mommy?"

Several years ago he came to me with the realization of knowing what is going on for him and he told me he was transgender. I of course said that I knew. It was quite a moment we shared. Different than the times before.

We have spoken about being transgender since that time, but we are now in the need for some really good therapy.

My main objective for Danny is that I want him to try to find contentment in himself now . . . Daily, Danny is happy, very, very social, loving caring, moody, a good friend and son and beautiful.

We live on the east coast just outside Boston and were wondering if you know anyone who we can see. . . . Any books that we should read. We need smart guidance and advice.

Can you help us?

Thank you,

Ruth

It of course may not have passed you by that each of these e-mails is from a mom. Indeed, mothers seem to be both the messengers and mediators to the outside world and often the first in a family to grab hold of the rope and begin climbing the wall of gender challenges. But in families where there are fathers, they are often close behind, sometimes in the lead or alongside, and in each of these e-mails the parents reflect the same creative journey with their child, regardless of the gender of the parents:

1. Learning from their child, early on, that he or she is not gender normative
2. Acknowledging in positive terms that their child is special
3. Recognizing that they want to do the best by their child, which means to get, not just for their child but for themselves, the help they need to traverse this unknown and potentially precarious terrain, to allow their child to blossom rather than wilt

4. Repudiating help that presents itself as intolerance in sheep's clothing
5. Searching for a community of parents and a culture of acceptance.

And unbeknownst to each of them, there is a public out there that laments their suffering and cheers their efforts, as in the following e-mail that signifies the spirit of so many that I received:

SUBJECT: *Kudos*

Dear Dr. Ehrensaft:

I heard you on the NPR story today and I am happy that Jona's family found you. I am so disturbed about the path that the other family in the story has taken under Dr. Zucker's recommendations. It just broke my heart to listen to how the other parents had to take away "Bradley's" toys one by one. It sounds like child abuse.

If Jona's family ever needs to hear any extra comments, just tell them that a stranger on the East Coast loves them.

Sincerely,

Mary Katsumoto

Could I dare be so trite as to simply state that it truly takes a village to support our gender-creative children?

MIRRORS AND MUSES

When children are born, they have no inkling of their gender. It is you, a parent, who will receive this information. The first thing you may hold, in addition to your baby, is the baby's birth certificate, with the gender stamped in clear lettering. From that moment on, you serve as a mirror to the baby, reflecting back a vision to your baby as being either a boy or girl, based on the information you have been given and your assumptions, beliefs, and behaviors, conscious and unconscious, about what it means to be a boy or girl.

For each parent, the announcement that their baby is a boy or a girl may mean something very different, and so no two parents— not even each parent within the couple—will be exactly the same in how they mirror their children's gender back to them. Yet, some general patterns have been uncovered. Researchers have found that parents will talk in a different voice to boy babies than to girl babies. They will hold girl babies longer and more often encourage boy babies to strive to do something on their own. They dress their babies differently, depending on whether their baby was assigned "boy" or "girl" on the birth certificate. All of this goes into the gender mirror that parents hold up to their very little babies. From that mirror, in a gender-binary culture, each baby begins the lessons of gender: "Who I am—boy or girl?"— and then later, "How are people going to treat me, dress me, play with me, talk to me, based on my being and/or being seen as a boy or a girl?" Soon every baby will absorb those lessons into his or her own gender identity and gender expression.

For a vast majority of families, there is a synchronization between the gender stamped on their baby's birth certificate and the gender that baby will later affirm as his or her authentic one. But for some babies, there is a mismatch. The stamped gender on the birth certificate and the parent's use of that information to create a gender mirror seem distorted and wrong to the baby, as earlier as the last quarter of the child's first year. As time goes on, the baby can grow frustrated with these reflective distortions. Imagine Hannah: "You people have got it wrong. You keep dressing me in pink frills and they don't fit who I am." Now Billy: "You give me all these vroom-vroom trucks, but all I want is my sister's dolls." As more time goes by, these babies begin to develop language and start to protest, "I'm not a boy. I'm a girl," or "I'm a boy/girl," and so forth. Here comes a critical moment in parental gender creativity: You can put down your first mirror and create a new one that accurately reflects rather than distorts what your child is trying to tell you about his or her gender self. Alternatively, you can force your child to act like the baby in the reflection that you have already created for your child, one that may match the gender on the birth certificate and the environment and expectations you have created for that child, but which for the baby has proved to be a grotesque fun-house mirror rather than a true reflection of his or her true gender self.

It is no mean feat for a parent to switch mirrors, particularly when it comes to mirroring something as bedrock as gender is in our culture. Patrice and her parents sat in my office for a first consultation. Patrice is in her last year of high school and recently announced to her parents that she is transgender. Her parents had always easily accepted that she was a tomboy, and then later a lesbian. But to transform their basic notion that their child is not a girl but rather a boy was daunting, if not overwhelming. It took two professionals, myself and the psychiatrist to whom I had earlier referred the family, to help them imagine the new gender mirror, one that indeed more accurately portrayed their child, who now asked to be called Patrick. Patrice/Patrick, with empathy and respect, said to her/his parents about her/his transition, "Of course, I know it's hard for you. You've only known for four weeks and I've known for almost a year. I just ask that you accept that it's real." But Patrice/Patrick wasn't just asking for acceptance. S/he was asking his/her parents to hold up a different kind of mirror and show that they could reflect back their own vision of Patrick as a boy, not a girl. S/he wanted them to start calling her Patrick and asked that "he" be the pronoun the parents used.

In another family, Nathan's mom, Josephine, sat on my couch with tears streaming down her face. Nathan, age five, was about to enter kindergarten as Nattie, a female. Josephine was on board with this transition, fully accepting the assessment that

Nathan was an affirmed female who would live more comfortably in a girl's skin. She did this after recognizing that a female identity was actually the one Nathan had been insisting on for the previous two years. Again, with the help of an outsider's professional eye (that would be me), she now saw more clearly the clarion call of Nathan's recent protests as he threw himself to the ground and wailed every time he was told that it was okay to be a boy who played with dolls, "No, no, I'm a *girl* who plays with dolls."

These parents needed time to mourn—in Josephine's case, the loss of the son that she had held in her arms as a baby and thought would always be her little, then big boy; in Patrice's parents' case, the loss of the daughter they had known for more than seventeen years. They had to carve out an inner place where they could let go of the child they held in their mind, to be able to embrace the child who stood before them. Without that space to mourn, parental gender creativity might easily transform into psychic collapse or, alternatively, parental gender mania, where there is a frantic leap into action ("Let's just say yes to the transition and get this going as quickly as possible") that misuses the time that should be spent digesting the situation and discovering new ideas. Along with psychological space to mourn, both Patrice's parents and Josephine also needed to take time to switch mirrors, which of course they all had been doing for years at a gradual and perhaps unconscious level as they sensitively adjusted to their children's gender-related presentations. Yet gender expressions and gender identity are not one and the same, as Nathan reminds us all when he cried out (although not in those words), "I'm not a gender-fluid boy, I'm a girl." For you as a parent, the challenge is greater and the stretch longer when you're refocusing your vision to see your child as your son rather than your daughter, or your daughter rather than your son, or perhaps a more gender-creative individual who doesn't have an easy label, rather than simply getting used to your child being a boy with a tutu or a girl in a football uniform. In all cases, whether a child is four and protesting or turning eighteen and protesting, be that child transgender or gender nonconforming, the call from such children to the parents is the same: "Throw out the old mirror and craft a new mirror, one that will reflect back to me my true gender self."

Crafting the new mirror is where the creative muse comes into play. Let me illustrate again with two families, one who was successful and one who was not. Annie and Charles first came to see me when their son, Alex, whom you've already met as the boy with a "secret," had a meltdown because he wasn't allowed to wear a skirt and blouse to his school chorus performance. Over our time together, Alex showed us all—through his fantasy play, and his choice of activities, playmates, toys, and clothes—that he was a gender-fluid child. During that same time, I published a book on child-rearing in the United States and other Western countries, which Alex knew about. One day, he walked into his therapy session, made himself comfortable in my therapist's chair, crossed his legs just as I always do, and announced, "Nice book, but your next book should be about discrimination toward boys and girls who want to be 'gender free,'" (i.e., free to express their gender any way they want). It took me some years to get there, but here I am, Alex, hopefully honoring your request.

Over the next several years, which spanned the last decade of the twentieth century and the first years of the twenty-first, Annie and Charles came to my office as a place to explore their feelings while they faced the possibility that Alex might grow up to be gay, or perhaps was transgender. At first, they reflected that they could accept a homosexual but not a transsexual outcome for Alex—that is, one that would include surgical transformation of his body. To them, transsexuality felt like a repudiation of Alex's own body and self, and simply "just too weird." A year later, through reading, talking to others, and exploring their own internal conflicts, anxieties, and biases, Annie and Charles seemed to have mourned their losses, worked through their squeamishness, and felt they were now prepared to accept that Alex might become a transsexual, if that was truly where Alex was headed and if that is what would make him feel whole and happy.

In a session during that period, Annie reported the following experience. Alex was now eight. She was shopping for him at a secondhand store and found a pair of jeans with embroidery at the waist, 1970s style. She debated buying them for him. She knew he would love them, but she scrutinized her own motives and did not want to be in the position of reinforcing problematic cross-gender behavior—problematic, that is, in his social world outside the home, particularly at the public school he attended. I should note that Annie was going through these emotional conundrums before the era in which such organizations as Gender Spectrum offered educational programs to both teachers and students in schools across the nation to promote gender acceptance and understanding for all children and youth. How different her own thoughts might have been just a mere five or so years later, when she might have felt more bolstered by community and educational supports and an emerging paradigm shift that would more easily allow Alex to present himself to the world as he saw gender fit.

So back to the 1970s embroidered jeans, in the 1990s. Annie decided to buy them. She gave them to Alex, whose first response was an angry one: "Mom, I can't wear those to school!" Alex, like Annie, was also a product—or perhaps we could say victim—of his time, when such clothes would be a red flag for harassment or embarrassment even in a liberal town like Berkeley, and might as readily be the same red flag today if Alex were to find himself in a more conservative community with little gender tolerance. But that's not all Alex was feeling. Before Annie could answer him, gender-creative Alex's face lit up and he added, "But I could wear them on the weekends!" From that moment on, the jeans became his favorite pair of pants, carefully laid out on his bed for weekend wearing. Annie still was not sure whether she had done the right thing, but the look of delight on her son's face convinced her that she had created a deeply happy moment for him, not just because of the acquisition of his gender-fluid jeans, but because of the recognition that his mother was attuned to and mirroring his true and creative gender self.

Charles and Annie were walking the parental gender creativity tightrope on a daily basis, mindfully trying to balance Alex's exuberant self with their concerns for his social and even physical safety. They made the choice to alert their child to the parameters of social constraints on gender expressions, but not without pain and sadness. They themselves railed against the gender-constricted norms of their community and felt somewhat duplicitous hoisting those norms on their son against their own beliefs. But when they looked over the schoolyard fence they saw a vision of Alex being hassled, teased, or even physically attacked by some of his classmates, were they to give him full rein to bring his gender-creative self to school. So they made a decision: They decided to protect him from such harm by educating him about the culture and setting limits on his public actions. They explained to him that there was a time and a place to push against the "not fair" parts of the culture, but school was not yet the time or place when it came to dress code. When he grew to be a teenager, he would be old enough to make his own gender choices about such things, but until then, as his parents, they would be making the decisions for him.

I am so aware that many gender-creative parents today would take issue with Annie and Charles' restrictions, feeling that it is more important to challenge the social norms and demand that the school shift its practices to both protect and meet the needs of their child, rather than asking their child to swallow or hide his or her spontaneity and gender spirit to accommodate or succumb to the nonaccepting or pejorative gender stance of the social milieu. I am telling you Annie and Charles's story not to advocate or to critique their approach but to highlight the individual path each family takes to be gender creative with their child within a specific social context and historical time, in that case the 1990s. As with Annie and Charles, many of these paths will have potholes carved by compromises made or unease felt regarding their parental practices with their gender-nonconforming child, but nonetheless all their paths will be situated outside a main highway paved with conventional gender expectations, prescriptions, and proscriptions.

A gender-creative parent can only exist in relation to a gender-creative child. So let's look at the whole system together. Alex had come to know, given the previous coaching and limit setting from Annie and Charles, that his embroidered jeans would never touch the seat of his desk at school. For a moment, he resented his mother's decision. He yelled at her, "Why would you tease me with these jeans when you know I can't wear them?" But in the next breath he stopped yelling and a lightbulb went on: "I'll turn them into weekend jeans." He came up with his own creative solution. On Annie's side, she did some internal balancing and came to realize that if she were to outlaw Alex's gender-fluid clothing desires completely, maybe they would just go underground, frustrating him completely and turning the desires into a highly charged secret stash. Or maybe she would end up turning Alex into a smoldering bomb ready to explode as his true gender self was forced into hiding or seclusion. So *together,* Alex and his mom found their footing on the tightrope—balancing Alex's gender authenticity against social proscriptions by adopting Alex's made-up category of weekend jeans. Neither Annie nor Alex was fully happy with this solution—Annie worried about sending mixed messages to her son; Alex still longed to wear his jeans 24/7. Yet overall, Annie had facilitated Alex's positive sense of himself as a boy who liked girl things in a 1990s world that was leaving little room for such desire or behavior.

Reading this now in the second decade of the twenty-first century, as well as from within the context of your own cultural upbringing, you might come up with an alternative plan or question some of Annie's inner motives for her purchase, given the strength of her ambivalence. In the spirit of gender creativity, I invite you to ponder what you yourself might have done in this same situation, if you were one of Alex's parents *in their time and place*. Given her situation, I would say that Annie's actions qualify as an example of parental gender creativity, as we watch her reflect and weave a tapestry that combines the threads of the social pressures and proscriptions with threads not just of Alex's but of her own psychological experiences of Alex as a boy with a not-so-secret secret: that he wanted to be a girl.

The second set of parents, Margie and Ted, were not so fortunate when it came to parental gender creativity. They contacted me when their son, Jacob, was nine years old, in about the same period that Annie and Charles had been coming to see me. They worried because Jacob was always playing dress-up with his friends. Jacob kept a special box in his closet filled with his mother's old clothes. He loved to put them on and prance around. When his friends were over, they happily joined him in this play. Like Alex, Annie, and Charles, Margie, Ted, and Jacob were residents of that bastion of liberal values—Berkeley. But unlike Annie and Charles, Margie and Ted readily accepted the social prescriptions for male and female gender expressions of their time. They told me that they were worried there was something wrong with Jacob because he engaged in such "girly" play. They didn't stop him, but they wondered if they should. What if he turned out gay? As they shared their concerns, I was aware that my mind kept drifting to my own question about Ted, "Are you sure *you* might not be gay?" I think my own "gaydar" might have been up. I did not share that thought, but tucked it away for later musing and proceeded to acknowledge their worry. The more they told me about Jacob, the more I began to think that Jacob might indeed be a protogay boy, exploring the margins of gender on the way to affirming his sexual identity. With that in mind, I later revisited their question, "What if Jacob turns out gay?" and asked if maybe it would be helpful to think about the possibility, "What if he *did* turn out gay?" They did not want to go there. They just wanted to fix the situation now.

Two years later, Margie and Ted came to see me again. Jacob had entered middle school and was socially isolated and unhappy. He wouldn't sign up for sports activities. He would just retreat to his room and to his computer. He no longer played dress-up; he hardly did much of anything. Jacob sounded as if he had hit the doldrums of early adolescence. Yet I was worried about him. His isolation and lackluster air seemed more extreme than what I usually see in an average youth his age. Margie and Ted simply wanted some advice about how to pull him out of his shell. When I wondered with them what happened to the joyful Jacob they had described previously, they frankly felt relieved that the box of dress-up clothes was gone and the gender-bending Jacob had disappeared from the scene. They saw no connection between that disappearing act and the new appearance of the listless Jacob. Regarding Jacob's social isolation and misery, they chalked it up to the adjustment to the social pressures of middle school, and wanted to go no further than that.

A year later Ted and Margie called me again, this time with a crisis on their hands. Ted had discovered that Jacob had stolen Ted's password to the Internet and was visiting S&M gay porn sites filled with violence and torture. What should they do? They came in for yet another consultation. We identified three major parenting tasks before them: (1) to communicate to Jacob that sneaking behind his parents' back and stealing Internet passwords was not acceptable; (2) to begin talking more openly about sexuality and share their own values about portrayals of sex fused with violence or abuse, leaving space at the same time for Jacob's experiences; and (3) to finally address the elephant in the room and open their eyes to the evidence before them, that Jacob had moved from gender-fluid expressions to exploring his homosexual feelings. Regarding the third of the three tasks, their job would be to make links to the boy who liked to play dress-up and find a way to help Jacob establish his authentic sexual and perhaps also gender identity in a positive way, while exploring their own conflicted feelings about it. I had already gotten to know Ted and Margie over the three years of their drop-in appointments. I made a guess that expressing their disapproval of pirating pass codes and having a general conversation about sexuality would be fine with them. But I wasn't so sure about the elephant in the room: Jacob's gender expressions and emerging sexual identity. Sure enough, both Margie and Ted were on board with the first two tasks, and sensitively thought about ways they could talk to Jacob about sexuality without shaming him, as well as trying to figure out what reasonable consequences they should enforce for stealing passwords. But when it came to the third task, opening up the possibility both to themselves and with Jacob that their son might be exploring his feelings toward boys and his unfolding sexual or gender identity, neither Margie nor Ted wanted to return to work on this more challenging task. I believe they declined because they did not have a fund of parental gender creativity to draw from to do that work, and also work through the loss of the child they wished they had, in order to greet the youth before them.

With sadness, I realized that without that fund or any desire to try to build it, Ted and Margie were also squelching Jacob's own gender creativity, forcing him to hide, suppress, even steal for his own authenticity. With a foreclosure of his parents' gender creativity, Jacob was driven underground in both his fantasies and actions, with no parental oasis or anchor to help him explore and establish his own unique gender and sexual self. Margie and Ted, in turning away from creativity and allowing themselves to be governed by fear and proscription, may certainly have been quasi-successful in suppressing Jacob's *expression* of his gender uniqueness. But it is far more difficult to squelch internal desires. I never had the opportunity to follow Jacob's development any further, but I remember being left with the worry that if my speculations were accurate, Jacob may well have been left in constant turmoil between inner desire and outer behavior. Perhaps Jacob was secretly exploring his own sexual wishes or attractions through his Internet forays, or alternatively, was turning to the darker side of underground sexuality as his own authentic gender or sexual self was blocked from the light of day, all of this contributed to by his parents' failure to embrace gender creativity (either their own or his), consequently imbuing shame, rather than pride, in Jacob's true self. As a footnote, it came to my attention years later through another source that Jacob did come out as a gay man, and is now happily living with a partner in another state. That gave me relief from my worries.

GENDER ANGELS, GENDER GHOSTS

When I first started thinking about parenting the gender-creative child, I sorted out two categories: *obstructive parenting* and *facilitative parenting*. I thought of obstructive parenting as those acts that condemn or break the spirit of children's gender identity or expression. I thought of facilitative parenting as those acts that make it possible for children to express themselves in their own unique gender way while helping them to adapt to a world that will not necessarily embrace that way of being. Facilitative parenting can be equated with parental gender creativity. Obstructive parenting is synonymous with a collapse in parental gender creativity, and instead consists of behavior often governed by rigid thinking, unbendable beliefs, fear-based knee-jerk reactions, and inability to mourn the loss of the child the parents thought they had. In my own experience, no one is a purely facilitative or purely obstructive parent; we are all a combination of both. The difference between a gender-creative and non-gender-creative parent is thus a matter of degree: If facilitative parenting can prevail over obstructive parenting, our children will receive parental gender creativity; if it is the other way around, the children will live at risk of being blocked in the development of authentic gender identity and expression.

Facilitative and obstructive parenting in many ways are shaped by our own childhood, personal history, and individual psychology. Over time I have come to think of obstructive parenting as dictated by what I have dubbed our "gender ghosts," and facilitative parenting governed by the opposite, our "gender angels."

Let's start with gender ghosts. Just as racism affects all of us, so, too, do gender stereotypes and biases. None of us has grown up in a genderless culture. In fact, we have grown up in one replete with gender stereotyping and demands for gender normativity, with all the biases that go with that. Even when we believe ourselves to be free of stereotyping and both gender sensitive and gender creative, "ghosts from the nursery"[50] may surface. These gender ghosts consist of the etched memories and experiences we had as children growing up in a gender-binary world—experiences with our parents, siblings, peers, teachers, pediatricians, and so forth. For example, I have a colleague who is an excellent clinician and a staunch feminist, someone who has lived her life with tremendous outward respect for people of all sexualities, identities, and gender presentations. One evening, we were having dinner together and she confessed that she found herself wincing when the mother of a gender-fluid little boy recounted to her how she had let her son march in the Halloween parade, decked out in flowing chiffon, the mother beaming with pleasure as she described how much her little boy just loved the experience. The thought floated through my colleague's mind, "You can't do that. It's too fem." Given her commitment to gender freedom, she caught herself and chided herself for such arcane thinking, but her self-abrogation alone will not suffice to will such thoughts away. To borrow words from social analyses of racism, we are all susceptible to internalized genderism and transphobia, given the culture in which we live. Those are our gender ghosts.

I, the mother of a girlyboy, unconsciously revealed my own "gender ghosts" in my professional writing many years ago. My book *Parenting Together: Men and Women Sharing the Care of Their Children* was written in the 1980s while my son was still a child. In it, I talk about expanded gender possibilities for children when they are raised by both men and women as their primary parents. One manifestation of the children's evidenced gender fluidity was cross-dressing among the little boys. In making sense of this finding, I wrote:

> Observers and parents alike begin to grow squeamish when they see boys dress up. It is not just what the neighbors think, but also stirrings within themselves about possible perversions. . . . Homophobic worries surface, such as when one grandfather warned his daughter to forbid her son from ever wearing a dress again or he would be in danger of becoming a homosexual. . . . In fact, boys donning women's clothes in their fantasy play is not at all related to later sexual identity. . . . Cross-dressing in boys' play is merely a manifestation of their cross-sex identifications and the ease with which they express the developing feminine aspect within them in their early years.[51]

It is not that this passage was either misinformed or wrong. But rereading it many years later, I had to ask myself why I was so adamant in discounting the possibility that cross-dressing in a little boy may indeed mean that he is on his way to being gay. After all, it was true for my son. What would have been so bad about preparing parents for the possibility that if their son likes to cross-dress, he might indeed grow up someday to be gay or transgender? This is something I definitely would do now, particularly given the research to support it. Quite possibly I was defending against something I was already beginning to know but was not ready to face—that not just any little boy who pranced in frills, but my own son and his whimsical dress-ups, signified early developmental stages in his gay identity. Over two decades later, times have changed and a host of my own gender ghosts have been shooed away by new experiences—as a professional, as an advocate, but perhaps most important, as a PFLAG mother of a son who I believe has established his true and creative gender and sexual identity.

Both my professional life and personal experiences as a parent have taught me that facilitating our children's unique gender development is not simply a matter of purging ourselves of our gender ghosts. In fact, some of them may remain so deeply buried that we don't even know they are there until they pop up in some spontaneous reaction, as when my colleague had the thought, "That's too fem." The challenge of gender-creative parenting, then, is to have the stamina and patience to allow those gender ghosts to come into the light of day—to be thought about, examined, and neutralized so that they don't become obstructers of the children's healthy and authentic gender development. It is not so easy to do this on one's own, but some parents have been able to go inside themselves and explore their own feelings and reactions with an empathic but self-scrutinizing reflective eye that allows them to push away the ghosts, refocus, and create new visions of children who go against the grain. If there are two parents, each can become a sounding board for the other. Even if they don't see eye to eye and have a relatively uneven playing field when it comes to gender ghosts, their bond with each other and their mutual love for their child can hopefully supersede those differences. If the bonds and the mutual love do prevail, the two parents can discover with each other a rich and fertile ground for sharing their doubts, fears, and deeply etched negative reactions. They can then work through them as they experience their gender-creative child's pushing the limits or challenging the basic building blocks of gender provided to them in their own growing-up years. But sometimes even this will not be enough, particularly if the partner bonds aren't strong enough or the gender ghosts are taking over with their howling. Then, finding a parent support group or meeting with a knowledgeable therapist can be the best insurance policy to work through the conflicts and protect against the gender ghosts, wiping out parental gender creativity.

There is yet something else that can come to the rescue of gender-creative parenting: our gender angels. Like gender ghosts, gender angels come from the parents' own gendered past, showing up in the present to help parents facilitate rather than obstruct their child's gender authenticity. Here is my definition of *gender angels*: those gender-creative and possibly gender-transformative experiences we ourselves may have had as children or as adults, which allow us to escape the constructions, constrictions, or restrictions of a gender-binary culture. Those experiences then get internalized and woven into our present personalities and gendered selves. Some will have carried these angels from their earliest childhood; others will only first have access to them later in adulthood. Either way, the important feature of gender angels is that they be given a strong voice in our gender ministrations to our children.

I've thought quite a bit about my own gender angels. What allowed me to embrace my gender-nonconforming son and to support rather than suppress his gender-creative self, particularly in an era that was not yet quite there with public supports for gender nonconformity? Not that I was perfect at it, and not that I didn't have my own gender ghosts, but something positive seemed to prevail, so that when people gave me questioning looks as they caught sight of my tutu-donned son in the swing, I responded to them with a big smile while I contained but whispered silently to myself my more negative and protective Mother Hen response, "You want to make something of it?" Was it my active participation in the feminist movement beginning in the late 1960s that gave me this ability to hold and support my son's gender nonconformity in the face of public scrutiny? In part. Was it my own dissertation on gender social-ization in young children, completed only two years before my son's birth, that also bolstered me? In part. But the fact that I joined the women's movement and the fact that I chose to write a dissertation that uncovered the unconscious, unequal treat-ment of little boys and little girls by their preschool teachers in turn need to be traced further back to the gender angels from my childhood.

As a child, I was always a combination of fem and tomboy—baking cakes and embroidering napkins under my mother's tu-telage, batting balls and competing in the classroom arena of straight As and academic awards under my father's. At the same time, my mother was also a straight-A student and my father, the son of a tailor and a seamstress, was the one who would show me a sewing trick or trim my bangs and ponytail. So be-cause of who they were, each of my parents provided me with a model of their own gender fluidity, given the norms of the time. I remember some other things from my childhood. When I went out with my mother, I would dress to the nines in 1950s frills and love it. When I played with my older brother, whom I totally idolized, I would sometimes tuck my long ponytail under my sailor hat in the hopes that someone would mistake me for a boy. I loved it if they did. My father would remind me periodically, "You can do anything your brother does. Don't let anyone tell you a girl can't." And I took that for my mantra. As I got older, my mother gave me a somewhat opposite, or at least contradictory message: "Don't tell anyone your grades. Boys won't want to go out with you if they know." So I didn't tell, but I persisted in getting good grades. At age ten, when my little brother was born, I wanted nothing more than to pretend that I was his midget mother, with all the dreams of 1950s mother-hood that went with that fantasy. Weaving together these mul-tiple parts of my gender self was no easy feat, and did not come without pain or conflict. And it took me well into my adulthood to do it. When I think back, what I will always remember most

about my childhood gender experiences are the moments of going against the grain, and it is to these moments, along with
my parents' support, that I attribute the strong presence of my
gender angels.

If I go back even further, I might need to mention my ninety-
seven-year-old aunt, my father's older sister, who was the only
girl on the neighborhood baseball team in the early 1920s. She
tells me now that she just couldn't understand why more of
the other girls didn't join, too. So maybe some of my gender
angels are just in the genes. If I go forward in the other direction, we could say that my son's gender nonconformity is also
in part a matter of genes or in part a result of my own gender-
nonconforming experiences, as well as my husband's, transmit-
ted to him, influencing or even determining his emergence as a
gender-nonconforming little boy. All of that is possible, but suffice it to say for the moment that my own gender angels, taking
the form of "tomboy" gender fluidity, helped me meet the son
who was presented to me and hold him in a way that facilitated
his gender development "outside the box."

Let's revisit our two couples. Annie and Charles, particularly
Annie, seem rich in gender angels, and also willing to bring
their gender ghosts to the light of day so that they could do
their best to support Alex in his gender journey. Margie and
Ted seem pretty much devoid of gender angels and instead governed by their gender ghosts, old demons from their own past
that dodged examination and played havoc with the couple's
capacity for gender-creative parenting, which in turn created
tremendous road blocks in Jacob's own gender trek. Alex's and
Jacob's parents represent opposite ends of the spectrum. Alex
was fortunate that his parents were able to reflect on their inner conflicts and use their gender angels to nurture and support him. Jacob was not so fortunate, with parents whose inner
conflicts and gender ghosts drove them into hysteria and denial
even as Jacob sent out direct messages and then smoke signals
about his evolving gender and sexual identity.

Each reader of this book will have gender ghosts, as no one is exempt from absorption of the culture that bred them, but as we can see with Annie and Charles and Margie and Ted, it is the addition and superseding of gender angels, whether formed in the past or crafted in the present, which become the critical variable in differentiating facilitative from obstructive parenting and ensuring parental gender creativity. Gender angels will give you strength in walking that tightrope between keeping your child safe and allowing that child to flourish in his or her own gender authenticity. For the time being, gender-nonconforming children still are somewhat strangers in a strange land and your gender angels and facilitative parenting will be crucial in helping your son or daughter negotiate being that stranger with resilience and creativity and a consolidated, rather than a fractured, sense of self.

HALLOWEEN: WHEN GOBLINS, GHOSTS, AND ANGELS COME OUT TO PLAY

When Halloween arrives, it is not just the goblins that come out of the closet. So do children's wishes to be all that they may not be allowed to be the other 364 days a year. And so do parents' gender angels and gender ghosts. For gender-nonconforming children, it is the awaited day when they are truly "free to be me," if only their parents will allow it. The boy who dreams himself a princess can beg for the costume—just for this one occasion. The girl who really is Batman, if only everyone stopped to notice, can step out and for just one night truly be the flying male hero that resides within her. Even in communities where there is little option for gender freedom, even in families where gender ghosts have squelched gender creativity, on Halloween children can revel in the once-a-year opportunity to be who they really are or who they dream themselves to be. Ironically, the masquerade of the holiday may be the one portal to authenticity for children struggling toward their true gender selves. And for their parents, the holiday may be the test of the strength of their gender angels and their gender ghosts in action as well as a testimonial to their parental gender creativity.

Let me illustrate with the story of just one such family in the midst of this test—the Morgans. Cheryl and Cecil Morgan are an African-American couple living in a small industrial city in southern California where they are active members of their local church. Their little boy, Brandon, is almost five and attends the local kindergarten. Cheryl contacted me after Brandon threw a colossal fit when she tried to give him a haircut. He wanted it long and curly, not short and ugly. She had also been informed by Brandon's teacher that he had announced to his classmates that he would like to be a girl, and that maybe he was one. He never made such declarations at home. His favorite color was purple and his favorite activity was to draw butterflies.

Halloween was coming. Brandon begged to be a purple butterfly for Halloween. Cheryl was open to considering it, but Cecil would have none of it: "No way—the kid'll get creamed as soon as he walks out the door. I've got to be a guide for him and teach him how to be a boy. Otherwise, he's dead meat. Do you know what they'll do to a swishy black boy out there?" As Cheryl hears Cecil say this, she gets a pained look on her face. She knows he's right, yet—why shouldn't Brandon get to do what would make him happy, especially on Halloween? She accedes to Cecil's prohibition of a purple butterfly, agreeing that it would not play well in their community. But she didn't feel good about saying no to Brandon. No better than she felt when she went to the local Target to buy Brandon clothes, when she froze at the sight of child-size purple glittery pajamas with painted butterflies that she knew Brandon would die for but just weren't right for a little boy. It didn't help to call Cecil on her cell phone from the store to ask his advice. Even when he said, "Absolutely not," she still lingered in the store aisle, not able to make up her mind—"Should I, shouldn't I?"

Cheryl continued to brood about Brandon's Halloween request. She finally came up with a totally creative solution, not without some soul-searching and attempts to balance the psychological scales—her child's wishes, her neighborhood, her husband's own misgivings about swishy purple butterflies, her own confusion about Brandon's gender wishes. Their family is religious and Brandon attends Sunday school regularly. At home they have a collection of illustrated Bible stories. She found a picture of the three Wise Men. There they stared from the page with long robes, bejeweled bands around their head and waist, and long headdresses draped around their faces. Lo and behold, the headdresses looked just like the towel Brandon loved to drape around his head when he was pretending to be a girl, which he now did more regularly in his mother's presence, but not his dad's, because he knew his dad got too upset about it. Now recall that purple is Brandon's favorite color. Factor in that Cheryl is an excellent seamstress. A trip with Brandon to the fabric store, a reading of the Bible story with illustrations in full view, and voilà, Brandon was transformed into a Wise Man— draped in purple robe and headdress, with brightly colored glass jewels bedecking his forehead and waist. What neighborhood critic or bully could possibly fault a Wise Man of Bethlehem on Halloween night? And how did Brandon feel about being a Wise Man instead of a butterfly? Judging from the photo Cheryl and Cecil showed me, you never saw such a happy person and a more beatific, beaming smile than Brandon, the Purple Wise Man, looking out at the camera in his beloved costume on Halloween night. Probably as ecstatically happy as that other little boy marching in the Halloween parade in his pink frills, despite my colleague's reaction that it was "just too fem." Everyone else might have taken Brandon for the Purple Wise Man, but as far as he was concerned, he was the girl with the long hair, jewels, and purple dress, whom he always dreamed of being.

The experience of crafting Brandon's Purple Wise Man costume led Cheryl to do more extensive exploration to learn more about children like Brandon who said they wanted to be or were the other gender and, most important, to learn more about her own son. She ordered Stephanie Brill and Rachel Pepper's book *The Transgender Child*. Even before she read it, she came up with her own creative experiment with Brandon. She had received a toy catalog in the mail. She asked Brandon to go through the catalog and circle the toys he would like, to see what he would pick. She thought he might go straight for the Barbies; he didn't. Instead, he circled all the creative art kits. She was pretty sure he wouldn't go for the guns and trucks; on that, she was right. For the most part, Brandon made choices that we could label "gender neutral"—board games, art projects, and electronic learning devices. Having told Brandon that his teacher had shared with her that he was telling his friends at school that he wished he were a girl, Cheryl asked him, "So Brandon, if you were a girl, what would your name be?" Brandon looked at her in surprise: "Mom—why Brandon, of course." Cheryl then asked Brandon: "If you were a girl, what would you want to do?" Brandon again looked surprised, even a little exasperated, and informed her: "Why, the same things I do now." Cheryl was now learning from Brandon that he was perfectly happy with many aspects of himself, but yet he also wanted to be a girl. Cheryl used her parental gender creativity, led by her gender angels, which involved her own upbringing in a household that emphasized that both men and women could be simultaneously strong and gentle, to try to learn more about who her son was. And through his toy choices and his answers to her questions, he told her—"Why, Mama, I'm a gender-fluid little person. I like being Brandon and I want to get to wear purple and have long hair." We can wonder whether Brandon is keeping a lid on his more ardent desires to be more like a girl or actually a girl because he has picked up Cecil's gender ghosts that exude tones of disapproval and unease about his son's gender bending, but in the meantime Cheryl is opening a path for Brandon to begin speaking up as she listens.

Although we began talking about Halloween, I'd like to take the liberty to jump forward to Christmas in the Morgan household. Just a little over two months after Brandon reveled as the Purple Wise Man, Cheryl and Cecil began unpacking the boxes of Christmas decorations. And there in the pile on the floor was the crimson jeweled and sequined Christmas tree skirt. When Brandon discovered this exquisite cloth, he grew apoplectic with joy, grabbed it, wrapped it around his waist, tied it with a belt, and starting twirling round and round in his self-designed dress. From Purple Wise Man to Christmas Angel. Cheryl could marvel in the joy this created for Brandon, but when she looked over at Cecil, she could see the lines of worry quickly surface on his face. So she intervened with a compromise—"Brandon, you can keep dancing for ten minutes, and then we have to put the skirt around the tree and begin decorating." Cecil, governed by his own gender ghosts that whispered loud in his ear that it was his responsibility as a father to coach his son how to be a man, did not have the freedom to revel in the gender creativity of his son, although he was trying his best. Cheryl was better able to allow Brandon the space to explore his true gender self, not burdened by the same gender ghosts that are particularly weighty for African-American fathers as mentors, protectors, and strengtheners of their sons in a world that might not receive them well. Which is not to say that Cheryl was totally free of them—she still put limits on what he can wear or do outside the house; she still dreads going to the store to buy Brandon clothes, because she can't bear the conflict between buying Brandon what she knows he would love and buying Brandon what are "appropriate" boy clothes. The crux of both their parental gender creativities will come from putting their heads together to sort out their little Purple Wise Man in all his gender wisdom and growth.

NAVIGATING PARENTAL GENDER CREATIVITY WITH AN EVER-CHANGING MAP: FROM TIGHTROPE WALKING TO OFF-ROAD DRIVING

A child's gender development is always a work in progress. As much as we know about how the gender web works, much still remains a mystery. To be creative is not just to allow yourself room to roam and ruminate. Being creative is also to be able to tolerate suspending yourself in a state of not knowing. That is not easy, but this suspension is one of the most critical components of being a gender-creative parent, and one of the most challenging, given that we are taught that gender is the very first thing we will know about our child and that gender is supposed to be bedrock henceforth.

Brandon may want to be a girl this year, but next year he may shift to affirming himself as a boy who likes girl things. Alex may have a six-year-old secret that he, too, wants to be a girl, but by age fifteen he may simply want to be a sensitive man who falls in love with other men. A child who may tell us she is absolutely sure of who she is at one point may begin questioning at another point. This sounds like potential chaos, but it is actually the evolution and creativity of the spinning of the gender web over time. So how are you supposed to know if your child is transgender rather than gender experimenting rather than protogay rather than gender fluid, and so forth? There is no temperature reading or blood test that can give you a definitive answer, and with the general public and maybe your own family breathing down your neck, it is a challenge to remain in a state of not knowing and allow your child to follow his or her muse. Your best tool to accomplish this is your own gender creativity. It means dispensing with linear thinking. It means dispensing with gender boxes. It means recognizing that there is no one right way to be, but there is always one right thing to do—and that is to listen very carefully to your child and heed what he or she is trying to tell you about his or her gender self, as your child grows.

We all know that it is hard to drive without a map or a GPS system, particularly when the roads are twisty. It's even harder to do off-road driving, particularly if you don't know your destination. There will be times when you will want to dispense with parental gender creativity and cut to the chase by carving out an immediate and clear gender destination for your child. For example, you may leap too quickly toward a transgender solution, because in many ways, it's a simpler trajectory—you just trade one gender box for the other and then live within the new box with all the rules that apply to it—and no one ever need know your child started in the other box. That's a lot easier than having to deal with, "Excuse me, but isn't that a dress I see on your son?" If your child is truly transgender, there is no problem with giving him or her space to transition. But if your child is in the process of trying the other gender on for size to see how it fits, you may collapse that expanse of exploration if you jump too quickly to gender-switching.

Parental gender creativity will hopefully correct this tendency by allowing time to explore and not yet know, keeping in mind that the destination is always your child's true gender self, whatever that might be and whenever that might be clear. No doubt your creativity will be easiest to maintain if your child is consistent, clear, unbending, and declarative regarding his or her gender self, whether it be conforming or nonconforming. For example,

▸ The child with an assigned male gender who is a Batman and that's that
▸ The child with an assigned female gender who is a princess and that's that
▸ The child with an assigned male gender who is an affirmed female and a confirmed princess and that's that
▸ The child with an assigned female gender who is an affirmed male and a confirmed Batman and that's that.

No doubt, parental gender creativity can be stretched to the limits in the face of a child who is changing, fluid, and hard to decipher, such as these children I quoted on the first page of my introduction:

▶ "Can't everyone see I'm a girl? I'm a princess with a penis."
▶ "I'm a boy in the front, and a girl in the back. Kind of a Prius—a hybrid."
▶ "They got it all wrong. I *do not* want to be a girl. I'm a boy who just likes to dress up."

Parental gender creativity has one final feature not yet mentioned: processing anxiety. To be a gender-creative parent is to be able to metabolize the anxieties of

▶ ambiguity or confusion regarding what your child feels or is trying to say about his or her gender self
▶ anger or frustration that may come your way from your child for "getting it wrong" or "not making me come out the gender I want to be or know I really am" or "not letting me be who I am *everywhere*"
▶ the disquieting feelings that pop up within you when your child goes against the grain of how you were raised or how you thought gender was supposed to be
▶ crafting a path for your child to walk on in a world that may not be friendly to who he or she is.

When you factor in that final piece, parental gender creativity is exactly how the transgender woman in the opening quote of this chapter described her parents: having the grace and wisdom to move forward and do what you recognize is right.

CHAPTER FIVE

One Pill Makes You Girl, One Pill Makes You Boy

"When is it my turn to be a boy?"

—A LITTLE GIRL WHO LONGED TO BE A BOY[52]

T he little girl was very young when she first posed the above question to her mother. Then she grew a bit older. By age nine, she decided she had waited long enough and her turn had come. With her parents' support, she became a boy named Marty. Marty was quite pleased to be living as his true gender self, which was all fine and good until Marty grew a few years older and the very first signs of puberty began to surface. For a girl, the first signs of breast buds can be a moment of scary excitement—"I'm starting to become a woman." For Marty, it was a nightmare. When his second breast bud popped up, alarm bells went off. Marty ran to his mother and cried in distress, "Mommy, feel this lump. You have to do something!" It seemed worse than having cancer, this breast lump. Marty's parents were already prepared and paid heed to his calls of distress. They made an appointment with a pediatric endocrinologist and arranged for Marty to begin taking hormone blockers to put a halt to the terrible thing that was happening to his body—it was turning into a woman's. This would stop his breasts from developing and his periods from coming. Later, assuming he remains steadfast in his affirmed male identity, Marty will begin cross-sex hormones that will allow him to go through the puberty of the gender that is his—male. His voice will deepen, his face will grow hair, and his muscles will thicken. Of course, ingesting testosterone will not turn his vagina into a penis or erase his internal female organs. Later, Marty will need to make further decisions about whether he wants to undergo surgical interventions to match his body even further to his affirmed male gender. Some transgender people do that. Particularly regarding "bottom surgery," however, at this moment in history, the large majority do not.

Marty and his parents alert us to a specific challenge to both children's and parents' gender creativity that we haven't yet addressed. That would be puberty. The physical changes that accompany adolescence can truly be the day of reckoning, particularly for the child whose assigned gender is completely mismatched to his or her affirmed gender. Some transgender children move happily through middle childhood, finding creative ways through dress and presentation to affirm their authentic gender. Then puberty hits and their changing body reminds them how the doctors, God, and whoever else got it wrong in delivering them into the world with a body that does not feel right. Some children have been fully prepared for this moment, as their parents have done their research and alerted them to the choices they will have when puberty arrives. These children may have known for several years that there is medicine they can get to stop their body from turning into the gender that is not them, and then later, if they want, they can get some other pills or shots to help their body be like the gender that *is* them. Some children have kept their own gender wishes and desires tightly under wraps throughout their whole childhood, either because of their own discomfort or from fear of their parents' negative reactions if they let the secret out of the bag. For them, it is only when adolescence hits with its first signs of body changes that they may almost leap out of their skin as they cry to their parents or to some other listening party something like, "Help me. Something horrible is happening, and I have to come clean with you. I'm not a boy. I'm a girl. Do something to get this peach fuzz off my face or I'll kill myself [literally]." So for both parents and children, the day of reckoning can often boil down to an Alice in Wonderland "Eat Me" moment—one pill makes you girl, one pill makes you boy—should we or shouldn't we?

Maggie is seven years old, light-years away from when she will ever have to think about pubic hair, breast buds, and menstruation. Maggie is not just any little girl. She is the girl who introduced me to the concept of a Gender Prius. With a swing of her long blond single braid cascading down her back, marking her as a girl, she does a swivel turn and presents herself in the front with basketball shorts and athletic T-shirt, looking just like any other member of a boys' basketball team. While she loves being mistaken for a boy, she is yet not ready to say she *is* a boy. That's how she came up with the creative idea of a Prius—"I'm a hybrid: boy in the front, girl in the back." Drew is Maggie's father. He is sitting in my office with his wife in our first consultation together. Suddenly, he explodes at me in angry tears, "Don't talk to me about hormones and making my daughter take things that we don't even know what they'll do to her. I can't let that happen." No one had been talking about hormones at all, but the future possibility with all its medical risks was an ever-present torment for Drew. In his angst-filled mind, I represented the professional who was going to crystal ball the gender path Maggie would take and direct him and his wife to push toxic potions down their daughter's throat, which would cause her to grow a beard and moustache before our very eyes and maybe make her sick or even shorten her life from heart disease, strokes, or cancer. Here I was, saying that perhaps we needed to slow down and would not know for a while where their young Prius would land regarding her gender identity; there was Drew, foreseeing a future with a terrifying foregone conclusion that Maggie would be a transgender child whom the doctor would poison with drugs.

Any one of us who is a parent may have at one time or another rolled our eyes, and groaned, "Oh boy, I can't wait until she's a teenager. It'll be living hell." But Drew's reactions were a stark reminder to me that the trials and tribulations of living with an adolescent are very different from the specific angst for the parents of a transgender or gender-nonconforming child, who are aware that someday not so far in the future the biological clock of puberty will be ticking. In this modern era, with its advent of hormone blockers and cross-sex hormones (assuming you can afford them), you may face daunting parental decisions about medical interventions for your gender-nonconforming child that may permanently affect the course of that child's life. And what if you get it wrong?

Marty and Maggie—two children, two sensibilities about puberty. For Marty and his parents, access to hormone treatments in puberty was a perceived blessing, warding off a potential crisis. For Maggie, puberty and the possibility of hormone treatments wasn't even a blip on her screen, but for her dad, it was like a 3-D horror show and a potential deadly curse. It's a newfangled notion for chemical interventions to be administered in childhood to alter the course of a child's physical gender development. And when we associate drug treatments with childhood, our mind immediately goes to the stimulants, antidepressants, and mood stabilizers that have been (over)prescribed to change how children act and feel. All of these drugs are controversial at best and have gotten a bad rap among many who are wary of injecting children with potentially harmful drugs that have nasty side effects, just because we want them to be happier. Then, add to that recent discoveries that the hormone replacement therapies thought to be so beneficial to women's well-being and longevity turn out to have potentially lethal side effects. And that's at far lower doses of estrogen than a transgender female has to take. So it's no wonder that Drew would be in a tizzy. And it's to Marty's parents' credit that amid this cultural noise level, they could weigh benefits and risks and come to a decision that providing hormone blockers was a positive intervention for their transgender son.

We cannot have a full understanding of transgender and gender-nonconformity issues unless we consider not just the changes that come with puberty but also the new forms of medical treatment ushered in by the advances of neuroscience and endocrinology: gonadotrophin-releasing hormone analogues (aka hormone blockers) to suppress puberty, and cross-sex hormones (estrogen for transgender girls, testosterone for transgender boys) to help a child's body match its affirmed gender identity. These treatments, taken in tandem, suppress unwanted secondary sex characteristics and introduce wanted ones, facilitating the transition of youth under the age of eighteen from the gender assigned to them at birth to that with which they identify. Proponents like myself say that the treatment saves children from the anguish of continuing to develop into a gender with which they do not identify while giving them the opportunity to be their genuine gender selves.[53] Opponents argue that children should be helped to accept the gender assigned to them at birth, and are not yet emotionally or cognitively capable of making such life-changing decisions.[54] One medical professional has gone so far as to call such treatments "a modern form of child abuse."[55] How can you know which course of action (or nonaction) is best for your child?

LEARNING FROM THE DOCTORS: UNDERSTANDING TRANSGENDER HORMONE TREATMENTS

When I was working as an academic at the University of California, I took my then four-year-old daughter for her regular checkup with her pediatrician. With her big brown eyes, Rebecca looked up at her beloved doctor and explained, very matter-of-factly, "My mommy's a doctor, too. But she can't make anybody better." Over the years, as I moved into being a clinician, I hope to have proven my daughter wrong, but she spoke a profound truth in that I was never drawn to go to medical school to learn about bodies and medical treatments that are the requisites of being an MD. Yet when it came to working with transgender and gender-nonconforming children and youth, I felt it was essential that I bite the bullet and educate myself about pubescent bodies and the new medical interventions that only recently have been made available to children and youth to support them in the emergence of their true gender selves. I would like to stop to share with you my laywoman's learning about hormone blockers and cross-sex hormones as they apply to true gender self-development.

Marty's story alerts us to the problem for transgender youth: The experience of a puberty based on gender assigned at birth can prove to be a stressor, a nightmare, or even a trauma for a child who is already clear and firm that his or her true gender is the opposite of the one listed on the birth certificate. A small group of pediatric endocrinologists have also been aware of this problem and have educated themselves and offered services that involve prescribing gonadotrophin-releasing hormone analogues to put a temporary arrest to puberty, after careful and thorough evaluation to confirm a child's gender status.

This treatment was originally developed in the 1970s for a completely different purpose: to suspend precocious physical maturity in children who begin showing signs of puberty as young as age seven or eight. For these children, the administration of these analogues stalls their physical maturation until they have the psychological capacities to deal with an emergent adult sexual body. While using the drug, they will continue growing, but without the signs of puberty. The treatment saves these children from feeling either totally out of sync or like freaks among their very young peers; it also provides prevention against traumatic pregnancies in very little girls if they should fall prey to a male's sexual advances. The endocrinologists discovered that the treatment was fully reversible—when discontinued, a child would resume his or her natural pubertal development within six months of termination of the medication. To date, neither major side effects nor changes in fertility have been reported; similarly, no drug-related increase in birth defects in the offspring of youth who have been treated with hormone blockers has been observed.

The rising incidence of young children who were declaring themselves as transgender was met by an exciting realization among the pediatric endocrinologists. They could borrow the hormone-blocking treatment for premature puberty and apply it to children who were not going to be happy with the emerging secondary sex characteristics of a gender they did not wish to be. In addition to avoiding the trauma of experiencing an unwanted puberty with irreversible results (such as body size), providing transgender children with puberty-inhibiting drugs allows families to buy time, during which the children can grow to fuller emotional and cognitive maturity and, with the help of their parents, make more informed life decisions about their gender identity and expressions and their wish to undergo drug (and perhaps later surgical) interventions to have their body match that identity.

Puberty is marked by five stages, known as Tanner stages. Tanner stages have been developed as a way to classify the time, course, and progress of changes that occur during puberty and are based on attainment of the so-called secondary sex characteristics, which include genital development in males, breast development in females, and pubic hair development in both genders. Ideally, treatment with hormone blockers for transgender youth and youth in process of sorting out their gender identity is administered during Tanner stage 2 of puberty, when early signs of sexual maturity—breast buds in girls, testicular growth in boys—become evident. Beginning the treatment in stages 3 and beyond can be too late to achieve the intended effect—stopping the unwanted secondary sex characteristics.

The drugs work by preventing the pituitary gland from sending signals to the ovaries and testes to produce estrogen and testosterone. The drugs are administered through injections, nasal spray, or annual implant. Requirements for the treatment typically include (1) parental consent; (2) a mental health evaluation documenting psychological stability and assessing longstanding gender dysphoria and evidence of an increase of those symptoms with the onset of puberty; (3) a gathering of medical history and physical screening, including bone age and bone density scan, overall blood panel, tests for hormone levels; and (4) in some clinics, the child's living in accordance with his or her stated gender identity prior to administering puberty-inhibiting hormones. At present, the treatment is very expensive. In the United States, the cost is somewhere between five and six hundred dollars per month and is not typically covered by health insurance.[56] That means that even in families who know this treatment would be best for their children, many will not be able to afford it. To date, therefore, hormone blocker treatment is primarily an option for children whose parents have the financial means to pay for it, except in places that provide public or private subsidies for the treatment.

In addition to the prohibitive costs, the administration of hormone blockers for transgender youth is not without its side effects. The main known downside to the treatment is that the child will become a "late bloomer." Unlike the children with premature puberty for whom the drugs were originally designed, who were way-too-early bloomers without the drugs, the transgender child who begins to take hormone blockers upon reaching a natural and age-appropriate puberty may find him- or herself younger looking than his or her age peers who are developing more adult characteristics. It is not just physical appearance that will be affected. Puberty, with its hormonal changes, is associated with significant advances in cognitive de-velopment, leading, for example, to a greater capacity for ab-stract thinking. The transgender middle school– or early high school–age youth taking hormone blockers may be stalled in developing those new capacities, as the brain changes associated with the hormones of puberty will not yet have occurred.

Hormone blockers are only the first step in medical treat-ments for transgender youth. If transgender youth decide, after taking hormone blockers, that they are still clear that their af-firmed gender is the opposite of what was listed on their birth certificate, they can begin taking hormones to induce physi-cal development in line with their affirmed gender. If these youth did not take hormone blockers and missed the Tanner stage 2 window of opportunity to stop the puberty associated with their assigned gender, they can still benefit from hormone treatments that will alter their physical presentation, just as transgender adults do. In contrast to the hormone block-ers, hormone treatment is relatively inexpensive, somewhere between twenty-five and seventy-five dollars per month.[57] A transgender youth with a female assigned gender takes testos-terone, a transgender youth with a male assigned gender takes estrogen.[58] The drug treatment produces the desired second-ary sex characteristics. Both testosterone and estrogen can al-ter a youth's facial and body bone structure, muscle tone, and voice pitch. Estrogen can cause breasts to develop. Testosterone can cause facial and body hair to grow, and can also increase a youth's height, if he is still growing.

Many think teenagers cannot possibly know, while going through the expected identity crises of adolescence, whether they really want to impose permanent changes on themselves that they may later deeply regret. Surely, according to this thinking, youth should be asked to forestall hormone treat-ments until adulthood, when they have the mental wherewithal to make such monumental decisions. Let's switch to the other school of thinking, which says that if you really listen, children will be able to tell you their authentic gender—they do know. Let's apply that thinking to young adolescents who are sure of their affirmed gender but who are asked to wait until adulthood to do anything about it—no hormone blockers, no cross-sex hormones. What is the future that awaits them? If they maintain their affirmed gender identity, which will be a transgender one, they may find themselves undergoing numerous surgeries in adulthood to adjust their body to fit their affirmed gender. Transgender men will undergo mastectomies, which will leave permanent scarring. Transgender females will undergo electrolysis to remove unwanted facial and body hair and may possibly elect to have their Adam's apple surgically reduced in size. Both men and women may choose to have facial reconstructions. Even with all these interventions, they may still find themselves stigmatized by their ambiguous gender presentation in which features of both sexes are concurrently visible. They might grow frustrated, even depressed, that the world still fails to sees them as the gender they know themselves to be and instead always stares at them, questioning and wondering, "So what are you? A man or a woman?" As one endocrinologist said to me about his adult transgender female patients, "Let's face it. If they don't get to me by puberty, when I open the door to the waiting room, all I see is Tootsie in size 13 high heels, and there's not much I can do about it." All of these painful experiences and costly procedures can be avoided if we allow transgender youth to have access to both hormone blockers and cross-sex hormones before they reach Tanner stage 5, which is the full adult sexual body.

Nonetheless, if you are a parent, it may be a tremendous weight on your shoulders to authorize your child to enter upon a life-altering treatment that has irreversible effects. Some parents may be inclined to avoid taking responsibility for the monumental decision of administering cross-sex hormones to their child by envisioning starting the hormone blockers when Tanner stage 2 arrives, and then simply keeping their son or daughter on the hormone blockers until their child reaches the age of majority and will make his or her own legal decisions. Unfortunately, such a plan is contraindicated medically. After extended time on hormone blockers, a child may be at risk for osteopenia or osteoporosis, potentially irreversible, if he or she continues on the blockers. And there are also salient psychological variables that should disabuse parents of this strategy. First, such youth will not only become late bloomers, they may begin to feel like never bloomers—totally out of sync developmentally with their cohort of teen peers who have fully emerged into their post-pubescent full adult body and mind. Second, we should all be alerted that many transgender youth thwarted in their desires for medically administered hormone treatments will, in desperation, take to the streets—purchasing from friends or vendors hormones that are untested and of variable dosages and then ingesting them with no medical monitoring, sometimes with dire if not deadly results. So a too-long delay, more than a few years, in moving forward from hormone blockers to cross-sex hormones comes with high risk. Standard practice is two years, at most.

Far more than hormone blockers, cross-sex hormones, even when medically monitored, are not without side effects or untoward outcomes. A transgender female taking estrogen is at increased risk for venous thrombosis and depression. A transgender male taking testosterone is at increased risk for cardiac stress, cerebral vascular accidents (strokes), and polycystic ovarian disease.[59] Fertility is also compromised, and because of the risk factors I just mentioned, life expectancy may be foreshortened. Some medical experts have also questioned whether moving teens directly to cross-sex hormones without first shutting off the body's pituitary gland through the administration of hormone blockers could present its own set of medical risks, to date not documented. Yet, as one twenty-three-year-old transgender male explained to me, "I know I may be shaving off some years of my life by taking testosterone, but when I considered the alternative of living my entire life miserable and depressed, it was an easy choice." This young man spoke for many in declaring that living a shorter, authentic life that matches one's true gender identity is far preferable to enduring a longer, futile one as a gender mismatch. Someone we may live in such a gender-free world that one's biological body will be far less relevant in declaring one's affirmed gender—a girl with a penis will be no anomaly, a boy with a vagina will be just one of many variations of male. Some already live their life this way, and have no desire to make any changes to their body. But at this moment in history, and perhaps through eternity, some people, both adults and children, will not find peace and harmony in their life until they find a better match between the body they were born with and the gender they know themselves to be. With the advent of hormonal treatments and surgical interventions, they now, more than ever, have that possibility.

Regarding surgical interventions, however, teenagers are asked to wait. Although there are no laws dictating that surgery cannot occur until age eighteen, and in a few instances it has been done on a youth under eighteen, particularly when it comes to genital (versus "top") surgery, it is standard practice for surgery to be forestalled until the age of eighteen or after. It is believed that, at that age, transgender young adults will have the maturity to make their own decisions and they will have the readiness to deal with the physical and psychological intricacies of such surgeries. It also takes the parents off the hook regarding legal permissions and responsibilities. Recently, however, some parents of transgender youth have begun pushing for a reexamination of this eighteen-or-older policy, particularly if they have children who have been living in their affirmed gender since early childhood. These children may have already been waiting for years and years for the time that they can fully achieve their full gendered self, which would include a vagina for a transgender girl and a penis for a transgender boy. To ask these youth to keep waiting and waiting when they are ready, both in body and in mind, and when they could have better harmony in their life if surgery were performed seems an unnecessary precaution, the parents say. And I think they have a point.

And so ends my laywoman's lesson on the medical treatment available to children and youth to support their authentic gender identity, which brought me to two conclusions: (1) The use of hormone blockers for questioning and transgender children and cross-sex hormones for youth who are affirmed in their transgender identity are definitely positive and gender-creative interventions; and (2) surgery may also prove beneficial. To deny these medical treatments could cause undue suffering, both in the present and the future.

PUBERTY, PILLS, AND A CRY FOR HELP

When Sammi first came to therapy, she was Sam. Sam had just turned sixteen. A late developer, Sam looked in the mirror and noticed the beginning of peach fuzz on his face. So did his parents, who began publicly acknowledging, with pleasure, the physical signals of his budding, albeit somewhat late, transition to manhood. Rather than feeling buoyed by his parents' glowing praise, Sam was wracked with agonizing anxiety. He silently contemplated suicide. Instead, in a state of desperation, panic, and turmoil, he confided to his mother that he did not want to become a man; he was actually a girl. For years prior to this startling announcement, Sam had hid in his room painting his nails, looking in the mirror, and envisioning his girl self. He had known since preschool that he was "different" but mostly kept it from view, particularly in the context of the strict religious school he attended. His parents noticed some of the behaviors, such as his interest in dolls, and simply told him that he could not do those things because he was a boy. Sometimes they even punished him when he persisted in his "girl" play. As he grew older, he became a social isolate and began to get in trouble at school. By the time he entered high school, he was showing signs of major depression, spending most of his time in the basement doing chemistry experiments or locked in his room surfing the Web for transgender sites and joining chat room discussions with other transgender youth.

Puberty broke Sam's code of silence. Before that, he took his parents' disapproval of his cross-gender interests as a signal to hide his true gender, both because of shame and fear of parental rejection. Yet he still held on tenaciously to his authentic gender self; he simply kept it behind closed doors, living out his fantasies of his girl self in the privacy of his bedroom. But now his body was betraying him and destroying his dreams. As with Marty, the first signs of puberty were met not with delight but distress. Masculinity felt so wrong to Sam. Praying to God to turn him into a girl had clearly fallen on deaf ears—his pubescence was a clear reminder. Peach fuzz not only threw him into a panic, it was beginning to plummet him into a deep depression.

Much to Sam's surprise, his mother listened carefully rather than reacting with alarm. Like many other transgender teens, Sam felt comfortable confiding his secret to his mother, but felt awkward around his father. With Sam's okay, his mom then talked to his dad, and the two of them decided to seek professional help. They first took him to a local mental health clinic for an evaluation by a psychiatrist, a gender specialist who, after a number of visits, assessed Sam as transgender. The psychiatrist then referred Sam to a pediatric endocrinologist for consideration of hormone blockers and to a psychologist for psychotherapy, as Sam seemed in a state of acute anxiety. Sam's parents, although supportive of their son, were also reeling from the shock of his disclosure that he was actually a girl. Sam had kept it so under wraps that they hadn't noticed a thing, except that he was growing increasingly solitary and lonely. So they, too, met regularly with the psychologist as they sorted out their feelings about their son who was apparently now going to become their daughter.

The endocrinologist, as did the psychologist, concurred with the psychiatrist's assessment that Sam was transgender. The endocrinologist started Sam on Lupron, the most commonly used hormone blocker in the United States. Fortunately, the endocrinologist caught Sam while he was still in Tanner stage 2 of puberty, when in addition to peach fuzz, Sam's testes were just beginning to enlarge and redden and his pubic hairs were beginning to grow. The Lupron stanched any further male development, and then four months later, Sam began taking estrogen to allow him a female puberty.

During this time, Sam returned to school after a summer break as Sammi, a girl. After some months of taking estrogen, she began to grow small breasts. Her hips began to widen, and her voice remained just as high as it was when she had started taking the Lupron, with no cracking or deepening. The peach fuzz disappeared. Sammi stopped growing any taller, and in every respect she appeared just like all her female classmates, albeit one with relatively large hands and feet, and a bulge between her legs that she took every precaution to hide. Sammi had every intention of someday having surgery to transform her penis into a vagina, which for her would at last bring her body and her psyche together as the female she knew herself to be.

Sammi is part of a cohort of children and youth who do not evolve into a transgender identity. They rather explode into it. And typically it is the visible signs of puberty that become the flame that ignites the loaded cannon. Before that, some children, like Sammi, are consciously hiding their transgender self from the world, fearing either shunning or reprisal from the world around them. Some children hide their true selves so deeply that even they can't find it. The circumstances of their lives have been such that their false gender self becomes so thickly encrusted around their true gender self that the latter gets buried in their unconscious, maybe surfacing in dreams as their nighttime mind frees them to dream and play, but never making an appearance in the light of day. Then comes the unwanted breast buds or the pernicious peach fuzz, and all hell breaks loose in these children's psyches, when they suddenly seem literally to be running from a fire, yelling as they go. Depending on how their cry for help is heard, these children will meet up with either emotional relief or a potentially deadly blow.

PUBERTY, TRUE SELF, FALSE SELF, LIFE AND DEATH

As I said in earlier chapters, I borrowed my notions of the true gender self and the false gender self from the pediatrician and psychoanalyst D. W. Winnicott. I'm now going to borrow again to help make sense of the seriousness of a potential crisis of puberty for the transgender child. Winnicott explains that if the true self is really in danger of being destroyed and the false self takes over completely, a person might just rather die than go on living an artificial life. Those people might want to bury the true self alongside their own dead body, choosing death over a false life that forecloses any chance for being authentic. As transgender children confront the dreaded body changes of puberty that they fear will strike down any potential to grow up as their true gender self, they may find themselves trapped in the fantasy that death is the only solution. Even though it is becoming increasingly clear that our gender lies in our brain, not our groin, the external body still counts heavily for many transgender youth who urgently feel the need to match their physical appearance to their inner sense of self. For them, breasts on a boy and whiskers on a girl are a terrible mismatch, one that they can avoid only until the moment when they involuntarily go through puberty.

Prior to puberty, children can be creatively playful about their gender presentation albeit within the seriousness of their gender affirmations. They play with how they wear their hair, the clothes they choose, their toys, their activities, the way they walk and talk. When it comes to their body, except for their genitals, the rest of them is pretty much androgynous. Boys and girls are both flat-chested. Boys and girls both have hairless faces. Boys and girls both have relatively high-pitched voices. Get the right haircut and buy the right clothes, and you can be any gender you want. But the adage that "clothes make the man" (and certainly the woman as well), so vital to transgender children, suddenly collapses under the weight of puberty. When the clothes come off, and even with them on, pubescent transgender youth are suddenly confronted with new indelible and highly visible body signs of an assigned gender that may have been discarded long ago. For the children like Sammi who have kept their true gender under wraps, the body changes of puberty might shockingly remind these children that the world is closing in on a permanent body casting of a gender that just feels wrong, even if it is a perfect match to the false gender self they have been living in up to that point. If you have never had that experience, try to imagine waking up one morning to find that an elephant trunk had grown where your nose used to be, and that is going to be your face for the rest of your life. I don't know about you, but for me that would be quite a horror. That horror of a freaky body transformation is exactly what I hear from some transgender youth as they open up about the dread and panic when confronted with unwelcome facial hair, breast buds, and so forth. It is not just a bad dream. It is a full-fledged trauma.

Now let me offer you a quote from Winnicott about the true self and the false self: "Whereas a True Self feels real, the existence of a False Self results in a feeling unreal or a sense of futility."[60] He goes on to say that if that feeling gets too intense, a person might actually resort to suicide to put a stop to it. Without support from their parents to do something about the unwanted puberty, this is exactly what can happen to transgender youth. The feelings of futility and unreality, in a swirl of panic or isolation, can lead to thoughts of dying or even active suicide attempts as they helplessly watch the seemingly unstoppable approach of these dreadful changes to their body, which for them marks the death of any chance for the true gender self to emerge or sustain itself.

Dr. Norman Spack, director of the Gender Management Services (GeMS) Clinic at Children's Hospital Boston, is a proponent of the use of hormone blockers and cross-sex hormones for transgender youth, to allow them to live in their "correct" gender, the one with which they identify. He reports that by 2007, of the two hundred adolescents treated at the clinic with these drugs, not one later regretted their choice. Further, although some entered the program suicidal, not one left the program after treatment with any suicidal thoughts.[61] In support of hormone treatments for transgender youth, Dr. Spack spoke on National Public Radio: "You start to realize what's really important in this world. . . . And I don't think there's anything [more important than] . . . who you are."[62] If what Norman Spack means by "who you are" can be equated with the true gender self, then hormone blockers and cross-sex hormones are vital facilitators that allow the true gender self to trump the false gender self, permitting a child to physically grow into the gender that is the "right" one, not by society's definition but by the child's.

TIME IS OF THE ESSENCE

We've already identified the dangers of jumping in too fast to declare a child's authentic gender identity instead of taking some time and recognizing it as an evolving process. Before puberty, the child should be encouraged to explore and unfold at his or her own pace. But as puberty approaches, the parents of such a child experience a psychological urgency not dissimilar to the sudden high alert for women who want children and hear their biological clock ticking, reminding them that their era of fertility is quickly drawing to a close—they feel a palpable need to rush into action.

Typically, hormone blockers are presented as an opportunity to buy time—a few years—for the child and for the family, until a child has developed the greater maturity and self-reflection to make an informed decision about whether to begin cross-sex hormones, which will have more permanent effects than hormone blockers, as well as to consider possible surgical procedures. Less typically addressed is the opposite pressure that comes earlier—not to buy time, but to seize the time before it is too late. The pressure is on the parents, not the child: "When do I start talking to my child about hormone blockers? *Do* I bring up the subject if I'm not at all sure my child is transgender? How will I know when my child has entered Tanner stage 2?" You now know how important it is to bring up the topic with your child before it is too late. But what if your child isn't ready?

Ruby was a child who always dreamed of being a boy and loved it when people mistook her for one. She has two moms, and each of them has struggled to make sense of Ruby's true gender self. She dresses just like a boy but plays mostly with girls and a few "nice" boys. She avoids the loud, rowdy ones. She says she'd like to be a boy, "mostly, kinda." If given a choice, she'll go into the single-toilet public restroom marked MEN, but she chooses the women's restroom over the men's when there are several stalls in each. Overall, she is shy and not very talkative, particularly about feelings, so even though we say that if you stop and listen carefully, the children will tell you, with Ruby, it was hard, because she wasn't talking. Not to her moms, not to the therapist they brought her to so that she could have a room of her own to sort out her feelings. Both moms were easy with giving it some time to see where their nine-year-old daughter was headed. But then Ruby turned ten, and with her birthday came the first signs of breast buds. Both moms decided it was time to sit down with Ruby to introduce her to the idea of hormone blockers and explain to her how they would work to stop her body from continuing to develop while she sorted out who she was, a boy or a girl. To them, Ruby was still just a young child, so they hated having to raise such grown-up things with her. But they also knew that within months, their daughter would be fully in Tanner stage 2 of puberty. For that reason, they felt they had no time to spare.

Ruby's moms talked to Ruby in a very age-appropriate, sensitive manner about gender, puberty, the possibility of taking hormone blockers and how they work, and their acknowledgment of Ruby's own expressed wishes to be a boy. They also let her know that they had noticed that she was just beginning to develop breast buds. Ruby listened, but she clearly started to get fidgety. As they talked more, Ruby appeared more agitated, which was an unusual state for this very laconic child. She mumbled to her moms: "Yeah, maybe I could take that medicine." There was a moment of silence, and then before her moms could respond Ruby blurted out, "But girls are nicer than boys," and ran to her room and shut the door. End of conversation.

A week later she came to one of her moms, upset and worried. She did not want to grow up. As a matter of fact, she hated the idea of growing up. Indeed, Ruby was caught in a Peter Pan moment where all she wished for was to stop the clock and stay a ten-year-old kid forever. But more important, the idea of taking medicine, or worse, getting shots that would stop her body from the changes of puberty, totally freaked her out. She needed her moms to back off and not talk about it anymore, at least for now. They obliged. They also had new information to work with—this typically taciturn child, suddenly blanching at the thought that someone would change her body to be a boy's, expressed in her clarion call, "But girls are nicer." Perhaps Ruby's flight from the conversation was not because she wasn't ready, but because she was a girl, period. Or maybe Ruby was a gender hybrid or gender fluid, unwilling to settle definitively into a single gender. Did Ruby's moms do her harm by bringing up hormone blockers—disrupting her childhood with sobering news about impending adulthood? Perhaps, but their only other choice was to let the time go by without giving Ruby a chance to weigh in on taking hormone blockers if she wanted them and without giving her mothers a chance to get a reading of where she was at on the issue. If the alternative was to wait and bring it up later with greater urgency, as Ruby moved more definitively into Tanner stage 2 and almost beyond, the moms would take the risk of suddenly dropping a bombshell with no time to retreat to a bomb shelter to think it over for a while. It was the breast buds that catapulted the moms into action, not impulsively but with an extensive consultation with a gender specialist first. I would say that although the conversation may have incurred some momentary stress for Ruby, it might also have given their daughter the opportunity to finally express her feelings about her own gender identity.

Some parents, knowing the clock is ticking, consider avoiding the disruption that Ruby experienced by administering the hormone blockers without the child's knowledge. One mother is caught in a custody dispute with her ex-husband. She believes their son may very well be transgender. She has sought out support groups and therapeutic consultations to help her sort this out and ensure that she can make room for her child to express his true gender self. The father thinks she's crazy and has even threatened to take her to court if she persists in indulging their son's "gender-inappropriate" behaviors, which he believes are both induced and encouraged by the mother. This dispute has been going on for a few years. Now, lo and behold, their son at age nine is beginning to show the very first signs of puberty. That's really early for a boy. Her strategy: To buy time by giving her son the hormone blockers but not to tell him what they are for. I do not know a pediatric endocrinologist who would go along with this plan, as it would be without the child's acknowledgment of the treatment and, more important, without the informed signed consent of both legal parents. But it is this mother's fantasy itself that concerns me here, reflecting the ethical compromises a parent may make and the flights of imagination a parent might have to resort to in order to afford his or her child the full advantage of the new medical interventions available to transgender and gender-nonconforming or -questioning children—and the knowledge of the potential negative lifelong consequences if the child is denied that opportunity.

Time plays its hand in one other important way. Let's turn to adult transsexuals for a moment. In the standards of care established by Harry Benjamin for adult transsexuals, a person is asked to live a certain amount of time in his or her affirmed gender before either cross-sex hormone treatment or surgery, as a real-life test of the authenticity of the person's expressed gender. This is a cautious and wise approach, to enable an individual to make informed decisions that may have irreversible outcomes. There are three caveats, however, when the real-life experience standards are applied to youth under the age of eighteen. First, the standard is not applicable to hormone blockers, which do not have a permanent effect. Second, the requisites of real-life experience should not apply to a youth such as Sam, who never had any real-life experience as a female but at age fifteen suddenly showed physical signs of puberty. That was a wake-up call, cracking open the shell around his true gender self and putting him urgently up against the clock if he was to benefit from hormone blockers. Third, youth operate under different time dimensions than do adults. Think how often we ask teenagers why they are in such a rush—to drive, to stay up late, to get to the mall, and so forth. It is not just that they are impulsive and impatient. It is their brain. The wheels of development are moving at a far faster pace than those of young or older adults. Three months or a year in the life of adolescents feels to them like an eternity. Granted, they are in the throes of identity formation that looks very much like a moving target. The monastic intellectual at age fourteen may convert to the dope-smoking spoken-word poet at age fourteen and a half, who will then convert to the class basketball star at age fifteen, and so forth, until he finally lands at the consolidated identity he will know himself to be, perhaps by the time he leaves high school. But on the other side, youth also have a quick processing speed when it it comes to working through their experiences. This can be particularly true around gender identity. For a transgender or questioning teen, an "ah-ha" experience can be followed by a quick entrance and stable immersion in the gender the youth now knows him- or herself to be. So I am merely bringing up a cautionary note that although it is good to leave enough time for exploration and reflection before taking action, unnecessary angst can be foisted on young people if they are asked to keep waiting and waiting before being allowed to move forward with cross-sex hormones. For example, a requisite twelve-month real-life experience in their affirmed gender before being administered hormones might feel like more than a lifetime, and an agonizing one at that. With that said, as more and more teens are fully coming out as transgender and requesting medical services, the standards, particularly regarding the time required for the real-life experience living in their affirmed gender, may need to be adjusted accordingly to take into account the speed at which adolescents develop. Think of them as the express train, while their older cohort is the local train. They all have the same final destination—establishment of their affirmed gender; youth may just get there faster.

TOPLESS

Transgender boys and gender-fluid children run into a particular problem when they approach puberty. Marty ran to his mother screaming, "Do something about these things growing on my chest!" Children who are assigned females but transition to a male identity early in childhood have no problem wearing the same bathing trunks as all their male friends. With ease, they can present themselves to the world as who they know themselves to be—little boys who get to go topless. And little girls who are gender fluid and like to express themselves with a male presentation, have the same prerogative to scamper topless whenever they feel like it until they start to approach Tanner stage 2 of puberty, when breast buds begin to show. In a culture that prohibits public exposure of female breasts, they are suddenly supposed to cover up when they used to be able to run free.

The first people to know this are their parents. Jenna is ten years old and has two loving parents who are both perplexed about her gender presentation and identity. She only buys clothes in the boys' department, expresses a wish to be a boy, has always worn boys' bathing trunks, and sleeps with only pajama bottoms every night, even when it is cold outside. She thinks she might want to transition to be a boy, but she's not sure, and she wishes everyone would back off asking her about it and just call her by her last name, a genderless solution. And she wants to go topless to the local swimming pool, in her boys' swim trunks, just like she always used to when she was littler.

Like Ruby, Jenna is just beginning to develop breast buds. Recently, her parents have been less comfortable letting her go topless at the swimming pool, but they fudged it by insisting that she wear rash shirts with her swim trunks, using the excuse of protecting her very fair skin from the sun. The game is now up—the real reason they can't let her go topless is that very soon she will no longer be able to pass as a boy in various states of undress—specifically, going topless.

That's not the only conundrum that is up for Jenna's parents. Her mom and dad were faced with the same dilemma as Ruby's moms. Very soon, Jenna will be fully entering Tanner stage 2. Should Jenna take hormone blockers as she sorts out her gender identity—which could certainly be transgender, but also could be gender fluid or "butch lesbian"? Should they begin talking to Jenna directly about hormone blockers, given that the decision may be before them within the next year? How much leeway does Jenna need to sort out her own thoughts and feelings about the blockers before a decision must be made?

To my mind, which I shared with Jenna's parents, there were two answers: no and yes. No, Jenna can no longer go topless, given the culture in which we live. Yes, it is time to talk to Jenna about hormone blockers and how they work, including that they put a halt to developing breasts. The danger, of course, is that Jenna will latch on to the solution of hormone blockers to solve her more immediate problem—that is, if those hormone blockers will release her to go topless at age ten, she'll be all for it. Yet I still see the psychological necessity of preparing Jenna for the realities of a world in which her chosen gender presentations are no longer as free as they once were, once hormones start pumping in her body. The unstoppable changes that accompany puberty out-weigh the risks of flooding her with too much information about gender and medical interventions. Explaining to her the option of hormone blockers offers her the opportunity to begin mapping out possible paths to her authentic gender. If that gender should be male, Jenna would still have a little time to ask questions and make an informed choice about embracing a "topless puberty."

In the same week that Jenna's parents consulted a thera-pist with their questions about toplessness and about blockers, Jenna was scheduled to attend her first gender-divided work-shop at school on "becoming a woman." As I write this, I'm recalling my own grade school sex education program, provided by my Girl Scout troop, in which we watched a film produced by Kotex in collaboration with Walt Disney. The film's narra-tor warned us that once you got your period you should never take cold showers or you would get terrible cramps, highlighted for us with a cartoon image of a Tinkerbell-looking naked girl shivering under a shower spigot as ice cubes poured down on her. I can only hope Jenna's class will be more enlightening than this. Ideally, both parents will decide that the aftermath of her workshop would be a perfect opportunity to sit down and talk to her. First, they would talk about why people born girls in our culture can no longer go topless in public once they start to grow breasts. They would give her some time to digest this and then add, maybe in the same discussion or at another time, how puberty is a time when children who do not want to enter the puberty that accompanies their assigned gender can take some medication to stop that from happening and give them some time to figure out if, later, they want to take some other medications that will help them have a body more like that of their affirmed gender. For Jenna, this would mean that her breast buds would stop growing as long as she took the "stopping" medication, and she wouldn't menstruate.

Jenna is just a little girl, but Chris is already eighteen and missed the boat on hormone blockers, as she did not discover herself to be transgender until well into high school, after first situating herself as a boyish-looking lesbian. Now Chris is absolutely clear that he is male and cannot wait to start hormones and have top surgery, maybe followed by bottom surgery down the line. He finds it uncomfortable binding his breasts everyday to achieve the appearance of the boy he now is. But the burning desire to remove his breasts is actually driven by the topless issue—when he's working out or at the swimming pool, he finds it nearly unbearable that he can't whip his shirt off like all the other guys he hangs out with. It is an agonizing reminder that he cannot yet fully live the male life he has embraced. His breasts betray him. They would obviously still betray him at a European beach where all adults, both male and female, are free to go topless, as he also does not want to be stared at as a freak—a boy with breasts. Both Chris and Jenna simply remind us that going topless is a particular conundrum for transgender children, youth, and their parents. The advances of medical technology offer solutions but also new complications for parents who want to give their transgender sons the opportunity to run bare-chested like all the other boys.

WHAT ABOUT WHAT'S BETWEEN THE LEGS?

Now let's go from top to bottom. As already mentioned, except for genitalia, prepubescent bodies are pretty androgynous. With that said, it is probably not an accident that in many cultures all young children are dressed the same, and only later, in preparation for their changing body, do genders part ways in clothing and physical accoutrements. (This was also true in some earlier eras.) But the one way they will always be differentiated by gender is by their genitalia. For example, gender-nonconforming children (and adults, as well) become acutely aware of this when it comes to public bathroom and locker room use—it is their genitalia, not their affirmed gender, that is assumed to dictate whether they enter the door marked GIRLS/WOMEN or BOYS/ MEN. We are a clothing-not-optional culture, and social practice is that our private parts are exactly that—an area of the body that is revealed only to intimate others, people of the same (assigned) gender, and medical professionals.

Throughout a lifetime, genitalia that do not match affirmed gender by our present definitions of male-female may become a "hidden" problem for a transgender individual who does not have bottom surgery. At adolescence, the problem can become especially acute. A vagina begins to expel blood, marking the onset of menstruation. A penis grows in size; has noticeable erections that bulge through pants, shorts, or bathing suits; and shoots out ejaculatory fluids. Cross-sex hormones can take care of some of this, eliminating menstruation and curbing ejaculations, but as mentioned before, the final step, genital surgery, is typically denied transgender people under the age of eighteen. Whereas most youth accept this as part of their pre-adult transgender self, some suffer from the agony of the unwanted private parts.

Nattie is not yet pubescent but has been living happily as an affirmed female since age five, except for one thing—you are not allowed to say the word *penis* to her; just say "private parts." Sammi, while benefiting from both hormone blockers and cross-sex hormones, still remained distraught that she was stuck with an unwanted "thing" down there. In a moment of desperation, she tried hacking at her penis in the shower with a bar of soap, an obviously harm-free but symbolic gesture—"Out, damned spot!" Jessie, who arrived at an affirmed female identity only at age sixteen, tried every form of tape and binding in her "battle of the bulge"—desperately intent on hiding the dimensions of her penis under her tight shorts. Meredith, age eleven and dreaming herself a boy, bought surgical gloves and converted them into penises, positioning them in her underwear every morning before going to school. (Creatively, she even started making them for some of her friends, who were intrigued by the idea of a portable penis.) When Freud came up with the idea of penis envy, he may have missed the boat in assuming that every woman would of course want what a man had, but he may have definitely been onto something about the strong desire of some people to have the genitalia that they don't have but should have. And what to do about the desire not to have the genitalia you were born with?

With the onset of adolescence, binding, packing, and in more extreme situations, attempts at genital mutilation can become the daily practices of transgender youth as they try to reconcile their changing body to their affirmed gender selves. Some transgender youth will deny the onset of menses, hiding it from their parents and also from themselves, and it is only when their parents dis- cover the hidden bloodied underwear that they grasp the distress of their children whose sexual organs are sending an unwelcome reminder that God or somebody else didn't listen to their pleas about their gender. Some youth of either gender will avoid any type of sexual behavior altogether, including masturbation—as it serves as a powerful and frustrating reminder that what is "down there" is not what they want to have down there.

We are not yet living in a world that accepts that gender can cross genitalia—why not a boy with a vagina, or a girl with a penis? We live in a culture in which youth begin to become sexu- ally active in their teens, yet one in which it is assumed that they must wait until the age of majority to make a decision as monumental as having surgery to convert their genitalia or remove internal sexual organs. Even though one surgeon to whom I spoke posed the question, "Wouldn't it make more sense to allow a transgender youth who is sure of his or her transgender identity to have surgery prior to age eighteen, while still having the support of the family, rather than asking a youth to do it only after leaving home and no longer having those supports?" this is not the standard practice. Adolescence is a time when living with ambiguity or nuance is a challenge, not only but especially when it comes to a teen's sexual self. In offering hormones to adjust secondary sex characteristics but leaving genitalia intact, that is exactly what we are asking of pubescent and postpubescent transgender teens—to live with nuance and ambiguity and accept their genitalia as they are. Many youth can rise to the occasion, fueled by their happiness to be allowed to live in their affirmed gender. But for some, the stress can be substantial. It therefore behooves all the caring adults in such youths' lives to be sensitive to those teens' feelings about "what's between my legs."

ETHICS

Asking parents to be legally responsible for medical decisions that could have lifelong consequences for a child's gender development is no light matter. It is also no light matter for the professionals who are assigned the task of assessing whether an individual child is indeed a candidate for hormone blockers or cross-sex hormones. What if you get it wrong? How can you know? Since children and youth are organisms in flux, wouldn't it be better just to put any medical interventions on hold until your child is of legal age and can make his or her own medical decisions regarding gender transitions?

To address these questions, I'd like to share a quote from a professor of pediatrics, Dr. Peter Lee. He was recalling an experience he had over twenty years ago, when treatments were not available for patients under eighteen. A young person came for help: an assigned female but an affirmed male, just under age eighteen. This individual was filled with "so much pain and agony in her development in the 'wrong direction' that she later committed suicide."[63] Dr. Lee hoped that he would never have to be confronted with such a painful experience again, which could easily have been avoided if the person had been given access to development in the "right" direction.

Chris, who lamented not being able to whip his shirt off at the swimming pool or workout room, was now approaching eighteen and began to dip into a deep depression when he imagined that the endocrinologist to whom he was referred would refuse his request to begin cross-sex hormone treatments because he had not had enough time in a real-life experience as a male. No parents would wish either suicide or depression for their child, so it would appear that it is most ethical to do no harm—to do good instead, by making sure that such youth have the opportunity to take advantage of medical treatments now available, which can ensure a solid true gender self. This medical intervention may prevent a toxic if not life-threatening false gender self-artifice that could become the teen's living hell and possibly a prelude to death.

Some say it is absolutely essential that a teen first have the opportunity to fully explore the sexuality of the body he or she was born with, before artificially altering the progression of sexual development through cross-sex hormones. I believe that Nattie, who won't allow the word *penis* to be spoken in reference to herself, and Sammi, who takes a bar of soap to her genitals, would take issue with this stance. If you force a child to live with the postpubertal body that matches the gender on the birth certificate but not the gender that youth knows him- or herself to be, just how is that going to contribute to a healthy and exploratory sexual life? It is common knowledge that most people, when overly anxious, tend not to have a great sex life. What could be more anxiety-provoking than suspending an adolescent in a protracted period of gender dysphoria, in which he or she is forced to live with the realities of a distressing and unwelcome developing body that possibly cannot be changed later? In fact, it has been my own observation that transgender and gender-questioning youth suspended in such a state, with no social or emotional supports to facilitate physical transitions through hormone blockers and/or cross-sex hormones, often forgo sex altogether. They retreat to their preadolescent selves when life was easier but also relatively sexless. Rather than giving transgender adolescents a chance to explore their sexuality in the body they were given, denying those adolescents access to cross-sex hormone treatments ends up blocking any opportunity to explore adolescent sexuality altogether within the identity that feels correct, true, and authentic—the transgender self.

PILLS TO MAKE YOU GIRL, PILLS TO MAKE YOU BOY

Puberty is a particular challenge for parents of transgender and gender-fluid youth. It may involve medical decisions that you must make on your children's behalf—hormone blockers, cross-sex hormones—which may have lifelong consequences. But here's what we know that might alleviate the load. The rates of depression and suicide are higher among transgender youth, particularly those who are not given an opportunity to expand into their true gender selves with accompanying social supports. No doubt playing with nature by switching the tracks of your children's physical gender development through drug treatments can generate anxiety: Is it safe? What does it do to the basic premise we were brought up with that a person's biological sex is immutable?

If a course of hormone treatment can significantly reduce extreme risk factors for your transgender children and stands the chance of making them happier as their true gender self is allowed to unfold, why wouldn't you facilitate that process? This is not playing God with nature; it is accepting that nature sometimes needs a human touch.

As adults, it is not for us to bend twigs but to recognize when a twig has been unwittingly twisted and help get it untwisted. We accomplish this not by forcing our children to accept a body they cannot embrace but by helping that body change to match the spirit of the individual within it.

CHAPTER SIX

We Are Family

Many parents shared journals with me that were filled with anguish. If they had decided to let their child live as the other gender, that meant cutting off ties with family and friends who weren't supportive, putting away baby pictures, mourning the loss of the child they thought they had. It meant sending their child out alone into a possibly hostile world.

—HANNA ROSIN, AUTHOR OF "A BOY'S WORLD"[84]

▼

Like the parents who wrote the journals shared with Hanna Rosin, if you are a parent who has a gender-creative child, you have embarked on a complicated and precarious journey—and so has your child, sent out alone into a possibly hostile world. What we also forget is that not just out in the world, but right at home, things can get complicated for such children, who will have to navigate among their siblings, grandparents, friends, schoolmates, teachers, and so forth. So let's stop now and look out from the perspective of the child who deals with all these "home" people.

• • •

SIBLINGS

In my field, so much attention is paid to parents and their effects on their child that everyone seems to forget about siblings. Think about it: Siblings are probably our most long-lasting relationships. For the transgender and gender-nonconforming child, siblings play a particularly significant role as either friends or foes. And for those siblings, such a child can present one of their most challenging and yet most rewarding experiences.

Tracy was now ten years old, living with her mom and dad in upstate New York. When she was a little boy, a long time ago, she told everyone they got it wrong; she was a girl. When she was four, and everyone still thought she was a boy, her mother gave birth to her younger brother, Quinn. Tracy insisted on a shirt that read, "I'm a big sister now." By the time Tracy was five, her pleas had been heard and she entered kindergarten as a girl, a gender in which she has happily remained ever since. Tracy has had a love/hate relationship with her little brother. Quinn siphoned away her mom's heretofore undivided attention and quickly evolved into exactly the kind of rough-and-tumble boy that Tracy loathed. By the time Tracy was nine, she was fulminating at her annoying little brother. As time went on, it became clear why. Tracy had established a happy social circle around her that knew her simply as a girl. It was her strong preference, honored by both her mother and father, that her transition from an assigned male to an affirmed female remain private and not be shared with anyone outside the immediate family. Quinn was part of that immediate family. He knew the whole story—that Tracy was transgender, had a penis, and a long time ago, before Quinn could remember, was a boy. Quinn was a feisty, outgoing little boy, a bit like Tigger in his exuberance and lack of personal boundaries. Over time he became Tracy's worst nightmare—the brother who could "out" her at any moment. Through malice, power-mongering and sheer immaturity or spontaneity, occasionally he did—with seemingly innocent offhand remarks when a friend was over, such as, "You know, my sister has a penis." Definitely a showstopper. Or sometimes, just to get revenge when no one else was there, he'd put his face in Tracy's and taunt, "You have a penis, you have a penis," sending Tracy into an emotional tailspin. She cannot stop ranting, "My brother is socially retarded. He's a total misfit. A complete nerd. He doesn't have a friend in the world. Who would want to be his friend? I hate him. I want him dead." I doubt Tracy is seriously considering fratricide. Tracy's real and understandable beef is that her little brother, a total wild card, holds the power to turn her life on end and transform it into a living hell. From where Tracy stands, her affirmed girlhood could be shattered into a sham girlhood in the eyes of others. She could be rejected by all of her newfound friends. She'd become the weird girl with a penis. And there is nothing she can do to stop it—short of entertaining murderous fantasies of putting an end to her brother's life.

For the moment let's leave aside the question of what it is like to feel like you are a gender fugitive, having to hide the truth about your gender transformation or your life might just as well be over. For many, what is between their legs is nobody's business but their own. After all, we don't walk down the street and stop everyone to ask, "Hello, do you have a vagina or a penis?" And for transgender children who have not yet reached puberty, their genitalia are really the only identifying feature that would belie their affirmed gender. So why does anyone else need to know? It is a matter of personal privacy. The violation of that privacy is precisely where siblings can end up being the bane of transgender children's existence—brothers and sisters who are simply incapable of keeping secrets; who want to tease or taunt or get back at their sibling for past transgressions; who because of their own anxieties, discomfort, or confusion about their gender-nonconforming sib turn on that sib whom they consider the bane of *their* existence. The siblings' trump card: telling the "truth"—that their sister is not "really" a girl or their brother is not "really" a boy.

It is not just the transgender children who may become wary of their siblings; so do gender-hybrid or gender-fluid children. Eight-year-old Jeremiah loves to play with dolls and dress up in princess costumes and always has, but he has also recognized that it doesn't go over so well in the school he attends, so he keeps much of his gender-fluid play within the four walls of the family playroom. He has a younger sister, Francesca. When Jeremiah and his sister are riding in the car with other friends on the way to or from school, Francesca will seize the opportunity to blurt out, "You know, Jeremiah likes to play with girl things." Fortunately, Jeremiah's mother intervenes, calling back from the driver's seat, "Hey, it's okay to play with girl things." Then later, she confronts Francesca: "Is your name Jeremiah? Then you don't share things about Jeremiah's business." There is, of course, some additional work to do with Francesca. She needs room to talk about her own experiences, confusion, and worries about her brother who is not like all the other kids she knows. Maybe Francesca has been teased herself after playdates with friends at the house, with such comments as, "How come your brother wears princess costumes? That's really weird. Why does your mom let him? You're all weird." And Jeremiah will need some coaching so that he, himself, is prepared to respond, either to Francesca or to anyone else who challenges his gender presentations or identity. It is good to know that his mother is his ally, but she will not always be there to step in, so he needs help to find a way to say with confidence, "Yep, I do, but they're anybody's things, not just girl things." The challenge to Francesca and Jeremiah's parents will be to support their son in his gender creativity while also acknowledging the discomfort it might cause their daughter, so they can help her transcend that discomfort to become Jeremiah's ally rather that his enemy.

With that said, it is important to remember that siblings are not merely evil forces to contend with. They can also be a gender-nonconforming child's strongest support, maybe even stronger than the parents, because they're the ones who will more likely be around to witness the taunts and teasing. I'm recalling my own children's experiences in grade school. Jesse would have dressed up in some outlandish outfit with layers of chiffon or ruffles or would have organized some elaborate fantasy game with a bunch of Cabbage Patch Kids and his bevy of girlfriends. Kids would run up to my daughter in the playground, stop her, and spit out, "Did you see what your little brother's doing. What's up with that?" I think you get the drift. Rebecca would stare down the inquisitors and retort, "Nothing's up. And what's it to you? My brother's just playing." Now, to be honest, that was never the end of the story, because sometimes my daughter would come to me and say, "Mom, do you know how embarrassing it is to always have to make explanations for Jesse?" Like Francesca, Rebecca also needed a private place for support and understanding, but for the moment let's just stay with the point that siblings can be a tremendous source of loyal protection for their gender-bending sister or brother. This is never an automatic process. It necessitates parental intervention to ensure that a strong ethos of gender freedom and fairness starts in the home, with parents and children respecting each other's gender presentations. These may include butch, fem, fluid, cross-, and emo. (The latter has been adopted from a type of rock music, a style of dress—skinny jeans, tight T-shirts, long bangs, kohl eyeliner—and a cluster of personality traits—shy, sensitive, emotional—among male youth that cross-culturally defied gender lines.)

What happens to children when their sibling violates this ethos? Like Tracy, they may wish their sibling dead. But most won't engage in fratricide. More realistically, there will be a tremendous breach in trust and a potential unraveling of a child's emerging self-esteem as a gender-creative little person—"If my own siblings won't accept me, how will anyone else?"

Lou is a transgender boy with a younger sister, Miranda. He can be really mean to Miranda, but only in retaliation for her outing him. They just moved to a new neighborhood, and Lou came home from school ranting, "She told. Someone came up to me and said, 'Are you a girl?' I hate her." Lou and his parents were planning to attend a conference for gender-nonconforming children and their families. When Lou found out that his parents were also intending to bring Miranda, he was furious. "Why should she come? She doesn't even support it." Miranda is clearly having her own issues or confusions about Lou's being transgender. Which is exactly why she *should* go to the conference—to get some help sorting out those issues, hopefully receiving empathy for her experience while developing greater compassion for her brother. And Lou will have to make some space for his sister to do that. Which is not so easy, because from his point of view, it is hard enough to go into the world as a transgender child who might be looked at askance by peers or adults in a transphobic culture— if you can't even trust your own sister, the world can start to feel pretty bleak, or alternatively, you can start to hate that sister. In blowing Lou's cover at their new school, Miranda has betrayed her sibling in a most sensitive and core part of his self. So she has some work ahead of her: Miranda will have to earn or re-earn Lou's trust. To do that, she will need to learn the same thing that Francesca learned from her mother—that her brother's business is her brother's business, not for *her* to disclose.

But let's think about privacy, secrets, disclosing, outing. I'm recalling an account by a mother of a six-year-old transgender daughter and a three-year-old son. The daughter had chosen a new name when she transitioned to female. Her three-year-old son was resistant to using the new name, and insisted on calling her by her old boy's name, James. The little brother said, "I miss James." When Meredith, who used to be James, reassured her little brother that she was the same person as before, he relaxed some and never called his older sibling James again. But now their mother was bumping up against a new problem. For the first time, both children would be attending the same school in the fall. The mom wanted to ensure Meredith's privacy, but wondered, "How am I going to teach my younger son that some conversations are only for home, not for school? Isn't it hard for an almost-four-year-old to understand that we have family secrets?" The answer is, "Yes, it won't be so easy for that little guy to understand that." From a four-year-old's perspective, secrets are about birthday presents or about things you might get in trouble for. Children of that age have not yet developed a sense of nuance regarding issues of privacy or nondisclosure of very intimate aspects of life.

This brings me back to the question dropped before—the meaning of keeping private one's assigned gender history. Is that really good for children in a situation in which they are living with potential informers all around them—their sisters and brothers, and also their old friends—who knew them in their earlier gender identity? In round-robin fashion, if a four-year-old is asked to keep private the facts of his older sibling's gender status (that she was born a boy, and transitioned to being a girl), how can that four-year-old possibly understand that that is nobody's business yet also a good thing? If it isn't a fun and temporary secret, such as about a birthday present, then it must be a bad thing, maybe something to be ashamed of, which is exactly the opposite of what we want to communicate and instill in the children about their sibling's authentic gender self. So the problem with the "right to privacy" approach within a family with young children is that although from the transgender or gender-nonconforming child's point of view it provides a circle of care, it simultaneously can be transformed into a ring of fire. Family secrets are rarely healthy for family life, and if not carefully framed as private family issues to be respected by all, they can also easily become fodder for sibling attacks. So for the gender-creative child who is not an only child, the presence of siblings must always be factored in when making decisions about disclosure of that child's gender status.

One last thing about siblings, from the point of view of a gender-creative child: The gender-nonconforming child will have a lot on his or her plate in negotiating a healthy-gendered childhood. Now we know that we also have to factor in siblings when we consider that plate. But it is not just siblings' effect on/reaction to their brother or sister that we must consider. Some transgender or gender-nonconforming youth have an extra burden: the worry that their own journey may harm their siblings.

Sarah was fourteen. At age twelve she transitioned to her affirmed gender. She and her little brother, Joseph, had attended the same school for years. Sarah had worked out her transition with her middle school friends and everyone seemed very accepting. But Joseph was only in fifth grade, and Sarah had already gotten word that some of Joseph's classmates had started giving him a hard time, teasing him about his brother who turned into his sister and how strange or "gay" it was. Sarah loved her little brother, who was somewhat shy and nervous. She lost many hours of sleep tossing and turning over the pain she was causing Joseph. She agonized that it was all her fault and Joseph didn't deserve it. Because they were now on separate campuses, Sarah could do nothing to protect Joseph during the school day. And besides, she was just learning, herself, how to respond to a world that wasn't always ready for her. She was still a bit wobbly in that, so fifth graders could definitely be her worst nightmare—they're old enough to know about transgender but too young to do anything but blatantly and maybe really meanly make fun of anyone who feels different. Sarah needed to be relieved of her burden by her parents, who would assure her that they would take care of Joseph and any teasing that might come his way. They could do this by coaching him directly and by going to his teacher to ask that all the children in the lower grades have an opportunity to meet with a community expert to learn about the many different ways to be boys and girls and the importance of everyone respecting those differences. But first, Sarah's parents, like every other parent of a transgender or gender-nonconforming child, must be alerted and at the ready to take care of their child's worries about his or her siblings and the siblings' worries about that child.

FROM THE SIBLINGS' POINT OF VIEW

We cannot get the whole story unless we also let the siblings speak. Dr. Michele Angello, a therapist who works with families that include a transgender or gender-nonconforming child, likened the experience of such siblings to that of siblings of a disabled child.[65] There are certainly parallels:

- Often both the transgender and the disabled child absorbs a great deal of their parents' attention, and perhaps also the family's resources, both financial and emotional.
- The siblings often have to explain to others why that brother or sister is the way he or she is or feel responsible for protecting him or her from harm.
- The siblings often have to deal with their own discomfort or anxiety about their sibling's developmental or gender status.
- The siblings may have to deal with the resentment from their brother or sister for having it easier in life.
- The siblings may feel pressure from their parents to be the ones who are "easy."
- The siblings are often forgotten by the professionals, who concentrate all their efforts on interventions to aid the disabled or gender-nonconforming child.

At the same time, language is a powerful tool, and likening gender differences to disability has the risk of reinforcing the notion that those differences are *deficits* in need of repair, while under-cutting the principle of transgender or gender-noncon-forming identity and expression as a positive sense of self with no defect implied. So I might dispense with the analogy but extract from it the need to pay attention to the similar burdens felt by the siblings in the context of their family and out in the world.

When a sibling has grown up with a sister who evolves into a brother or a brother who evolves into a sister, the transi-tion can be a pretty dramatic change for that sibling. This is especially true for older teen and young adult siblings with a brother or sister who does not affirm his or her gender until well into childhood, adolescence, or early adulthood. There are just too many years of knowing it one way—"I have two brothers and a sister," or "I have a younger sister," and so forth. There is a tendency, by both professionals and parents, to underplay this change, to reassure the sibling by pointing out that their brother-now-sister or sister-now-brother is still the same per-son. Well, yes and no.

Phoebe is twenty years old and home from college for the summer. While she was gone that school year, one of her younger teenage siblings transitioned from male to female. That sibling had begun cross-sex hormones, and the estrogen was having the effect of inducing raging hormonal imbalance. Phoebe's mild-mannered gentle brother was now an emotional roller coaster of a sister, a constant PMS nightmare as far as Phoebe was con-cerned. So when Phoebe was told that her transgender sibling was still the same person, she exploded, "Don't tell me it's the same person. Because it's not." She went on to lament how she had lost the brother she had loved so much, and now found her-self with a whirling dervish of a sister. She wanted her brother back. If parents need space to mourn the loss of the child they had so they can better embrace the child they now have, that can only be even more so for the siblings of a transgender youth or young adult. After all, they have grown up with the map of their family as the foundation on which they build all their outside relationships, and within those parameters, a sister is a sister or a brother is a brother for the rest of your life. Phoebe's outburst alerts all of us to be sensitive to the distress or sadness that might come the way of siblings as they witness what to them can seem like a science-fiction transformation, temporarily leaving their family map in shreds.

Part of that family map has to do with rules, regulations, and privileges. When a child is questioning his or her gender identity or affirming a transgender identity, parents have to make accommodations to facilitate that process. For example, they might allow that child to go on the Internet to make contact with other youth who are also going through the same process, especially if there is no access to other youth in their own city or town. The time allowed and the free access to the Internet might be in direct violation of the parents' set policies about their children's computer use. So a sibling pokes his or her head in the study and erupts, "Hey, how come Frankie gets to go on the computer after nine o'clock when the rule is, 'No screens after nine o'clock'?" "Different strokes for different folks" is not going to go over well with that sibling. Instead, he or she may grow resentful, and that resentment might be taken out on Frankie, a more ready target than the parents, who are really the ones responsible for the perceived double standard. That kind of resentment could easily happen in Phoebe's family as well, if her transgender sister's PMS outbursts are tolerated or overlooked by their parents while Phoebe's own crabby premenstrual moods are met with annoyance or rebukes. Like Joseph's brothers in the Old Testament, the siblings in such situations could grow so resentful of the favored child's perceived elevated status and privileges that they might feel ready to sell their gender-creative sib to the first slave trader who came along.

One father had indeed witnessed that happening in his family—not the sale to a slave trader but the rising fury of his other children as they watched their transgender sibling get what to them seemed like unconscionably favored treatment. They organized a sibling protest. This father took notice and learned his lesson. His advice was simple, to be heeded by all of us: *Be careful that all the children get the same attention.* I would attach an addendum: If your gender-creative child is in need of special things, simply explain to the other children in the family why this is happening. For example, "We only let Frankie go on the Internet after nine p.m. because, given the time difference between where we live and where other kids who use this site live, it's the only time Frankie can actually find other kids to chat with who are going through the same thing Frankie is." In general, siblings who feel there is enough to go around for everyone will have latitude to embrace those inequalities if parents explain to all their children *why* they are acting one way with one child and another way with the other children. It also helps to communicate and to demonstrate that special treatment will also be given to the other siblings as needed.

MAKING SUPPORT A FAMILY EFFORT

It takes a family to launch a gender-creative child. But it might also take support groups, conferences, workshops, or picnics. And those take a fair amount of time. And sometimes they require the whole family going together. But that's not necessarily how the siblings of a gender-creative child want to spend their free time. Here comes one more potential arena of resentment. I'm recalling one teenage sibling of a transgender girl being asked how he felt about attending a local gender conference with his family. While he was very supportive of his sister, he had this to say about his own participation: "I'm cool, as long as I don't run into any friends who think it's about *me*." We could hardly call this a supportive sibling comment, and it does reveal his own discomfort with the trans thing—"Okay for my sister, but I'd rather die than have someone think that's who I am." But we must also remember that his family was asking him to step well outside his comfort zone—if it weren't for his sister, he'd probably be out on the soccer field, not sitting on a folding chair with twenty or so families of gender-creative children. An older brother of another transgender boy refused to come to this same conference when he learned that he would not be allowed to wander in and out of workshops. For him, that's the only way he could imagine going—knowing there was an escape hatch if he began to get too uncomfortable. I could certainly understand the conference organizers setting a policy that workshop attendees commit themselves to participating in a workshop from beginning to end, out of respect for the presenters and other participants. Yet I think we also need to tailor situations to accommodate the feelings and needs of the sibs, to support their own emotional journey or turbulence and make room for them to become their brother's or sister's strongest allies.

AND WHAT ABOUT MOTHERS AND FATHERS?

We have already spent a great deal of time talking about parents' experiences and thinking about how you can become gender creative and facilitate your child's true gender self. But now I want to come around from the other side—how you may be experienced by your gender-nonconforming child. If you offer empathy, understanding, and support, your child will feel emotionally secure and remain confident that you are right alongside in his or her journey. But let's now consider the opposite—what happens when children don't feel that support?

Franny is an eighteen-year-old who is sorting through her gender identity and is pretty much convinced that she is transgender, although she had been identifying as a "butch lesbian" since middle school. Like many youth who have an assigned female gender and transition first to lesbian and then to transgender, in her earlier adolescence the only place she could find in her community that fit her desire to cut her hair short, wear boys' clothes, and happily be mistaken for a boy was in the lesbian subculture, where she was welcomed and embraced as butch. But as her high school years progressed, this didn't feel right. When she imagined herself with a partner, it indeed was with another female, but in her imaginings there would be only one girl, and that would not be her. Increasingly, she came to realize that she was a boy under wraps, and as a transgender culture began to grow around her, she discovered that this was where she belonged—as a heterosexual transgender young man.

Her parents were dubious. They saw Franny as very young and suggestible, and believed that she was being unduly influenced by a transgender counselor at a summer program she attended. As far as they were concerned, they saw *nothing* "boy" about Franny, which was somewhat shocking to me, as the young Franny who walked into my office looked like nothing other than a teenage boy yet to grow whiskers. But now Franny had to convince her parents that she was really a he. Franny tried writing her mom a note explaining that she knows her mom has told her to go slow on the trans thing, but that she needs her mom to know that she has wanted top surgery since ninth grade and has never changed her mind. Franny went on to say that she is thinking of changing her name, too, but she can go slow on that, because after all she has been Franny for eighteen years—and that most of all, she just wants to talk.

Her mother was trying her best to do what was best for Franny, and, right after she got Franny's note, she confided in me that she was glad Franny was opening a conversation. She could even understand why Franny was doing it in writing, as Franny has never been good with face-to-face conversations that might end up in a confrontation. Franny's mother wanted to do anything she could to support her, but she also admitted her real feelings—that, truth be told, "I do want to keep my daughter."

Having met both Franny and her mom, I know that her mom is trying her hardest, but I also know that Franny ended up feeling frustrated and unheard. She doesn't agree that she is sensitive to being confronted even gently—she just gets unglued by what she experiences as her parents' unrelenting refusal to hear what she is trying to say: "I'm not just going through a phase. I've been sitting on this for years. Yeah, I may be shy, and I may have gone through some ups and downs in high school, but did my parents ever stop to think that it's because I was always living in a skin that feels uncomfortable, and with breasts that I detest? Look at the way I look. That's not new. What is it that they can't see?"

I have every confidence that Franny's parents will come around and be able to see, and it was certainly my assessment that Franny's transgender affirmation was not a fleeting phase or temporary quirk but an expression of her true gender self. I understand Franny's mother's concern to take it slow, particularly when it came to a move as permanent as a mastectomy. But recall what we said about the time lines of adolescents and the trauma that their (unwanted) gendered body can become to them. Right now, as far as Fanny is concerned, her parents aren't coming around soon enough, and Franny is not only getting impatient, she is also beginning to feel let down by them. Franny's mom wants to keep her daughter, but Franny keeps trying to tell her that there is no daughter to keep. To mourn the loss of a daughter is definitely Franny's mother's work; but to deny Franny's authentic identity to avoid that mourning process will do no one any good, and it is already leaving dents and bruises on Franny's psyche. She doesn't simply want to open up a dialogue with her mom. She wants to feel her mother's love and support.

Like I said, I'm optimistic that there will be a good outcome for Franny with her family. Others do not fare so well. Thomas was an older adolescent living in a small conservative town. In the recent past, he came to realize that he was a transgender female. He did this with no support or dialogue with his family but on his own through his connections on the Internet. Even though he was petrified, he had decided that it was time to come out to his family. He chose his cousin to start with, as he believed this cousin would be the most likely to accept him rather than condemn him:

> Tomorrow I am planning to tell my cousin about my situation. I do have to admit that this is the hardest thing I have ever tried to do. Hopefully I can gather enough courage by then. I have even rehearsed what I want to say. I have been reading some information on the Internet about telling your family and it said to always stay confident. I am one of the shyest and least confident people you will ever meet, but after living for 19 years as someone who is not the real me, I know I have to do this.
>
> I have also been trying to bring up conversations with my parents about things that they do not want me to do like getting my ears pierced. They have let me grow my hair out for a few years and I can tell they do not want to give any more "freedom" than that. My dad said that if I get my ear pierced (keyword: ear; not plural) I would have to shave my head. But he said when I move out I can do whatever. He then proceeded to give me a speech about how bad the economy is and how hard it would be to live on my own. I fear that that day may be approaching faster than I hope.

Thomas is not being paranoid when he fantasizes being asked to leave or making the choice himself to leave the family home after dropping the "bombshell" that it is not just a matter of pierced ears or long hair, but the realization that he is an affirmed female. We have to remind ourselves that gender-nonconforming and transgender youth, along with gay, lesbian, bisexual, questioning, and queer youth, may be the only group of minority children who cannot count on the love and support of their own family in their minority identity. Black parents will teach their children to have pride in their race, prepare them for the racism that is other people's problems, not theirs, and watch their children's back if they should meet up with prejudice or violence. The same is true for children of ethnic or religious minorities. Trans, gay, and queer youth cannot count on this. The parents and children in a minority families share their minority status, which is rarely the case for trans, gay, and queer youth and their families. So it is no accident that the ranks of homeless and foster care youth are disproportionately filled with transgender, bisexual, gay, lesbian, questioning, and queer youth—they didn't become transgender, bisexual, gay, lesbian, or queer because they lost their family; they were thrown out of their family or fled violence and abuse *because* they were transgender, bisexual, gay, lesbian, or queer. Thomas is brave to face the potentially explosive reactions of his parents when he spills the beans about his true gender self. From the point of view of transgender or gender-nonconforming youth, we must always keep in mind the fear and anticipation of total family rejection when we think of the journey they go through.

Franny, Thomas, and all the other older youth and young adults who are only first telling their parents about their true gender identity will also need to do their own work in having compassion for their parents and giving them time to adjust to this breaking news about their child—that their daughter hopes to become their son, their son their daughter. Nancy's teenage child Morgan had recently disclosed to her that he was actually a she. Soon after, Morgan transitioned to female. Nancy was doing her best to keep up with this quick change of events. She took Morgan to buy new clothes. She did okay until they got to the underwear department. She looked around at the bras and panties and suddenly it all hit her. With tears in her eyes, she tried to share with Morgan what was happening: "This is just all very new for me." Morgan stiffened, looked her mother in the eye, and spoke with conviction: "Well, it's not new for me." As Nancy recounted this incident later, she broke down sobbing. Both Morgan's and Nancy's experiences are poignantly real. Morgan had been sitting on a new gender identity for what felt like eons; she needed a mother's blessings. Nancy was still feeling the aftershocks of what felt like a major earthquake in her life—motherhood had been her central identity, and now its contents were suddenly torn asunder.

Emotional adaptations take time, and children old enough to have a sense of time and the ability to imagine being in another's shoes will need to extend that understanding to their parents. If you are one of those parents, this can only happen if you truly listen to your children, understand the urgency of their claims to an authentic gender self, and recognize that although you are entitled to your own feelings, some of these feelings will need to be shielded from your children and worked out in your own private space so as not to overload them with your emotional upheaval. The golden rule of parenting prevails: Your job remains to take care of them, not ask them to take care of you.

THE SEVEN T'S

Let us return to the formula of the seven T's. First, the seven T words:

▸ Transgender
▸ Transgression
▸ Transphobia
▸ Trauma
▸ Transcendence

▶ Transformation

▶ Transition

Now the formula of the seven T's: The *transgender* child who *transgresses* binary gender norms may face *transphobia* and psychological *trauma* within the family while leading the way to the family's *transcendence* of that transphobia by creating a *transformation* in the family's thinking, feelings, and actions as the child *transitions* from the gender assigned at birth to his or her authentic and affirmed gender identity. Depending on how that process unfolds, the child will either come out with a true rather than a false gender self or with a bruised and battered psyche.

As an undergraduate psychology major I remember being totally taken by the concept of *cognitive dissonance*: a mental conflict that occurs when beliefs or assumptions are contradicted by new information. So, for example, you have always believed that people who are devout Catholics are not able to think for themselves, because they're asked to surrender to the teaching of the Lord. Now Gloria is your new roommate, a devout Catholic, yet she is the most free-thinking person you have ever met. How do you resolve that contradiction? One side of the equation has to give: Either what you believed about Catholics is wrong or Gloria really isn't the free-thinking young woman she appears to be, or maybe she's just the rare exception to the rule. I have discovered that cognitive dissonance, with the accompanying need to resolve conflicting beliefs and feelings, runs rampant in many families of transgender and gender-nonconforming children and youth.

We've already established that the family is the place where a child first develops a sense of self as boy, girl, or other. Remember that it is the parents, not the child, who first "know" that the child is a boy or a girl. What happens to parents who, over months or years or even decades, "know" their child to be a boy or girl—only to be confronted with new information when they hear from their child that they have it wrong? What happens to the siblings when they discover the same thing? And to the grandparents, and so forth? What do we have here? A potential collision between transphobia and baby love. A perfect storm of cognitive dissonance: "I believe that transgender people are sick or deviant and to be despised or feared. I love my baby/child/ adolescent who I now learn may be one of those people." How does the family resolve this?

From the child's point of view, she or he can only hope that baby love will trump transphobic fears, and that the bonds that have already been built will guide the parents away from their negative beliefs to a more positive sensibility about gender creativity and gender nonconformity. This may take several years and necessitate headaches and heartache, but it can indeed happen. For example, recall Brandon, who pranced through trick-or-treating in his Purple Wise Man costume. When Brandon first showed up with his "girly" interests, his dad felt repelled. He admonished his son and tried to redirect him to more masculine pursuits. Hard as he tried, he couldn't help himself from withdrawing somewhat from his son, who was causing him a considerable amount of pain and whom he was beginning to experience as weird. Brandon sorely felt his parent's withdrawal, and clamored for more of his father's attention and positive regard. Brandon worried that maybe Daddy didn't like him. When Daddy realized this, it pierced him like an arrow to his heart, and he did a sudden turnabout, stopping to explore his negative reactions to and beliefs about "sissy boys" and making every effort to stay connected to his son. Brandon reinforced his dad's positive efforts by his squeals of sheer delight when his father returned home from business trips, just wanting, "Daddy, Daddy, Daddy" and running into his arms.

The most powerful moving force in resolving the cognitive dissonance is the children themselves. It is my belief that the vast majority of parents love their children, and that the parent-child bond may be the strongest one we experience in our lives, even trumping or at least running equal to our bond with our partner. Parents may not be so powerful as to shape their children to an authentic gender self, but children surely can shape their parents in getting them to come around to embrace their gender bending, despite the parents' prior convictions or beliefs that it is all just plain wrong. Remember what we discussed about gender angels and gender ghosts. For parents or other family members filled with gender ghosts but lacking gender angels, the cognitive dissonance between their negative beliefs and the opposing love they have developed for their children creates the perfect breeding ground for brand-new gender angels to come into being. This transformation is rarely a point in time but may unfold over many years of family life, with much back-and-forth as specific issues challenge the family's long-held beliefs. The best strategy is to return each time to the seven T's formula, to transcend each difficulty as it arises.

SHAM STRATEGIES

Sometimes parents think they have successfully worked through the seven T's formula and have come through wholly embracing their transgender or gender-nonconforming child. In an attempt to be gender-creative parents who shield their child from the transphobia they recognize as running rampant all around them, they will orchestrate a seemingly protective strategy for their child. When you investigate a little further, though, you might discover that the strategy is built on a shaky foundation of untruths or a scaffolding of unresolved transphobia in the parents themselves.

In November 2008, Hanna Rosin's "A Boy's Life" appeared in *The Atlantic*. We learned about eight-year-old Bridget, a child who had transitioned from being Brandon in a rather conservative community. Bridget was feeling fairly anxious integrating herself into her social world, where everyone had always known her as Brandon. One day, she and her mother, Tina, were on an excursion several miles from their home. They thought this would be a pretty safe outing, as no one there would ever have known Bridget as Brandon. As luck would have it, her geographical safety net tore when she spied a fourth grade friend of her stepbrother's. She was nervous, wondering how he would react to her. Tina sat Bridget down on a bench and gave her the following advice: "If anybody says anything, you say, 'I'm not Brandon. I'm Bridget, his cousin from California.' You want to try it?" Bridget: "No. I don't want to." Well, of course Bridget didn't want to try it. It was a bald-faced lie. And how angry would that kid Bridget was worrying about be if he felt himself being played for a fool? And what would then be heaped on Bridget's head in retaliation?

Tina was only trying to protect her daughter; in her own words, "I want her to be known as Bridget, not Bridget-who-used-to-be-Brandon." But the fact of the matter is that Bridget *did* used to be Brandon, and it is only magical thinking or delusional fantasies that could lead us to think we could dupe another child by coming up with this story of the cousin-double and presenting it in the name of the "right to privacy." When Bridget refused this strategy, Tina coached her with an alternative response if this boy or anyone else gave her a hard time about her gender transformation: "Well, if someone keeps it up, you just say, 'You're crazy.'" Now most probably that wouldn't be the truth, either. More likely, that someone would be confused, anxious, or perhaps hostile about gender nonconformity or gender transformation. I understand Tina's impulse to toughen Bridget up so she can feel more comfortable navigating her peer world. I also understand her anger at anyone who would give her beloved child a hard time. But meeting up with bullying by bullying in return is rarely a good strategy. Casting aspersion on another child's character by calling him or her crazy because that child questioned Bridget's gender status is what I would call a sham strategy. Why not instead coach Bridget to give a positive response about herself, such as: "Well yes, once I was a boy, yeah,

Brandon, but now I'm a girl. My name is Bridget. That can happen, you know." If the situation is potentially violent or persistently hostile, the alternative strategy is to teach your child to recognize the danger, stalwartly leave, hopefully find adult help, and know that it is perfectly normal to feel threatened or scared as well as angry. It is a very smart strategy just to leave. And if that is not effective, and a child is indeed in consistent danger, some families have seriously considered moving to another area that would be more accepting or where the child will not be haunted by his or her gender history. That, too, I would endorse. But I cannot emphasize enough that creating smoke screens or attempting to press the Delete button on history merely promotes a sense of a shameful past to be hidden and a false belief that our present selves have no history. In the words of Hanna Rosin, "[Tina] wanted things to be easy for Brandon, for him to disappear and pop back as Bridget, a new kid from California, new to this town, knowing nobody. But in a small town, it's hard to erase yourself and come back as your opposite."[66] And Bridget shouldn't be asked to erase herself. Instead, she needs help from her parents to communicate a positive sense of herself and her own past, even when others feel differently.

Then there is the unresolved ambivalence that can leak out in the name of a parent's gender-creative strategy. Angelina is a gender-fluid child and has been for a long time. Actually, she qualifies as a seven-year-old gender hybrid. She says she's half boy, half girl. Since she was very young, she has only worn boys' thigh length briefs. She explains that girls' skimpy panties gives her wedgies. This is only one of her many "boy" gender expressions. Joanna is Angelina's mom. Joanna definitely qualifies as "fem" by today's cultural standards. Joanna says that it's absolutely fine with her that Angelina is a gender hybrid. Yet she also feels it is her responsibility as a mom and as the "feminine person" in the family to expand Angelina's horizons so that she can also experience the positives of the female side of life, since Angelina identifies, in part, as a girl. Joanna has come up with a strategy. She zeroes in on underwear as a place to start. Joanna goes out and buys wonderfully soft, comfortable girls' underpants. Not a chance of a wedgie. She lays them out on Angelina's bed. Playfully, Joanna challenges Angelina: "Just try them and see. Tell you what. I'll give you a chocolate treat for every day you try wearing them." (Joanna knows that Angelina will practically die for chocolate.)

Joanna thought this was a very gender-creative strategy. I disagreed, and told her why: I thought the idea was a subtle form of reparative home therapy—we won't take away your football uniform and your boys' underwear, but we will skew the playing field by offering bribes for gender-conforming behavior, with the underlying message that we would prefer you to be gender conforming. With deeper exploration, it was not really Joanna's desire to expand Angelina's horizons but her own anxiety that she was not being an active enough force in shaping her daughter's girlhood, neglecting her duties as a good mother. With even deeper exploration, this anxiety was attached to Joanna's true feelings that it was not normal for Angelina to be so boy-like. It was Jake, Joanna's husband and Angelina's father, who blew the whistle on Joanna. He strongly believed that they should just let Angelina be who she was, who was a girl who liked boys' clothes, underwear and all. And by the way, Angelina never fell for the chocolate bait. It wasn't worth a wedgie.

Then there are children who find their parents asking them to duck and cover. Carolina was in college by the time she realized she was transgender. Before that, she had lived as a lesbian for many years. It was only when attending an all women's college that she came to know that she did not fit in, because she didn't feel herself to be a woman. Past the time when hormone blockers might have afforded her a male puberty, she chose to take testosterone, have a mastectomy, and change her name to Carlos. Carlos is now a young man with a beard, male physique, and a lower voice. Carlos's mother, Sharon, has had trouble adjusting to the transformation of her daughter into her son, and, like Franny's parents, insists that she never observed a single boy thing about her child, so she never saw it coming. Sharon's father is very old, frail, and somewhat senile, yet still the strong patriarch of the family. He is also extremely conservative in his values and lives in a Bible Belt town in the American South, about forty miles from where Carolina grew up. He and Carolina had a very close relationship. But since Carolina became Carlos, Sharon has barred Carlos from seeing his grandfather. She says it would kill him. In an inversion of the story of Little Red Riding Hood, he would be puzzling, "Granddaughter, what a deep voice you have. What big muscles you have. What short hair you have." He could never have made sense of his beloved granddaughter's becoming his grandson, and if he did make sense of it, he would only go to his grave early, with hate in his heart toward this abomination of a grandchild, or so Sharon thought. In the meantime, the grandfather asked over and over, "Where's my Carolina? How come she never comes to visit me anymore? Is she too busy to remember her grandfather?" In the past, Carolina would devotedly come to visit her grandfather every time she returned from college, and over the summers as well. As weeks turned into months turned into a year, the grandfather could only conclude with chagrin that Carolina had indeed forgotten about him. In the meantime, Carlos begged his mother to be allowed to see his grandfather. He missed him terribly and was horrified at the thought that his absence would lead his grandfather to think he didn't love him anymore. He was prepared to tell his grandfather in as slow and sensitive a way as he knew about his decision to transition from a female to a male, and he was even prepared for the rejection from his grandfather if that should be the outcome, although he desperately hoped it wouldn't be. The thought that he would never see his grandfather before he died weighed against his mother's warning that if he did see him, his grandfather *would* surely die. Sharon was definitely in a tight spot, trying to protect her father while seemingly sheltering Carlos. Interestingly, it was her extended family that challenged her duck-and-cover strategy. They were strongly opposed to barring Carlos from his grandfather. Without telling her, they took it upon themselves to share with the grandfather the story of Carolina's transformation to Carlos. And he didn't die.

George Hagen is the father of a school-age gender-fluid boy. He waxes positive about all the ways he and his wife have supported their young son in his gender-nonconforming expressions. They know they do not want their son to feel ashamed but rather proud of who he is. Yet they are plagued by the potential bad things that might come his way:

> Looking into his eyes, I know he's on his own. I can't be at his side on every playdate. I can't change his friends' attitudes, those of future teachers, or those of strangers who stare at him on the street. Already he knows he's different. He's not a girl, and yet he doesn't act like a boy. . . . We [he and his wife] wait anxiously for the stereotypes to catch up.[67]

As they wait, they will do right by their son if they are ever-mindful of avoiding falling into the trap of sham strategies to assuage their fears and protect their child. There is a lesson to be learned here. Falsehoods, bribes, and taking cover will not create a healthy child. What a child wants is honesty, forthrightness, and genuine coping strategies, not smoke and mirrors.

WHEN FAMILY MEMBERS AREN'T ON THE SAME PAGE

Sometimes not everyone in the family will have traversed through the seven T's formula. A mother may be completely at ease in supporting her child to be gender creative; a father may be adamantly opposed to encouraging any such "perverted" behavior. Or, the siblings are all fine with their gender-bending brother or sister; the parents are fundamentally opposed and threaten to ask the child to leave the home. Or, the grandparents think it's fine but the parents don't; or, conversely, the parents think it's fine, and the grandparents see the whole family as going to hell in a handbasket.

Tension between parents, parents and siblings, or parents and grandparents often becomes the central focus of mental health professionals working with the family of a transgender or gender-nonconforming child. Although it has been my impression that mothers and grandmothers have an easier time accepting such a child than do fathers and grandfathers, it is not an automatic equation. Sometimes you'll find tension between partners in a two-mother family, sometimes in a two-father family.

As in all other critical aspects of child-rearing, these children will do best when the parents, whoever they may be, are pretty much on the same page, but they are at risk for anxiety, depression, behavioral problems, or manipulative ploys if they find themselves wedged between two parents who are not. In the eyes of gender-nonconforming children, the parent who does not offer support can easily become the evil one, while the more supportive parent is elevated to angel status. That kind of radical splitting in children's sense of each of their parents is never good for healthy development. On the other hand, if one parent is truly rejecting or abusive to the child, developing protective barriers against that parent and turning to the more supportive parent for nurture and protection can be a necessary and even life-preserving strategy.

The tensions between the parents over what to do about children who go against the gender grain can mount to critical proportions—so critical that the relationship falls apart, leaving children feeling responsible for destroying a family just by trying to be their authentic gender self. If the tension erupts *after* parents are divorced, there is yet another potential risk for such children: they can become the object of a custody battle, with their gender affiliation used as ammunition by parents who are in disagreement about it.

Ava and Jordan met in college. In their senior year, Ava discovered she was pregnant. Although they had planned to wait until they finished college before marrying and starting a family, both decided that their love and commitment was strong enough to speed things up in the face of this unplanned pregnancy. The first few years with their daughter, Leila, were blissful for both parents. She was a feisty little girl, but despite the challenges, they found themselves in agreement on all the practical and more philosophical aspects of parenting—until Leila started exhibiting some unusual behaviors. If they put out one of her dresses to wear, Leila threw it on the floor and screamed, "I won't wear this—ever." She asked to have her hair cut short like her friend Mikey's. Both parents said no, Mikey had short hair because he was a boy; she had long hair because she was a girl. So Leila took fate and a child's blunt-edged scissors in her own hands and gave herself a lopsided shaggy meant-to-be-buzz-cut. When Jordan discovered her shorn hair on the bathroom floor, he, in Ava's words, "Totally went ape-shit." Ava, on the other hand, had just entered a graduate program in psychology. She was taking a course on gender. She looked at Leila's shorn head and began to connect the dots—Leila was trying to tell them that she was not the fem little girl they thought they had brought into the world; maybe she was even a boy. She began to ask Leila, "Do you feel like a boy or a girl?" Leila burst into tears, "Why couldn't you make me one?" Ava, confused, asked, "Honey, what do you mean?" "Why couldn't you make me a boy like Mikey's mommy did? Why did you make me a girl?" Ava thought it was time to consult with a gender specialist. She assumed that Jordan would surely agree. She assumed wrong. Jordan was furious: "You're just putting thoughts in her head. She's not a guinea pig for your psychology class. She's our daughter." Ava was outraged in return: "How could you possibly accuse me of such a thing?" So began the demise of their blissful partnership. Instead of their being able to resolve their differences about Leila's gender development, their marriage began to fracture. Three years later, they had separated and were in the midst of a bitter custody battle, Jordan accusing Ava of turning Leila into a boy because of her own agenda, Ava filing a countersuit that under Jordan's care their child would be emotionally harmed by being forced to abide by Jordan's gender policing.

If the family can stay together, roll up their sleeves, and work through their differences about what is to be done for a child who goes against the gender grain, the benefits to the child are enormous. If the family cannot or is never given the opportunity to do any of this, the risks to the child are equally enormous. Even if family members start from a place of being light-years apart in negotiation of the seven T's formula, I would say that they owe it to their gender-nonconforming child to let love for that child trump their differences, and if needed, seek out a mental health professional to guide them through the sometimes grueling process of trying to agree on what should be done for their child's health and well-being.

WHEN THERE IS NO FAMILY

So far, we have taken for granted that children have a family. But the reality is that a fair number do not. I mentioned earlier that gender-creative youngsters are one, if not the only, minority group of children who cannot depend on support from their immediate family. Sadly, if a family has not been able to transcend its transphobia, hatred and bigotry can sometimes override the bonds of love, if they were ever there at all. Gender nonconformity may be seen as an act of the devil or a sin against God. If a child will not or cannot match the parents' gender expectations, that child might be punished, abused, or even ejected from the family home. Indeed, a fair number of youth in foster care are grappling with their gender or sexual identity. They do this not because it is a means of adapting to life in a group home or a foster family placement, but because that may be the very reason they are there—their birth family did not want them anymore. For others, being gender nonconforming or transgender was not the reason they found themselves without a family; they find themselves in foster care for other reasons, removed from their family for such things as child neglect, abuse, or the death of a parent. And they also happen to be gender creative. But what that means in all cases is that these children and youth may very well have no consistent, open-minded parental figures to guide them through this process.

Over the years, activists have been concerned about the treatment of transgender, gay, lesbian, bisexual, and queer youth in out-of-home care with faith-based providers—so concerned that the Child Welfare League of America and Lambda Legal joined together to draft a policy statement and a tool kit for action, explaining:

> Faith-based organizations and individuals motivated by their religious commitment have long played an important role in providing unbiased charitable and social services. Indeed, many religious communities welcome and affirm lesbian, gay, bisexual, transgender and questioning ("LGBTQ") people, and many individuals are motivated by their religious faith to help LGBTQ youth in foster care. But the anti-LGBTQ beliefs of some religious traditions may create ideological barriers that undermine the professional obligation to create a supportive system of care for LGBTQ youth."[68]

The undermining comes from foster parents whose mission is to make good Christians of their wards. In the mind of these caregivers, gender-nonconforming or transgender children will never make good Christians. So the children who are transitioning from their original home into foster care are again met not with compassion and understanding, but with potential punitiveness and aspersion for pursuing "strange" ways that are against God's will, potentially repeating the children's original gender trauma.

In September 2009, I participated in the conference "The Experiences and Needs of LGBTQ Youth in Out-of-Home Care," held in Oakland, California, and sponsored by the Bay Area Youth Centers. Many of the speakers were transgender youth themselves, who resided in group homes or had been in foster homes with an individual family. They had experienced numerous challenges. They had to keep coming out over and over again—to new group home staff, to new social workers, to new foster parents. They objected to their transgender status's becoming part of their official records: Why did every new foster care worker need to know their gender history? Why couldn't they be allowed to come out in their own time, just like any youth in an intact family? If they did want to come out, some had a terribly hard time, because there was no one there to support them in that process. Some fled the placement they were in, in search of a group home or foster placement that would support rather than abuse them for being transgender or gender nonconforming. Some feared for their safety, not only from their peers, some of whom could be brutal in their transphobic harassment, but from the very substitute parent figures who were supposed to be caring for them. If sibs in intact families have a hard time accepting a trans brother or sister, you can imagine how hard it is for foster brothers and sisters who are simply thrown together by chance. The strategy of these foster youth was to persist in self-talk that reminded them that being transgender or gender nonconforming was not a bad thing, it was just part of who they were. They did best if they could locate supportive peers, staff, and trans activist groups (which is far easier to do in the San Francisco Bay Area than in a small town in Middle America).

What was amazing was that against great odds, these youth were so vital and deeply involved in building their lives, and also that they had found each other. This doesn't account, however, for the many other foster children who will suffer greatly while trying to find their own way with no parents or understanding foster parents to support them. I am a founding member of a national organization, A Home Within. We provide pro bono mental health services to children and youth in foster care. A fair number of the older youth we serve in the San Francisco Bay Area are gay or lesbian, trans, bisexual, questioning, or queer. And a fair number of those youth have gravitated toward our Fostering Art program, which brings them together to teach them photography skills and engages them in collective projects about their own lives, under the guidance of a caring, gender-sensitive instructor/mentor. What I have learned is that if gender-nonconforming children don't have a family, the community can help them build one—a collective family that will protect and promote their gender creativity.

AND YOU'LL NEVER WALK ALONE

If you are a transgender or gender-nonconforming child, you may have an uphill journey into a potentially hostile world. You will need to rely on your parents to advocate for you on many fronts:

▶ To pay attention to your siblings and how all of you are getting along
▶ To run interference with extended family who wonder why you are the way you are
▶ To know how to talk to your friends' parents, and even your friends, to explain to them who you are and how you got there

▶ To talk to your teachers about making sure school is a safe place for you

▶ To pick just the right pediatrician for you or know how to educate your doctor about who you are

▶ To recognize when you might need a therapist or counselor to talk to . . . or know when they might need a therapist or counselor to talk to.

If you don't have parents like that or any parents at all, our best hope is that someone else will step in to do those things for you so that you'll never have to walk alone.

CHAPTER SEVEN

The Gender-Creative Therapist

My description amounts to a plea to every therapist to allow for the
patient's capacity to play. . . . The patient's creativity can only be too
easily stolen by a therapist who knows too much.

—D. W. WINNICOTT[69]

▼

I thought it only fitting to open this chapter with a quote
from the man who provided us the blueprint for the true and
false gender self. Right now, the mental health field is in the
midst of a sea change about children's gender health. Those of us
who object to a model of therapy governed by professionals' and
parents' desire to "help" a child accept his or her own assigned
gender and all its culturally assigned accoutrements must pay
heed to Winnicott's pleas: *Let the children tell you, don't tell them,
and provide them space to be their fullest creative selves.*

In the fall of 2010, I conducted a workshop for parents titled
"The 'Good' Therapist?" at the annual Gender Spectrum Family
conference. Asked to provide a description of the workshop for
the program brochure, I wrote:

The field of mental health is a snarly place for gender non-conforming children and their families. Any one of you may have experienced a therapist wanting to "fix" your child and cast blame on you for your child's [inappropriate] gender. These are therapists who do harm in the name of help. But there are those of us committed to stopping that harm, replacing it with support for families to foster their child's true gender self and for children to discover that self. Dr. Ehrensaft will present a model for doing that work, outlining for what and when to seek out the services of a mental health professional; when to have your child be seen, when not to; how to know if a therapist is trained and committed to gender growth rather than gender conversion.

That is exactly what I'd like to do in this chapter.

Two mothers of transgender or gender-nonconforming children shared with me two diametrically opposed experiences with a mental health professional:

MOTHER ONE: We found that most of the therapists seemed to be there to impede progress rather than to assist.[70]

MOTHER TWO: Thanks, Diane. You helped us quite a bit last summer when we talked on a phone appointment. We live in Boise and keep your words in our hearts and minds daily!

It is no secret that there are good therapists and bad therapists. But that's not the point here. When it comes to gender growth and development within the perspective of a true gender self, the lines seem to be drawn in the sand with a regrettably stark contrast: therapists who help and therapists who harm the children; therapists governed by "genderism"—advocacy of a binary gender system—versus therapists who embrace gender freedom and a broader gender spectrum.

HOW TO DRIVE A CHILD (AND PARENTS) CRAZY

Ken Zucker and Susan Bradley, at their Toronto clinic, met with a four-year-old boy who told his parents he was dead and was now a girl (a particular girl in a popular children's film). Here is an excerpt of that interview:

INTERVIEWER (I): In your mind, do you ever think that you would like to be a girl?

CHILD (C): Yes.

I: Can you tell me why?

C: I don't know. . . . Because we get to sit around and talk and do everything girls need to do.

I: In your mind, do you ever get mixed up and you're not really sure if you are a boy or a girl?

C: I am a girl.

I: Tell me more about that.

C: (*No response.*)

I: Do you ever feel more like a girl than like a boy?

C: It's too late. Because I'm already a girl. Because I hate being a boy.

I: You know what dreams are, right? Well, when you dream at night, are you ever in the dream?

C: I don't have dreams.

I: Do you ever think that you really are a girl?

C: Yes.

I: Tell me more about that.

C: (*Runs out of the test room to return to his mother in the reception area.*)[71]

The recounting of this interview was placed under the subheading "Do Children with Gender Identity Disorder Manifest Distress?" You bet they do, in the hands of a clinician who asks them leading questions and then labels them with a disorder. How many times would this child have to tell the interviewer "I *am* a girl" before the therapist would even begin to listen? I'd have to say that the evidence suggests that yes, this child is distressed, but not because she is a transgender child. It is distressing to be mentally battered by an unrelenting professional with a bias and an agenda. If I were this child, I would run out of the room, too—to preserve my sanity.

So how should mental health professionals provide for gender-nonconforming children and their family? What can we do to make a consultation a welcoming experience, rather than one to flee from?

It is not just the children who flee. At this same clinic, therapy was recommended for both Ben, a gender-nonconforming little boy, and his parents. After giving it some thought, Ben's parents declined. The psychologists thought things had gone well with the parents; they were concerned about Ben's family's resistance to treatment. If Ben's parents were anything like many of the parents I have known, they went home, considered what it would mean to "treat" Ben—take away his girl toys; enforce playdates with boys; ignore, turn their backs on, or outright punish his cross-gender play preferences and expression; police his clothing choices; set up Dad as the masculine man for Ben to emulate; and, in short, do everything in their power to erase his wish to be a girl. And, at the end of the day, they just weren't willing to inflict that kind of regimen on their child. Now, I can only speculate about Ben's mother and father, never having met them, but I can say with conviction that parents often have an uncanny way of knowing when harm might befall their child. Under the circumstances, I would say that declining the clinic's services was a very sound strategy on Ben's parents' part.

Not all parents have the opportunity to flee treatment. Either because of the era they've been parenting in, the area they live in, their trust in the expertise of the doctors, or their own confusions about their child's gender uniqueness, it's pretty easy to fall into the wrong hands. Catherine Tuerk is a friend and colleague. She is also the cofounder of the Washington, D.C., Gender and Sexual Advocacy and Education Program (previously named the Outreach Program for Children with Gender Variant Behaviors and Their Families), which she started precisely to prevent the harm done to her son from happening to other gender-nonconforming children. Some time ago, she reported to a journalist her experience thirty years earlier of taking her gender-fluid little boy to see therapists. Deeply influenced by the thinking of the day, she worried, watching her son, that he might become gay or transsexual and that it would be her fault. She must have done something to have made him that way, she thought. She was told by mental health experts that her son could surely be "fixed," that they could extinguish his "effeminate" behaviors and get him to be a (heterosexual) boy's boy. So, following their advice, she and her husband put their son through years of psychotherapy and psychoanalysis to make him more "masculine." Lo and behold, after all those years of money, time, and aggravation, the treatment was for naught. At age twenty, her son announced he was gay. And he was angry about what had been done to him as a child in the name of mental health. As Catherine looked back on her experiences with the mental health field, she bitterly came to realize that "everything I had been told by professionals was wrong or harmful to him and our family."[72]

Therapies that attempt to shape children to accept their assigned gender and all the social accoutrements attached to that gender are on one side of the line drawn in the sand. Therapies that offer a place for those children to creatively explore and develop their authentic gender self, whether it is a match or mismatch between assigned gender and a uniquely spun gender web, are on the other. You already know which camp I belong to. From where I sit, I urge you to beware of doctors or other health or education professionals who want to employ behavior modification, reward-and-punishment programs, token economies, and other shaping and molding to "fix" a child's gender, to make it what those experts believe to be normal (i.e., the gender assigned at birth or the socially prescribed expressions that correspond to that gender). And beware of therapists who query parents about what *they* did to make their child that way, with an unrelenting search for a history of trauma, loss, or mental illness. I come here not to bash those people but to encourage them to rethink their practices to offer an alternative model of mental health services that aims to support families and facilitate rather than stifle children's gender creativity and authentic gender self.

PRIMER OF PRACTICE

Parents need to be aware that many mental health professionals—psychiatrists, psychologists, social workers, marriage and family therapists, counselors, and educators—have to unlearn what they were taught about gender development. We were educated to believe that a child is born and given a *sex* assignment, male or female. If that gender is ambiguous (*intersex*, known in earlier times as *hermaphroditic*), fix it surgically as soon as possible, because by eighteen to twenty-four months of age, children will be set in their ways, with a fixed core gender identity as male or female. Once children develop that core gender identity and enter their preschool years, parents, teachers, and community will demonstrate the behaviors, attitudes, and roles that go along with the sex assignment. They will do this either through direct instruction, role modeling, or by their sheer presence as a gendered figure in the children's life. The children will absorb that information, both consciously and unconsciously, while going through their own soap opera of shifting love affairs—with their own mother and father. Luckily, this will not last forever, and the children will emerge, at about age six or so, with a clear sense of their stable gender, recognizing that it is permanent, accompanied by a clear sense that they want to marry someone of the opposite gender someday. By this philosophy, gender identity and sexual orientation are considered inseparable, and if all goes well, the children's sex and gender will be in perfect alignment and they will be happily heterosexual. If all doesn't go well, the children require treatment, to correct homosexual tendencies or get boys to be boys and girls to be girls—thus the psychiatric diagnosis of gender identity disorder that is fostered by these teachings.

It is vital to your child's well-being that you locate a gender-creative therapist, one who has shaken off these notions and replaced them with an alternative model of gender development. First of all, gender is a weaving together of nature, nurture, and culture. This gender web concept allows for every individual to discover his or her own unique gender identity and gender presentation, which may have many variations beyond the traditional binary notion of male or female. That web can interweave with, but is a completely different entity from, sexual identity/orientation. An easy way to remember this difference: Gender is who we go to bed *as*; sexual identity concerns whom we go to bed *with*. Gender is not fixed by age six; it is a lifelong, evolutionary process for us all. There is no documented evidence to date that indicates that psychological harm will be incurred if a child transitions from one gender to another and then back again, and such switches are not necessarily a symptom of unstable gender identity, but may simply reflect exploratory gender creativity.

If you want to understand the biological underpinnings of

gender, don't look between the legs, look between the ears. The majority of people demonstrate a match between their assigned gender and their affirmed gender. But some do not. That does not mean they are disordered, any more than the minority of people who are left-handed are disordered because their brain dictates they use their left hand rather than their right, in contrast to about 90 percent of the people around the world whose brain says, "Use your right."

A therapist who hasn't done his or her homework will be working with a handicap, concerned not with allowing your children space to unfold but with wrapping them up in a package of what they are "supposed to be." In addition to acquiring compiled lists of gender-sensitive mental health professionals as well as word-of-mouth suggestions conveyed through the community, it would behoove you, before embarking on any therapeutic relationship for your gender-creative children or your family, to check out not just the credentials but the professional's notions of gender health, gender goals, and mental health interventions.

If we are to facilitate children's healthy gender development, we must give them space to discover and tell us who they are. They know more than any of us do. Gender-sensitive professionals offer services not to fix the child, but to build resilience, sort out confusions and conflicts, facilitate family and community supports, supply evaluations and recommendations to other health professionals, especially pediatric endocrinologists, and, most important, provide a private space when needed for children to explore and build their gender selves, selves that may radically go against the grain of the culture in which they live. At the same time, there will be times when children's gender presentation or exploration is a symptom of something else, not their search for their true gender self, and we will need to learn how to differentiate gender as a symptom from gender as an expression of self, probably our most challenging task.

WHEN AND WHO AND FOR WHAT? THE PARENT CONSULTATION MODEL

Much of the therapeutic work I do with gender-creative children is what I dub "behind-the-scenes" interventions. By that I mean that I meet with the parents either without ever seeing the child or for an extended period of time after which the parents and I decide collaboratively that it would be helpful for me to also see their child. In this parent-consultation model, I start from the premise that a child whose main "presenting problem" is that he or she is gender nonconforming may be no more in need of treatment than is a child whose main "presenting problem" is that he or she is gender normative. I know that the challenges of being such a child often fall most directly in the parents' lap. Opening up my office to parents without the presence of the child gives them an opportunity to work out their own feelings, conflicts, and confusions, while also giving them time to adjust their perspective about their child and explore all their options for supporting that child. They can then take those ideas home and help their child, who may never know that I exist and who can continue in the tasks of childhood without being put under the microscope of a "shrink," an experience that might mislead them into thinking that there indeed is something wrong with them.

The questions plaguing parents can include "Whatever is going on with my child?" "When do I tell my gender-fluid daughter that she can't go topless anymore?" "Just help me sort out whether we should send a letter to the school disclosing Sally's assigned gender or leave that as nobody's business" "Where have I failed?" and so forth. The tasks I and other gender-creative therapists can help parents with include:

▸ Putting together a clearer picture of their child's unique gender web

▶ Moving from burdensome feelings of responsibility that they are the ones who created this to a constructive sense of responsibility for the ways they can support their child's authentic self

▶ Working through all of their feelings—the good, the bad, and the ugly (not only for the parents' sake, but also to relieve the child of having to shoulder the parents' feelings)

▶ Facilitating a mourning process for the child they thought they had and opening up a place that can embrace the child they do have

▶ Learning how to respond to their child in a way that will best facilitate his or her authentic gender self

▶ Managing the balancing act of keeping their child safe while supporting his or her authentic gender expressions and identity

▶ Addressing fears about their child and the unsafe world out there

▶ Developing strategies for dealing with extended family, teachers, community

▶ If there are siblings, ensuring parental mindfulness for those children's experiences as well

▶ If there are questions about medical interventions (hormone blockers, cross-sex hormones, future surgery), linking parents with appropriate medical professionals. (Note: In those situations, I will at some point surely request to see the child as well, as he or she will need a mental health assessment to qualify for medical services.)

Any mental health professional taking on this work will need to grasp the psychological experience of parents who have a gender-nonconforming or transgender child. While no two parents will be the same, there are indeed some patterns. Even in the most supportive of communities, you as a parent will be hard-pressed to shake the images that have crossed the front pages of your newspapers over time—Matthew Shepard, left to die on a fence for being gay; Gwen Araujo, battered to death because she was a girl with a penis. In the words of Riki Wilchins, executive director of the Gender Public Advocacy Coalition: "Kids are dying out there because they don't meet narrow gender norms—the boy who throws 'like a girl' or the girl who is perceived as being too masculine."[73] The specter of violence or even death may become either a loud siren or a lurking shadow that can render clear thinking very difficult. And the anxiety about danger and negativity from the outside world can get all mixed up with a parent's own internal doubts or gender ghosts from the past, creating a rather noxious emotional potion. This angst is hard to escape, and should be held in mind by any mental health professional working with parents, with the aim of helping them embrace and protect their gender-creative child. Gender-sensitive professionals can offer a safety net to parents as they build up their own immunity against living in this state of worry or fear.

The mother of a transitioning transgender youth asked the workshop presenter at a gender conference, "What is okay for me to share with my son about my own struggles with his transition?" Now, that is a hard question to answer without knowing this particular child and family, as there are no boilerplate solutions. But the meaning behind the question itself leads me back to the value of behind-the-scenes work with parents. In chapter 6, I spoke of the need for parents to shield their children from their own psychological struggles in coming to grips with their children's gender-creative self. It is okay for a parent to remind a transgender youth, "You've had several years to be thinking about this, but I'm just learning about it for the first time. So you're going to have to give me some room for that." But when it comes to the surfacing of very raw and perhaps painful feelings, a mental health professional can prove invaluable, by providing parents with the privacy of a confidential relationship in which they can bring all their different feelings to the surface without dumping them on their children. Psychoanalytically speaking, I assume that even then, there is always the possibility of sending those feelings through the airwaves unconsciously, but I also believe that those feelings can be neutralized significantly before they ever filter through, and that it never helps any child to be directly exposed to a parent's sobbing, anger, or chagrin about him- or herself.

Many parents seek out concrete advice—"Should I let my son wear skirts to school?" "Do you think Aliya should get to say she's a boy? She's only five." "Should I let the school know Kenny is transgender?" and so forth. A good therapist will help parents develop a plan of action but will not dictate one. We professionals should never be in the position of telling people what to do; rather, we should position ourselves to help parents create their own strategies. For example, bathrooms and camping trips are sure-fire issues for which parents seek help. Disclosure is another.

Richard and Marlene came to me because they found themselves in a pickle. Their seven-year-old, Bets, was mostly living as a boy these days but sometimes slid over to girl, Bets's assigned gender. The school camping trip was coming up. For the first time, there were going to be gender-segregated cabins and the parents would not be accompanying their children on the trip. If Bets stayed in the boys' cabin, what would happen when it came time to take a shower? What about going to the bathroom? How would the other boys receive Bets? If Bets stayed in the girls' cabin, there would be no best friends and Bets would stand out as the girl who is also a boy. The teachers were okay with whatever Richard and Marlene decided about where Bets slept. But Richard and Marlene weren't okay about making that decision. My only role was to listen to Richard and Marlene, help them weigh the pros and cons of each decision on the scale, and share my reflections about what each of the decisions might mean for Bets. In the end, they decided on the boys' cabin, and all went well.

Creighton and Pamela were another couple seeking advice—should they tell their child's new kindergarten that Chloe was born a boy but transitioned to being a girl, or was that nobody's business? Again, there is no boilerplate answer to this question; it depends on specific circumstances. Yet the therapist whom the parents consulted was able to make the observation that the problem might arise later when children, themselves, began to discover that Chloe was a girl with a penis and would want some explanation for that. It might not come up in kindergarten, but at some point later there was a good possibility it would. The therapist was operating from the principle that denying one's gender history was not in a child's best interest; yet she also recognized that the family might feel otherwise and that there were countervailing arguments that articulated that expressed thoughts, feelings, and behaviors, not bodies, are all that are relevant to know about a child's gender identity. It was not the therapist's role to impose her own views on the parents but to help them sort out their own guiding principles in developing a plan of action. Creighton and Pamela took in the therapist's thoughts about potential problems down the line, but in weighing it against their perception that Chloe just needed to be a girl like all the other girls, they decided against disclosure. Two years later, a problem did arise, and Creighton and Pamela were able to use the therapist again to facilitate their next plan of action. They called on their parental wisdom acquired from their and Chloe's experiences at school to disclose Chloe's transgender identity to the families in Chloe's class, despite Chloe's protests. They now believed this to be a better strategy and more in Chloe's best interests than the previous nondisclosure strategy that left them living with the constant anxiety of Chloe being "outed" by curious or questioning little friends, especially because two of her old friends from preschool, who had known Chloe as a boy, were now going to be attending her grade school.

The mental health professional working with parents has to learn to combine listening to the parents with speaking up, and that means taking a professional stance and sharing what he or she does know about gender development and gender health. For example, parents may come to me and say, "I know my kid is toying around with being transgender. And when he's eighteen, he can do whatever he wants, when it's off my watch and my legal responsibility. But before that, absolutely not. He's a boy and he's going to stay a boy, as long as he lives in our house. And we'll ground him for a month if he even thinks of going out of the house in a skirt." I listen carefully, and explore what it would mean for the parents if their son was truly transgender and what they thought might happen to him if he actually did go out in a skirt in their community. Somewhere in there I would share with them the statistics on youth under eighteen who do not receive support for their transgender identity: their rates of depression are higher than the average teenager's. So are their rates of poor self-esteem, suicide or thoughts of suicide, drug and alcohol use, self-mutilation, and sexual acting out. I do this not to scare the parents but to communicate to them what we are learning about children and youth who are squelched in their gender expression or identity. I do this also because I believe that no loving parent would ever want those outcomes for their children, even as I weigh those outcomes against their own expressed fears about what will happen if they *don't* suppress their children's transgender expressions. I will do the same kind of sharing when I hear one parent say to the other, "It's all your fault. You never should have let him have all those dolls and dress-up clothes and let him play with your makeup. You turned him into a sissy and a weirdo." I will listen, and I will stay with each parent as they express what they are feeling, but I will also share my thoughts that the dress-providing parent might simply be responding to the child's constitutional predisposition to his gender self and that child's desires, rather than shaping their son's behaviors. I believe I would be shirking my professional responsibilities if I didn't speak up.

The dress-providing parent doesn't usually sit there passively while her husband accuses her of turning their boy into a sissy. She may look at me and sputter, "This is what I have to put up with. He has no idea what he's talking about—he's just a retro macho." At this point she might pull a book from her bag and angrily toss it in her husband's direction—not just any book, but perhaps Stephanie Brill and Rachel Pepper's *The Transgender Child*. "Why don't you try reading this and knock some sense into your head." Right here we have one of the most important functions of the behind-the-scenes mental health work: creating a dialogue between two parents who are at odds with each other. Many times, these parents hurl accusations and recriminations at each other to try to rid themselves of their own internal worries about their child. If the world is going to point the finger at the parents for making their child this way, and if such books as *The Transgender Child* are instilling opposite worries that they might not be gender sensitive enough, the overwhelming stress of all that might lead parents to lay blame on each other, when the real issue at hand is their common and shared worry about who their child is, how their child got there, and whatever are they supposed to do for that child. Alternatively, these parents may genuinely be in opposite camps regarding those gender lines drawn in the sand, and this dialogue could reflect the beginning, the middle, or the aftermath of a collapse of the couple's relationship, as occurred with Ava and Jordan. The opposite-camp situation is more evident in heterosexual than in gay or transgender/gender-nonconforming or feminist parenting couples, for most of the latter have worked through their own struggles in going against the society's gender grain, and will typically find themselves in the same camp. But whenever the opposite-camp tension shows up, in whatever combination of parents, it takes some finesse and training in couples therapy on the therapist's part to break their stalemate. It means giving space for each parent to air his or her worries and fears, but most important, it involves encouraging parents to listen to each other, while again stepping in to say what you know about children and gender health, always making it clear to both parents that you are not taking sides, you are just trying to prevent or correct a double exposure and help them find a single focus that will ensure the best strategies to raise their child.

Some parents benefit from hearing from other parents. In this case, the mental health professional can become a facilitator of parent groups where support, sharing of information, and provision of professional expertise can alleviate the angst parents feel about going it alone in a hostile world or the conflict they feel with each other, when there are two parents, as well as within themselves, as they try to sort out what is best for their child.

WHEN AND WHO AND FOR WHAT? TREATING THE CHILD AND/OR THE FAMILY

So I've met with the parents. When would I then want to meet with the child?

I'd like to quote from Ellen Perrin, Edgardo Menvielle, and Catherine Tuerk, as I could never say it better myself:

> Most [gender-variant] children will respond to parents' acceptance and encouragement. Referral to a mental health specialist is appropriate if the child is anxious, depressed, or angry, exhibits self-destructive behavior, or experiences significant isolation—especially if these problems do not improve with short-term counseling. Children who are victims of bullying can benefit from therapeutic approaches that teach skills to respond more effectively and provide strategies to reduce the impact. Children who are very shy or have difficulty making friends may benefit from training to improve social skills and reduce social anxiety.[74]

I recall a recent conversation with a respected colleague and friend who is a gay psychoanalyst. He is very committed to helping gender-nonconforming and transgender children and youth, and he expressed his hope that all these children could be afforded the opportunity of a child analysis. I was somewhat taken aback by his remarks but went home to think about it. I am not at all averse to psychoanalytic treatment, albeit the idea of a three- to four-times-a-week treatment for a child in the context of twenty-first-century family life and economics seems utopian at best, anachronistic at least. But that's not the point. Why should the child who does not conform to binary gender expectations, particularly the transgender child, be assumed to need treatment, but a cisgender[75] child (one who is living in accordance with his or her assigned gender) who does conform should not be assumed to need such treatment? Would my colleague want to have been referred for psychoanalysis as a child because the professionals or his parents knew that he would someday be gay? Merely being gender nonconforming, transgender, or gay does not make one a patient. The challenges of the developmental journey toward the true gender self for the gender-creative child in the context of a potentially hostile and genderist/transphobic culture might be fodder for an analyst's couch, but only under the specific conditions outlined so clearly by Perrin, Menvielle, and Tuerk.

The main reasons I myself move to invite parents to bring their gender-nonconforming or transgender children to see me are as follows:

▸ The parents are absolutely stymied about who their children are and would like me to help them bring their children into focus.
▸ The children themselves are asking for someone to talk to about "gender stuff."
▸ The children haven't asked but the parents recognize some of the signs of stress, including clamming up on the topic, and would like their children to have a place

of their own to sort out feelings and get help expressing wants and needs.

▶ The parents don't see stress lines, but when I listen to their descriptions of what is going on for their children and at home, I recognize them, and suggest that the child come in for an assessment.

▶ The children are suffering from bullying, teasing, and harassment, and need help building resilience to confidently be their true gender self in a world that is not inviting.

▶ The children are suffering the stress of being caught in a vise between two warring parents and clearly need a room of their own to find their voice.

▶ The children are not receiving much parental support and appear to be developing symptoms as a result. (This is a delicate one to present to parents, but I would be remiss if I didn't address it.)

▶ The parents' description of the situation sounds so confounding that it seems imperative to see the child to sort out if the child's gender issues are actually a symptom of something else or are truly a reach toward an authentic gender self, or some combination thereof.

▶ The family is contemplating going forward with medical treatments—hormone blockers, cross-sex hormones, or surgery in older teens. In this scenario, meetings with the child are provided either to assess and make recommendations for treatment to a pediatric endocrinologist or interdisciplinary medical team, or to help the child and the parents sort out whether such treatments would be in the child's best interests and to psychologically prepare the child for the treatment if the family decides to go ahead with it.

Often I meet with children only a few times, although sometimes I see them in ongoing intensive treatment or sometimes I become their gender consultant to whom they come as needed, somewhat like the pediatrician doing periodic checkups or the medical specialist who steps in only when an issue arises. I would say that in any of these interventions, I'm guided both by my own quest to understand the complexity of each child's unique gender web and by the principles of therapy laid out by the World Professional Association for Transgender Health, which involve helping each child attain "personal comfort with the gendered self to maximize overall psychological well-being and self-fulfillment."[76] With all children I treat, I first set up an evaluation period of one to three sessions, to give the child a chance to meet me, for me to meet the child, and to then come up with a treatment plan, where indicated.

I find that, of all the above reasons for children to be seen at all, I most often recommend ongoing psychotherapy when:

▶ It is so clear that the children are hungry for a place of their own to talk, play, and know there is someone who understands.

▶ The children are wracked with anxiety and worries even in the face of optimal family and community supports.

▶ The children have at least moderate anxiety and worries and are receiving minimal, conflicting, or compromised support from the family and/or the school.

▶ The children need help developing both a *self*-narrative and a narrative that they feel comfortable presenting to the world.

▶ The children need to build resilience to negotiate unfriendly interchanges or a blatantly hostile world, a world that could include parents, siblings, extended family, school, and neighborhood.

▶ My meeting with the children tells me that gender may be the reflecting pool for some other underlying issue and not the core issue, and I will need some time to help the child sort that out while providing ongoing psychological support.

I mentioned earlier that our hardest mental health challenge is to differentiate gender as a symptom from gender as an expression of self. There is one ex post facto test—if children are given permission to express their apparent true gender self and everything seems to settle down, that is a good indicator that the preceding turmoil was indeed about gender and was "cured" by removing the children from the straitjacket of a false gender self, demonstrated by the children's relaxing and appearing more balanced and secure in most if not all aspects of life. If the same children were to be prohibited from that expression, the turmoil might only grow worse—they may become agitated, depressed, or even suicidal. On the other hand, if the children become more agitated after being given permission to transition to a declared gender expression or identity, something else might be going on. Those children, if prohibited from that expression, may be no more or less agitated. But better not to wait until after the fact to garner that wisdom. Although surely not an exact science, protocols are presently available and being further developed to help clinicians access a child's gender status as well as differentiate gender dysphoria from psychiatric disorder.[77]

Additionally, if a mental health professional really listens, with an open clinical ear, the children themselves will tell you. The children searching for their gender self often provide a consistent narrative over time in which they report, or parents observe, a continuous thread of attempts at or successes in gender creativity. Children who hop onto gender as a gate to swing from to quiet other ills often lack a consistent gender narrative, and seem either manic, hysterical, nonsensical, or chaotic in describing their gender woes. At its most basic, it just doesn't sound real. There are also children who suddenly show up with a gender issue after a trauma and with no previous history of gender bending. Here, too, we may be seeing children who are expressing other troubles through gender. For example, the three-year-old who suddenly announces that he is a girl after losing his mother to sudden death may be in a desperate emotional search to reclaim his lost mother by becoming her, rather than in a journey toward discovering his true gender self.

Here are a few clinical examples to illustrate the difference between gender as an expression from gender as a symptom, illustrations that highlight the complex task confronting the mental health professional. A teen who has been diagnosed with Asperger's syndrome insistently tells his therapist that he must listen to his pleas to transition to living as a girl, or the boy might end up hurting himself. The therapist pursues the boy's wish to become a girl and the boy is quite forthright in his motives— he has no friends; he notices that girls have more friends; if he becomes a girl, he will be better at making friends, and then he'll have some. The wish to become a girl is magical thinking, and a creative but not a *gender* creative solution to the primary problem—social isolation because of his lack of social skills.[78] Another young man who has recently entered college begs his therapist to make arrangements for him to start taking estrogen. The therapist is not a gender specialist and has been meeting with this youth for other reasons, including family strife, so he refers his patient to a gender specialist to assess whether this young man is a candidate for cross-sex hormone treatment. The gender specialist discovers that this young man is very frightened of his own aggression—he fears that he might explode and hurt someone. He doesn't want to be a woman, he just wants to be a gentler man. Because women are less aggressive than men, and transgender women have reported that they feel less aggressive after taking estrogen, he wants estrogen. We could say that this youth, in desiring estrogen but also a continued male identity, was declaring his status as gender fluid, except that the goal is a smooth temperament rather than blended gender. In this situation, the gender specialist concluded that the young man should continue to work with his therapist on issues of aggression and fears about his own feelings, rather than turn to cross-sex hormones as a medical solution to temper outbursts.

Whether gender issues turn out to be a quest for the true self or a solution to psychological ills, if a gender specialist decides to see children individually and that therapist has been trained, like myself, to listen to the patients and wait until they bring up material they want to talk about, that therapist will have to unlearn the therapeutic "waiting game." In a culture laced with disapproval and judgmental attitudes toward girls and boys who go against the gender grain, a therapist might have to wait until hell freezes over if he or she expects the children to spontaneously bring up their "gender stuff." The therapist may risk being intrusive, but I cannot stress enough the countervailing benefits of initiating a dialogue about the child's gender, such as, "Tommy, I noticed you haven't mentioned anything, but your mom and dad told me that every night you cry and pray you'll wake up in the morning and you'll be a little girl." That child may well be relieved of the burden of "We don't talk about such things," a burden that he can easily carry even if his parents have given a pep talk about meeting "the nice doctor who knows about these things and is going to help you." Children may be relieved to meet an understanding adult outside the family who speaks up and shows interest and a desire to know more about their true gender self. And by the way, as the therapist shows that interest, he or she should make sure the playroom is equipped accordingly, with not only princesses and popguns but gender-fluid and transgender dolls and puppets with which children can find a likeness—a soldier in a dress, a princess with a penis (this would apply only to anatomically correct dolls, which many therapists keep in their office, traditionally for evaluations of sexual abuse, but now proving invaluable as a means to create transgender dolls, by a switch of clothes or a hair restyling).

I should mention that although some children want a very private room of their own to explore and establish their own gender authenticity, some children, like their parents, benefit from groups, where they can hear from other children about their experiences and feel a commonality with those children, rather than feeling like the outsider, which is so often their experience in other social settings. Many of these groups take place in psycho-educational or community support settings and do not necessitate the services of a mental health professional, but a trained therapist facilitating such a group can also be an extremely helpful adjunct or primary form of mental health intervention, especially for children who are trying to build resilience and self-confidence and strengthen the narrative of who they are. It can also be a place to find friends. Ironically, some children shun such groups, either because they are too shy or private and do not want to talk about their troubles "in public," or because they do not identify with the other children.

Some children may only find their true gender selves if their family does some therapeutic work as well. Therapists may choose to treat both the child and the family, alternating meetings with each. Or they may refer the family to another therapist with whom they will work collaboratively—one therapist will see the child, the other the family. And sometimes the therapist will decide that the child should not be seen in individual therapy at all, as the bulk of the problem lies in the family's negotiation of the child's unique gender web and the best thing is to bring in the whole family. Recall that in chapter 6, I spoke of the challenges for the siblings of the gender-nonconforming child. It is within the context of family therapy that these issues can often best be worked through. Alternatively, the child's individual therapist may want to attend to the siblings, or one or more of the siblings may also need a room of their own, their own individual therapist who will offer them a private and confidential place to sort through their own feelings and experiences.

Whenever I do general teaching on child psychotherapy, I warn students going into the field that the workload for child therapy will be at least three times the individual work with adults. By necessity, it will require regular meetings with the parents, both to fill them in on the progress in the therapy and to hear insights and observations from the parents while offering their own as well. But there might also be phone calls or meetings with teachers, school counselors, school principals, educational specialists, pediatricians, medical specialists, psychiatrists, speech pathologists, occupational therapists, family therapists, psycho-educational evaluators, custody evaluators, mediators, group therapists, and parents' individual and couples therapists. Quite a village. That village grows bigger when the children being treated are transgender or gender nonconforming. To become a child therapist working with these children is also to become a child advocate, for such children will only do as well as the school and community does in supporting them. It therefore behooves the therapist to use his or her clinical skills and extend his or her activities to work collaboratively with whole families—not just parents but grandparents, aunts and uncles, and siblings—and with relevant communities to ensure that the children are enveloped in a social network of safety, security, acceptance, and gender creativity. And the therapist will absolutely need to know how to work as a member of an interdisciplinary team of health professionals that may include at the very least the child's pediatrician, a pediatric endocrinologist, and a child therapist, plus a family therapist in situations where family therapy is recommended in conjunction with child therapy.

THERAPIST AT WORK: LISTEN, WAIT, AND PONDER

The therapeutic work should always be a collaboration between parents and therapist. Yet some of the work is totally in the therapist's domain. I'd like to take the opportunity to pull back the curtain and share with parents what should be going on within a therapist's head if the individual is doing his or her job.

First comes the mantra I keep repeating: "If you really listen, the children will tell you." You don't go on telling or interrogating children until you force them to flee the room. But that listening should not translate to having passive ears. While children are in the room (be it alone or in the presence of others), the listening involves paying attention to what the children are saying and accepting the children's gender expertise while having the translation skills to decipher the meaning of what the children are telling you in words or in play. We also must listen for what the children are *not* telling us about themselves, for that might indicate an anxious erasing of history and an inability to think and talk about the stream of their gender life from birth until the present.

If parents are in the room, the listening means hearing where the parents are, not where you hope them to be, and starting from there. It means acknowledging that the parents may not be on the same page as you regarding gender, or may not be on the same page with each other. It means balancing respect for a particular family regarding their own psychology, culture, and values with your professional understanding of healthy gender development, even when it is at odds with the family's practices.

So it is our professional obligation to combine empathic listening with expertise and observation. It is not a question of holding back on information or thoughts that might not sit well with parents, but learning how and when to deliver them in a way that the children and their parents can hear.

Yet how do you listen to a moving target? Would that it were so easy that a gender-nonconforming child or youth would come to my office, sit on my couch, and give me a perfect composition with introduction, major thesis, text, and conclusion, and all I had to do was take it in. Sometimes that does happen, but more often than not, it's a lot messier. Let me offer a snippet of an ongoing therapy with a gender-fluid, possibly transgender teen who came to me to sort out his/her gender conundrums. Michael was sparkly, literally and figuratively, and imaginative, with a mind that was almost always in high gear. He asked his mother if he could see me to sort out his confusions regarding both his gender identity and sexual orientation. One week, he sat on the couch across from me and declared, "I'm androgynous. Actually, I'm a Gender Smoothie: Just take everything about gender, throw it in the blender, press the button, and that's me." Just a week later he said, "If I want to have sex reassignment, then I'm just going to go ahead and do it." Okay, maybe we were getting somewhere, except the next week he did a turnabout: "I've never been the kind of person who knew I was a girl trapped in a boy's body." So perhaps we got that settled, and then the next week I listened to him tell me, "I'm just a gay boy. And you know what? I hate vaginas. They smell horrible. They're disgusting." But Michael as a gay boy only lasted seven weeks, and the following week Michael announced, "I'm just a chick with a dick," followed the next week by, "I'm just a woman with a vagina in the rear." So what good is, "If you listen, they'll tell you who they are," if the children tell you six different things in as many weeks and you feel as if you're an out-of-control moving sidewalk or caught in a revolving door? Fast-forwarding, I can tell you that eventually, with adequate time to explore, Michael sorted out his confusions and came to understand that he was a she—a heterosexual transgender female. But in the meantime, listening meant following closely what Michael was trying to tell me and holding a mirror up to reflect what I heard, accompanied by my voiceover as I shared with Michael my thoughts about all that he told me. Michael, on his own, caught his vacillations from one week to the next. I listened as he described himself as having two different brains that contradicted each other—one saying he was a gay boy, the other saying he was a transgender girl. He was absolutely clear about the difference between sexual orientation and gender identity. In his own words, "Sexual orientation is what you do with your clothes off; gender identity is what you do with your clothes." At the same time, he was absolutely unclear about himself. Michael made it easy to be a listener, because he hardly let me get a word in edgewise. But I'm pretty persistent, so after listening for quite a long time I was able to offer my observation: "Michael, I'm listening and what you're telling me is that you just don't know yet. So let's slow down and give you some time to explore without declaring. Otherwise, we're both going to fall on the floor dizzy."

As Paul Simon (and others) have counseled us, "Slow down, you move too fast." Beware the therapist who is all too eager to jump forward with solutions. It makes us all nervous to live in a state of ambiguity or not to know about something as essential in our culture as gender status. And some therapists might want to advertise their progressive thinking about gender by being avid advocates of gender-nonconforming or transgender children, leaping forward to carve a path for the children to immediately declare a new identity, regardless of whether those children are actually ready or even actually desire such a transition. And remember, children are fast-moving organisms. They develop at a quick pace, there is no tomorrow, and if they want something, they want it now. Waiting is not their forte. Whereas I would absolutely take issue with professionals or lay people who insist that a child is too young to know about his or her true gender self, I would also say that a child may be all too eager to just get on with life, and it is the mental health professional's role to slow things down and offer an opportunity for the child and for the parents to have a fully realized rather than a rushed journey, one that fully explores dreams, hopes, fears, confusions, disappointments, and coping strategies, as well as affirmations.

I offer another caveat here. Remember that some children experience puberty as trauma rather than celebration. And also keep in mind that some children may have been suppressed or blocked from expressing their true gender self for a very long time. For these youth, time may be of the essence, and fast must replace slow, as in any crisis situation. The sudden crisis of an unwanted puberty in children who only at that moment have experienced an epiphany, a recognition or acknowledgment of their possible transgender self, can be averted if a therapist facilitates quick action so the children can have access to puberty blockers. Youth who are about to crack under the pressure of living a false gender existence, to the point of being ready to take their own life, cannot wait for a slow response—they need swift and immediate intervention from a mental health professional who can participate in breaking the shackles of the false gender self that are about to do those older children or young teens in. So let me do some editing here: Slow down, except when the biological clock is swiftly ticking or in those crisis situations where it is essential that you move fast.

For professionals like myself, being a good gender therapist is being willing to grapple with our own gender ghosts. Because if we don't, they will surely get in the way of listening, thinking, and acting empathically and appropriately with the children and families who come to us. The ghosts can appear in the form of unexplored cultural assumptions that we just take for granted. Or they can take the form of the training I alluded to earlier, which taught us that children who make us feel anxious because they are violating gender norms are gender sick, because otherwise why would healthy people like us get anxious? Let me give you an example of gender ghosts subtly at play. Remember transgender Max, whom a therapist compares to an English child who tells everyone he is French. Despite the therapist's contention that his young patient only "wants to be" French, Max replies, "I don't want to be, I don't like to be . . . a boy." When another therapist participating in that session simply asks, "You are a boy?" Max's response is: "Yes."[79] The relationship between body, feelings, and culture in Max's gender web and authentic gender self has nothing in common with the English boy who pretends he is French. But the first therapist's attempts to label Max's gender identity as mere make-believe is a reflection of his own gender ghosts that tell him that a transgender male is not a "real" male but only an artifice of a male. Unless he receives help to rid himself of such assumptions and beliefs, which I assume were instilled from his own gender past, this therapist will be a danger to young people who are earnestly trying to establish their gender authenticity.

I mentioned earlier the importance of our having gender-fluid and transgender play equipment in our office. How many child therapists actually have transgender dolls available for our child clients? It is probably our own gender ghosts that make us overlook this. We may have gender-neutral dolls, but the mixing and matching that is the ilk of transgender children often are nowhere to be found in our office. How come? And how many of us have books with gender-fluid and transgender characters? *William's Doll*[80] is a start, but only that. I think the answer is that we never stopped to think about it, and our own gender ghosts confine us to preparing our therapy offices in a traditional binary way.

So a therapist's work is never done. We will need to continually scrutinize our own gender upbringing and the outmoded assumptions or practices that might slither into our therapeutic work. The good gender therapist will be the therapist who listens but tells, knows when to go slow and when to go fast, can live with ambiguity and not knowing, and is willing to confront his or her own gender ghosts.

Λ DΛY IN THE LIFE OF A GENDER THERAPIST—
BRADY GOT EATEN BY THE DOG

Now I'd like to give you a window into the daily work of the gender therapist. I met Philip at a community event where I was speaking on gender development and gender creativity. He asked for my business card and soon after I received a call from him. He and his wife, Amy, asked to consult with me about their four-year-old child, Brady. In our first sessions together, I learned the following things about Brady. Four months earlier, at Christmas, Brady had announced that he wanted to be called Sophie all the time and that he felt like a girl in the inside and a boy on the outside. Before that, Brady had given himself the nickname Rainbow Love Heart. Dad tried to talk more to his child about his gender feelings, but Brady didn't want to talk about it, saying that he felt he was a girl, but couldn't be, because he had a boy's body. Soon after, Brady/Sophie described him/herself as a girl with a penis and a boy's voice. Even before that Christmas, Brady had been longing for girls' clothes. At age three, Brady told his parents that he wanted to be a woman, not a man, when he grew up. Later, he asked if he cut off his penis, would it hurt. Amy and Philip were both concerned that Brady might actually try to cut off his penis to achieve his goal of being a woman when he grew up. During that same year, Brady saw a girls' shirt in a store, and begged his mom for it, but his mom said no, that was for girls, and he was a boy. A year later, Mom had done her research and worked through her own feelings and felt more comfortable buying Brady/Sophie girls' clothes.

Brady/Sophie was attending preschool when s/he first came to see me, after a series of meetings with his/her parents. His/her parents reported that s/he only wanted to play with girls, wanted to let his/her hair grow long but wear boy clothes, and wanted to be a princess. Most of the time s/he was in her own world, and both parents described him/her as having a bit of an Asperger's quality. S/he identified with an animated car from Pixar Studios whom s/he identified as Girly Girl, a car with boy paint but a girl engine. S/he glommed onto the idea of a Merman, a male mermaid. S/he seemed in turmoil, and Amy and Philip just wanted to make sure they were doing right by their child, which was to allow him/her to express him/herself as Sophie. So that is why we all decided together that they should bring Brady/Sophie in to see me.

Brady/Sophie arrived at our first session in what I would described as "unisex" clothes, a tie-dyed T-shirt, shorts, and sandals. Almost the first thing Brady/Sophie said to me when s/he met me was "I'm half and half. Half boy, half girl. A boy on the bottom [s/he points to his/her waist down], a girl on the top [s/he points to his/her waist up]." I asked what name I should call him/her. His/her response: Sophie, explaining, "My nickname is Brady, but in kindergarten we'll sign me up as Sophie and I'll want everyone to call me 'she.'" Brady/Sophie was intrigued by my sand tray, and spun a wild tale of a giant sandworm that scares people and then eats them. After the first visit with me, Philip called me to let me know that Brady/ Sophie said, "I don't want to have to go to school if they have to call me Brady."

In the very next session, Brady/Sophie arrived fully decked out as a little girl, with a headband, girls' shirt, and multi-colored Crocks. He/she announced to me that "I'm all girl now—Sophie. It just happened real fast. I'm not half and half anymore." I asked Sophie where the boy half went. Sophie's response: "Somewhere else." I noticed that Sophie kept sucking in her tummy—she thought that would make her more of a girl on top. When I meet with children I ask them to draw a person (any person they want) and to draw a self-portrait. "No way," replied Sophie. Instead, she drew the car named Girly Girl. On the front she carefully wrote out the number 53. She explained to me that 53 is a girl's number. Her old number used to be 95, and that is a boy's number—"8 is a boy's number, 76 is a girl's number, 6 is a boy's number, 70 is a girl's number." When I'm meeting with a child I'm always making mental notes to myself. As I listened to the number categories, that note was: "No gender fluidity for this little person. For Sophie, gender is as binary as her number system."

In a later session, Sophie was very excited and wanted to tell me the news. "Did you hear? There's no more Brady. I threw Brady in the garbage, and Brady couldn't get out because the garbage can's too high, and then all the garbage got thrown on top of him. But Brady climbed to the top and still couldn't get out. Then Corky [their dog] came and ate him. Actually, Mom fed Brady to Corky. He tasted good, like a human. But a dead human, because Brady was already dead when Corky ate him." This was a four-year-old's creative solution to get a better gender match between the outside and the inside.

Sophie wanted to draw new portraits. No more Girly Girl cars. Now she was drawing mermaids. In my work with transgender little girls and gender-fluid little boys, particularly gender hybrids, mermaids are indeed very popular. It makes total sense—one kind of body on the top, another on the bottom. But Sophie, in her newfound affirmed female gender identity, was not so sure yet that she was in a safety zone. How did I figure this out? Because Sophie moved to the sand tray, picked out little mermaid figures and a big toy shark, and had the shark chasing the mermaids around the beach, trying to savagely eat them. As I watched Sophie's play, I ruminated on an article I had recently written, "A Child Is Being Eaten,"[81] and remembered very young children's fantasies and mixed feelings about getting eaten: Either you are a yummy dessert that all would want or an innocent victim of a ferocious monster or wicked witch. And if you want to get rid of your enemies, feed them to the wolves. To Sophie I commented, "Bottom-boys and top-girls sure might get gobbled up around here, for better or worse."

My work with Sophie was now drawing to a close. Brady, now Sophie, was no longer exhibiting the inner turmoil that had brought her parents to me in the first place. Sophie's parents now had Sophie in clearer focus. My ongoing work with them helped them see what they already knew intuitively: Sophie was a transgender little girl. In one of our last sessions together, Sophie and I had the following conversation:

SOPHIE: You know what? Sophie is calm when she wakes up in the morning. But Brady, who got eaten, was wild.

D.E.: Does your mom know that? [Amy is in the room with Sophie. I should make note here that many parents of gender-creative children are hesitant to leave their child alone in a room with a therapist. If I were a parent, I might be, too, given the harm that has been done to a child's true gender self under the auspices of cure.]

SOPHIE: I don't know.

D.E.: Should we ask her?

SOPHIE: No, I just want to tell Diane. But if you weren't Diane, I wouldn't tell you.

I invite you to compare this dialogue with the dialogue on page 205, between the therapist and the fleeing child in the testing room in Toronto.

In that same session, Sophie later told me that Brady has never shown up again since Corky ate him. But I saw signs that "Mermaid Sophie" was still not in safe waters. If Brady was gone, his penis wasn't, as Sophie kept clutching her penis through her shorts, especially as she told me that some of the boys at her preschool told her she can't be a girl, because she used to be a boy. I asked Sophie what she did when this happened. "I just get quiet and don't say anything." In our parent sessions, I had worked with Amy and Philip to help Sophie come up with some language so she would have a way of responding to her friends. Amy and Philip were in the process of doing that, but emotionally Sophie was still like a deer in headlights when her friends said she couldn't be a "real" girl. So in our session, I wondered with Sophie if she could be a teacher to her friends, because she probably knew more than they did about how someone who used to be a boy could become a girl. She asked how I knew that she knew more. "Because," I said, "you are the expert of yourself." Sophie thought for a minute and answered by saying, "I have

eight baby dolls and nineteen race cars." Now how was I supposed to make sense of that? To the best of my clinical acumen,
I would say that Sophie was speaking in code about her expertise
concerning her own unique gender web. Throughout all her play
sessions, she interwove a theme that consisted of nurturing baby
doll play and violent race car mayhem—ergo: eight baby dolls
and nineteen race cars. She may have been binary in her thinking about gender and may have thrown Brady to his death in the
garbage can, but in her actual gender web, she had spun together
the threads of all the parts of her—Brady *and* Sophie.

The outcome of our work together was that Amy and Philip
decided to allow their child to go to preschool as Sophie, a girl.
The teachers reported back that Sophie's previous behaviors,
when she was confined to a male identity, now made more sense
to them. For the first time, they observed that Sophie jumped
right into the play. In the past, when she was Brady, whenever
a boy showed up in her vicinity, she would run and grab a baby
doll and carriage and remain frozen in her tracks. Sophie now
had her first real friend, a little girl named Gina. One little boy
at her preschool continued to give her a hard time. He belliger-
ently told her that he was only going to call her Brady, he would
never call her Sophie. Sophie was no longer a deer in headlights.
Now she could look this boy in the eye and say, "Well, that's
okay, but if you do, I'm not going to answer you."

In the initial period when Amy and Philip agreed that it was
time to give Brady/Sophie the green light to transition to being
a girl, we came up with a strategy for Sophie. Each morning,
Amy would set out three sets of clothes: girl clothes, "gender-
neutral" tie-dye clothes, and boy clothes that Brady/Sophie had
been wearing as Brady. Brady/Sophie consistently chose either
the girl clothes or the tie-dye clothes, never the boy clothes. The
first few days Sophie presented as a girl were not all that calm;
Philip and Amy noticed that she was wound up like a top. But
the anxious excitement seemed to dissipate, and after the first
week Sophie seemed to settle down, now that she was allowed

to wear girl clothes whenever she wanted, which was always. Sophie, usually a very understated child, suddenly burst out, "I'm the happiest I've ever felt in my life."

But now Amy and Philip were faced with another challenge—helping four-year-old Sophie come to terms with some body realities. As Brady was transitioning to Sophie, she had a lot of questions. She wanted to know if she would grow up to have "nomies" (breasts) just like Mommy. Because isn't that what happens when little girls become women? Her parents, in response to Sophie's questions, pondered what they should tell her about body change options for transgender females—either surgical or hormonal. Again, it was not my role to give advice but to supply Amy and Philip with some developmental guidelines. I discussed four-year-olds' cognitive and emotional capacity to absorb medical and scientific information, and the risks of overloading them with more than they can handle, versus the benefits of providing them with a clear and user-friendly gender road map, a risk analysis that of course will vary from child to child. After talking about it with me, they decided to keep things both general but also specific to the very question that Sophie had asked. They planned to tell Sophie something like the following: "There are many ways to be a boy or a girl, and no, if you are born with a penis, you won't grow breasts on your own." They would then wait to see what Sophie, who is very scientifically minded for a four-year-old, would do with that information. If she wanted to know more, they would tell her they would get back to her on that one (until we all had a chance to put our heads together again, although their inclination was to wait until she was a little older to fill her in about the possibilities of hormone treatment or surgeries).

Our work was now over and I remained in their family's life on an "on call" basis whenever they might need me. That summer, between preschool and kindergarten, Philip contacted me by e-mail twice. In the first e-mail, he reported that Sophie was adjusting to life as a girl and seemed to be enjoying herself,

although she was showing some signs of stress, particularly fin-
gernail biting. She had a worry that people would find out she
used to be a boy or think she was a boy. She also had a fear of
people who knew her before as a boy, who she thought wouldn't
be accepting. On the other hand, she beamed with pleasure
when she was acknowledged or recognized for her true gender,
as when a parent at the playground said to his own child, "Careful, there's a girl already on the slide," or when a sales clerk
commented, "I like your hair. It's cute." In this same e-mail,
Philip also requested that I write a letter for Sophie to carry
when traveling and for school and medical care, which parents
of transgender children are advised to have. Philip had done his
homework and had several thoughtful suggestions about how
he would prefer the letter to read, all of which I incorporated.
Here is the letter:[82]

> To Whom It May Concern:
>   I am writing this letter in regards to Sophie X, who has
> been in my care since _____. I am a clinical psychologist and
> gender specialist who is working with Sophie and her family,
> for the purpose of helping her clarify her gender identity.
> Sophie was assigned a male gender at birth but has shown
> signs of gender fluidity from early life. Under her care with
> me, Sophie (née Brady X) has expressed both to me and to her
> parents that she is an affirmed female. With the support of her
> parents, Sophie is now living fully as a female and self-identifies
> as such. To promote her well-being and emotional health, it
> is imperative that Sophie be seen and treated as a female by
> her parents, her educational settings, and the community
> surrounding her. In school settings and the community, this
> would include such things as bathroom use, participation as
> a female in sports activities or any other programs that might
> be designated as "girl" activities, and so forth. Both of Sophie's
> parents have supported Sophie in her transition to an affirmed
> female gender identity and are in full agreement, as am I, that

her well-being and mental health will be best served by recognizing and acknowledging her as a female.

Sincerely,

Diane Ehrensaft, PhD

In the second e-mail, Philip thanked me for the carry letter and reported the following story. They had gone to a picnic with other transgender children and their families. Afterward, Philip and Amy asked Sophie what she thought of the other kids. Her reply: "They were okay, but I was the only girl."

Our work was done for the present. Sophie entered kindergarten as a girl and by last report was doing remarkably well, both at home and at school. As Sophie grows older, she and her parents will have some important decisions to make—whether, when, and to whom to disclose that she had once been Brady; whether to take hormone blockers; whether to take hormones; whether to have surgery. Or, as Sophie gets older, Brady may make a reappearance, like Jonah from the bowels of the whale, but this time it will be from the stomach of Corky. And I will be on call as needed.

A SECOND DAY IN THE LIFE—I'M A COUNTERFEIT

Benjie was about to turn eighteen when he came to me for help in his transition from a lesbian teenager to an affirmed young man. I had begun the work with a family session with Benjie and his parents, and then moved to individual sessions with Benjie, with auxiliary parent sessions and parent contact. Our work would be brief, as Benjie would soon be leaving for college. Benjie was usually perky and upbeat, dressed casually in sweatshirts and shorts, but always well put together. But one day Benjie showed up to one of his sessions looking very distraught and definitely disheveled. There was a crisis with his girlfriend, Priya. Benjie found out that Priya had cheated on him and had sex with Robert, another boy at their school. Benjie came home so upset that he started throwing things around his room and punching the walls. He also erupted at Priya at a party and his friends had to pull him away. He had always looked up to Robert as the kind of boy he wanted to be—smart, funny, affable, tall, good-looking, buff. Now Robert had stolen Benjie's girlfriend, or at least her heart. How could Benjie compete with someone who had a real penis, rather than a strap-on? Surely Priya, or any girl, would prefer a real man, in fantasy one who can have everlasting erections, over him. Isn't that what all women want? Priya's betrayal was bad enough in itself, but this upset quickly bled into a larger distress that Benjie would never be a "normal" man because he wasn't born with a penis and would never have a "real" one. That made him hate everything about his life. He desperately needed to hold on to Priya because she loved him for who he was. He feared no other girl would, when he got to college. Because if Priya didn't, who would? These days, it is hard enough to be a man with a penis who has to compete with the Marlboro Man as the persistent icon of American masculinity. The feeling of being counterfeit because you don't have a penis at all only makes it that much worse, if not dire.

Benjie's troubles didn't stop there. When his parents witnessed Benjie tearing apart his room, they were quite taken aback. It wasn't the first time Benjie had had an outburst, but now there was a different matter on the table—Benjie had already met with an endocrinologist and was scheduled to begin testosterone very soon. His parents blew the whistle, fearing what testosterone might do to his already roller-coaster emotions. They wanted some further assessment before moving forward. (It should be noted that Benjie's father in particular was already extremely ambivalent about hormone treatment.) This is where the mental health professional comes in. I did see that there was more psychological work to be done before Benjie began a course of cross-hormone treatments. It was not a question of *if*, but *when*. I did wrestle with the chicken-and-egg question: Maybe Benjie was erupting with angst and anger because he couldn't afford to wait any longer to at least have some body semblance of being a real man. It's never easy feeling like you're playing God in these situations, but I made a clinical decision that it would be risky business to jump forward without giving Benjie some opportunity to find better ways to handle turbulent emotions before ingesting hormones in his body. The wait wasn't that long, and Benjie did go on to start testosterone, but only after he felt sturdier on his emotional feet. Benjie also taught me the importance of giving heed to the potential excruciating angst of feeling counterfeit. We can say that gender is between your ears, not your legs, but at the same time we cannot deny that what's between your legs may also play a significant part in affirming your authentic sense of self as male or female. Particularly for teens and young adults, sexual encounters can become fraught with anxiety when a transgender teen doesn't feel like a "real" boy or girl because he or she is lacking the proper sexual anatomy. And the counterfeit accusation comes from without, not just from within, which starts much earlier than the teen years. Seven-year-old Christie, who had been easily accepted as an affirmed female from kindergarten on, was confronted with a classroom group activity that was to be divided by gender, in which she began skipping toward the girl group. She was informed matter-of-factly by another little girl in the class, who knew that Christie was a girl with a penis, "Oh, but this group is for *real* girls." So a day in the life of a therapist will involve on-going sensitivity to the "counterfeit" feelings that may plague children and youth as they try to establish a unique creative gender self that might feel authentic to them but not to the outside world.

FROM THE COUCH TO THE COMMUNITY

Colette Chiland is a mental health professional in France who specializes in gender issues. In her book *Transsexualism*, translated into English in 2003, she wrote, "By treating children we might be preventing disorder of gender identity in adult life, which is the best thing we can do."[83] From where I sit, them there's fighting words. If we are talking about the disorder of an individual strangling within the grips of his or her false gender self, we should absolutely offer our mental health services to replace it with an authentic "ordered" one as the best thing we can do, whether that solution be transgender, gender nonconforming, or gender fluid. But if we are talking about a disorder defined as the psychiatric diagnosis of gender identity disorder, we should absolutely cease and desist offering any such services aimed at trapping that individual in a binary box based purely on their assigned gender at birth, for that would be the worst thing we could do.

If you are a parent of a gender-nonconforming or transgender child and are shopping for a mental health professional to help your family, beware wolves in sheep's clothing, or just plain wolves . . . or bulls in china shops—therapists who mean well but are untrained in true gender self development and treatment. If a therapist uses the diagnosis, informally or formally, of "gender identity disorder," other than to obtain insurance reimbursement or facilitate other needed medical services,[84] take heed. And when you do locate a therapist who meets the criteria of a gender-creative therapist, also make sure he or she is a therapist who is willing to step away from the couch and work with others in the community. Gender-creative psychotherapy must by definition be community psychology. If our therapeutic goal is gender expansiveness but also gender safety for the children, this will indeed take a village. Your child's therapist must be willing to be an active advocate for gender awareness, either for your own child or for all children through participation in professional and public gender advocacy activities.

CHAPTER EIGHT

Who Are the Genders in Your Neighborhood?

On what foundation should the idea of belonging to a sex be based?

—COLETTE CHILAND, *TRANSSEXUALISM*[85]

O n September 21, 2010, I opened my copy of *The New York Times* to read the front-page headline, "Where Boys Are Prized, Girls Live the Part."[86] To my surprise, I learned that a practice exists among families in Afghanistan to disguise their daughters as boys, one that has been going on for generations. These children are referred to as *bacha posh,* which means "dressed up as a boy" in Dari. Why do families do this? For economic reasons (boys can leave the house and help out, girls cannot), for social reasons (it is considered shameful not to have a son), and for superstitious reasons (a hope that masquerading your daughter as a boy will lead to the birth of an actual son—this hope occurs within a belief system that a mother-to-be can control the sex of her unborn). The decision to disguise the daughters as sons is the parents', not the child's. Missing a son, the parents make one up, dressing their daughter or one of their daughters, most often the youngest, in male clothing and cutting her hair in a boy's style. Typically, puberty brings an end to the masquerade—again decided by the parents, not the child. Parents without sons make the decision to transform their girls into boys under the umbrella of a tribal culture in which only sons can inherit family wealth and in which families without sons are to be pitied or treated with contempt. Even having a pretend son can garner some relief from this social aspersion.

Azita Rafaat, member of the Afghan Parliament, mother of a six-year-old *bacha posh,* and herself a *bacha posh* in childhood, explains to the Western journalist who interviewed her, "Yes, this is not normal for you. And I know it's very hard for you to believe why one mother is doing these things to her youngest daughter. But I want to say for you, that some things are happening in Afghanistan that are really not imaginable for you as a Western people." As I read, I thought to myself, "and there are some things that are happening right in our own Western country that are really not imaginable to our own citizens." In Afghanistan, parents purposefully make their girls boys. In the United States, parents are willingly allowing their girls to become boys, not because of the parents' needs, but because of their child's own expressed needs and desires.

Are these Afghan daughters who dress as boys expressing their true gender selves? Most likely not. They are conforming to their parents' expectations, consciously masquerading in a false gender self in the form of a cross-gender presentation. Their parents try to make it an alluring proposition, as when Azita Rafaat queried her youngest daughter, "Do you want to look like a boy and dress like a boy, and do more fun things like boys do, like bicycling, soccer and cricket?" What little child could turn that down? But the story doesn't stop here. Indeed, after living for many years as a boy with all its accompanying privileges in a culture where women have few, some daughters do not want to go back to living as a girl, and if you stare at their pictures, they look as "boy" as any other boy who appears alongside them in the photo. Zahra is fifteen and has been dressing and acting like a boy for as long as she can remember. Now, given a choice, she would never go back to being a girl: "Nothing in me feel likes a girl. For always, I want to be a boy and a boy and a boy." For the daughters who do not want to give up being boy, could this be their evolving true gender self? Possibly. Other *bacha poshes,* when called upon later to marry and be a wife and mother, just don't know how to be a female after several years of living as a male. Shukria Siddiqui, now thirty-six, lived as a male until early adulthood, when her parents planned an arranged marriage for her: "I had to learn how to sit with women, how to talk, how to behave. When you change back, it's like you were born again, and you have to learn everything from the beginning." And still others express discomfort about the masquerade. Miina is ten. Every afternoon after school, her parents have her change clothes and disguise herself as a boy so she can work in a store in another neighborhood and bring in some badly needed family income. Miina complained to her parents, "I'm not comfortable around the boys in the store. I am a girl."

If there was ever an example of the nature-nurture-culture three-dimensional gender web, it is in the story of these Afghan daughters made to be sons. There is no one end to the story, and it appears that each *bacha posh* emerges with her own unique fingerprint of gender. So which is the stronger determinant in the gender web—nature? nurture? culture? In the words of the wise old rabbis, "It depends."

Learning from the story of the Afghan *bacha poshes,* standing alongside the two-spirited of Native American culture or the *hijra* of South Asia (members of a third gender—neither man nor woman, many of whom are castrated males), we must be humble enough to say that we can never know for sure the genders in our neighborhood. Yet we must ensure that there is room for all and for every variation, and that our children grow and thrive in a gender-expansive rather than a gender-bound world.

GENDER FREEDOM IN AN UNFREE WORLD

Throughout the pages of this book, I have tried every which way to examine how we can promote children's true gender self by giving room for each child's gender creativity. Yet I can never forget that the world we live in may not be on board and that our job as parents and as citizens is also to serve as our children's protectors. I frequently get e-mails or calls from parents around the country saying, "You know, we don't live in the Bay Area like you do. There's not a snowball's chance in hell that I can let Thomas show up at school in his dress without the shit getting beat out of him. And he's only six. So now what do I do?" Or, "I know my child would be so much happier if I could allow him to be the girl he says he is, but my ex-husband threatened to take me to court and sue for full custody if I ever did that. What should I do?"

It is never good to tell children that who they are is not okay. Yet it is never good to send them into an unsafe situation without protection. This is the main tension we face as we try to make space for our children to be gender creative. The world we live in today is changing rapidly but is still nowhere near where it needs to be if all people are to have gender freedom.

In the present U.S. educational system, we know that some schools have sent boys home if they show up in a skirt, asserting that it is against school policy. More horrifying, we learn that Larry King, a fifteen-year-old boy in California, was fatally shot by a schoolmate; and Carl Joseph Walker-Hoover, an eleven-year old boy in Massachusetts, hung himself as a result of violence or bullying at school. Although both deaths were attributed to antigay bullying or harassment, with no effective school intervention, in each case it was not really the youths' sexual orientation but their "girly" gender presentation that brought on the wrath or aspersion of their peers and their ultimate death. We can wonder if the same was true for Billy Lucas, Asher Brown, and Seth Walsh, three young gay teens from different parts of the country who committed suicide within weeks of one another in 2010 after unrelenting bullying by classmates at school.

In the present U.S. court system, we know that a divorced father may very well have his day in court if he accuses his ex-wife of neglectful and perverse child-rearing behaviors, winning a change in custody if she allows their son to wear that dress. That same father can also use the court system to prohibit the administration of hormone blockers to his transgender child, making for a far more risky journey into adolescence for that child.

Educational policies need to be challenged and antibullying programs put into effect. Sensibilities of family court judges need to be radically retooled. But the wheels of justice move slowly and the halls of learning sometimes take years to reconstruct.

In the meantime, in this imperfect world, we know that children sometimes must craft a false gender self just to survive. We watch them take on their own self-protection, even when their parents are not demanding it. Lance is a seven-year-old boy who loves wearing dresses, the frillier the better, the more sparkles the better. His two moms are fine with this, and have supported his expressing himself however he wants in private or in public. They know that they will step in to advocate for him in any situation in which someone might look askance at his gender presentation. The staff and administration at his school are equally supportive, and have brought in gender specialists to do trainings on gender acceptance for the children and the teachers. But much to his moms' puzzlement, he himself is adamant that the dresses stay home. He went so far as to wear a tailored skirt to school one day in first grade, and happily wore it in the morning until it was time to go out for recess with the older children. Then came the transformation—he whipped out his shorts and discarded the skirt. He had already been taunted by some older children and did not want to face it again, even though his teachers assured him that the teasing was unacceptable and that they would be right there to support him. Apart from fortifying himself against teasing, Lance is also a very private child, and he found it excruciating painful to become the center of attention. So in a gender-bound culture, by his own choice his sparkly dresses may stalwartly remain part of his own private self, pleasurable to him only within the intimacy of his home, where he will neither be teased nor stared at. Would this be necessary in a freer world? I would hope not, but in the meantime we need to honor not only the parents' but also the children's efforts to balance gender freedom with gender protection in a world that continues to be unfree.

These efforts on either parents' or children's parts can work as long as the children recognize that their purpose is not to wipe out the true self but to protect it from harm or to preserve their privacy under certain very unfair circumstances. In the best of all possible worlds, we must do everything in our power to remove the harm and the unfair circumstances, and it is important for the children to know we are doing our best to make that happen—in our homes, in our schools, in our communities, and in public policies and practices. Yet meanwhile, in a homophobic, transphobic, genderist world filled with hate crimes and violence, we are sometimes called upon to ask our children—or sometimes they call on themselves—to put on a protective shield. This works as long as we can define it as just that—a protective shield rather than a defective self.

The transgender adult community has adopted the term *going stealth*. This means that a person decides to live in his affirmed gender without other people realizing that he or she once lived in another gender. Going stealth can be layered—a person may go stealth in public but not with family, partners, or intimate friends. The term originated in the adult transgender community but has been applied to transgender children as well. Our children may go stealth in two different ways: (1) transgender children may go out in the world and live as their affirmed gender without letting anyone know their assigned or previous gender;

and (2) gender-nonconforming children may hide their true self gender presentations from public scrutiny and "come out" only in safe, protected situations. So Sophie who was once Brady may go stealth if she presents to the world as a girl with no reference to her past life as a boy; and Lance goes stealth when he doesn't wear his sparkly dress to school, and puts it on only in the sanctity of his home.

Unfortunately, the word *stealth* has connotations of furtive, secret, or clandestine actions—negative and false qualities that go against the grain of gender freedom, gender creativity, and gender authenticity. In these final pages of the book, I wish to pose the question, "Wouldn't it be nice if there were a world where secrecy or stealth was not an issue and gender-nonconforming and transgender children could feel free and safe to express themselves in whatever ways felt most comfortable to them?" They could disclose their assigned gender, or not. They could slip into their dress, or not. They would do this depending on how they felt like expressing themselves rather than how others said they had to be. What would that world look like?

IMAGINE

In the mid-1990s Dar Williams sang out to us all to live by gender creativity in her song "When I Was a Boy."[87] Phyllis Rothblatt followed a decade later with a song and accompanying book for children, "All I Want to Be Is Me." It is written in the voice of a child. I invite you all to take a look at the book or listen to the song online, but in the meantime I wanted to share the refrain to the song that so poignantly opens our eyes to the gender-expansive world as children imagine it:

Don't call me he. Don't call me she.
Please don't assume who I must be.

'Cuz I don't feel like just one of these.

I want to be all of me.

All I want to be is me.[88]

Now let's listen to our own adult voices. Let us imagine to-gether this gender-expansive world where children can be accepted and permitted to be all of their gender-creative selves. Parents would no longer have to balance the safety of their children against the blossoming of their child's true gender self. Sophie might have an easier time connecting her earlier life as Brady with her present life as Sophie. Lance could more easily step out in his dancing shoes and dresses. Children would no longer have to worry about which bathroom to use or which cabin they would sleep in on their camping trips. To be a boy with a vagina or a girl with a penis would be just one variation on gender, rather than a shocking anomaly. If that came to be, some people might discover that surgery or hormones would no longer be necessary to overcome feelings of being a counterfeit gender because of a perceived mismatch between body and mind. Counterfeit feel-ings would fade or even disappear because bodies and the notion of binary gender boxes would no longer dictate the boundaries in which children would be allowed to explore their gender creativ-ity and discover their true gender selves.

Imagine a world where children would no longer be afraid to go to school and where school would never again feel like run-ning the gauntlet for a gender-nonconforming or transgender child. This would happen because the schools would be educated not just to tolerate but to fully accept gender in all its varia-tions, and children would no longer be frightened or threatened by those who are different from themselves. There would be room for everybody. Larry King and Carl Joseph Walker-Hoover might still be alive.

Imagine a world where we were ahead of rather than behind the game when it came to medical interventions for our children. We would have gathered all the information we could about the effects of hormone blockers and cross-sex hormones on youths' body and health. We would have revised our practices to be more developmentally sound. No longer would children be allowed to take hormone blockers for only a few years because of health risks if taken any longer than that but then be told that they were too young to begin cross-sex hormones and would now have to wait, maybe another two or three years, or even more. No longer would the age when they could start cross-sex hormones be set by practitioners who have unilaterally decided that youth younger than that age were not ready to make such lifelong decisions. Imagine instead that we had an integrative set of practices and standards so that children who were clear about their gender identity could have a smooth transition from hormone blockers to cross-sex hormones, at ages much younger than sixteen. Imagine a world in which we would have figured out that sixteen as the designated earliest age for cross-sex hormones just doesn't make sense when children as young as ten may be going on hormone blockers, particularly as the age of the onset of puberty keeps going down in younger generations. Imagine a world in which we would understand that putting children on hormone blockers for two years and then stopping because they are not safe but telling children that they will have to wait a long time to be eligible for cross-sex hormones may be excruciating for children who have been ready for over a decade. This would happen because we would have created interdisciplinary teams who would have put the time, resources, and research into thinking carefully about the full scope of medical practices that have become available to transgender children and youth, along with their physical and mental health ramifications.

Imagine a world where the professionals were no longer the primary gatekeepers of a child's gender development. At the Gender Spectrum conference in 2009, Stephanie Brill chaired the plenary "Be Yourself, Change the World" and shared with the audience a conversation she had had with a gender specialist at the international WPATH (World Professional Association for

Transgender Health) conference that took place in Oslo earlier that year. The professional approached her with this question about a family with a transgender child: "We have a family who has not complied and has allowed their child to transition before age sixteen. What should we do about them?" Stephanie had a very brief response: "What makes you get to decide?" Imagine a world where it's not the doctors but the family that gets to decide a child's gender presentation, and where no aspersion is cast on parents who facilitate their child's transition to his or her true gender self. This will happen when people recognize the rich variations in children's gender development. It will happen when we acknowledge that the primary expert in determining an authentic gender self is the child him- or herself. It will happen when parents, not professionals, are recognized as the main facilitators of their child's true gender self. It will happen when *gender identity creativity* truly replaces *gender identity disorder.*

Imagine a world in which we will have scientific answers rather than biased reports about the outcomes for children who are allowed to carve out their own gender paths in comparison to those who are being directed along paths determined by others. In 2009, Darryl Hill, Edgardo Menvielle, Kristin Sica, and Alisa Johnson reported the findings of their comparative study of children whose families participated in the Gender and Sexuality Advocacy and Education Program through the Children's National Medical Center in Washington, D.C. In this program, parents were affirmative of their children's gender nonconformity. The researchers concluded, "It is certainly the case that for at least some parents and gender-variant children, an affirmative approach is a route to a healthier child. Thus, good adjustment in a child can be achieved without the anti-humanistic rejection of a child's gender choices and enlisting parents in gender policing and behavior modification. More research, of course, is warranted."[89]

Yes, more research is in order. We have so much more to learn about the gender web. Just a few research questions come to mind. How many children who transition from male to female or from female to male at age five show consistency of gender identity over time? For those who do not, is there any evidence of harm to their personality or psychological functioning if the children are fluid over time, transitioning from one gender to another over the course of their development? Do the children who are given access to hormone blockers, regardless of their final decisions about their gender identity, show greater relief from stress, anxiety, and depression as a result of being allowed the time to think about their gender journeys before entering into a puberty that might potentially be an unwanted one? Answers to these questions and so many more will happen when we move beyond our preliminary studies to well-funded comprehensive longitudinal studies of development and psychological outcomes for gender-nonconforming and transgender children and youth—in all their variations.

Imagine a day when mental health professionals would no longer pathologize children who defy assigned binary gender boxes. Jennifer was a seventeen-year-old transgender male who sought out the services of a renowned gender clinic in England. Although Jennifer had kept his assigned name, he was identified in the therapist's written account as a male transsexual. Yet the therapist kept referring to the patient as "she." The therapist found that when he tried to explore the roots of "her" "atypical" gender identity development, the patient disrupted the treatment. The therapist attributed the retreat to the patient's resistance and fears of having the foundation of "her" gender identity revisited. Rather than seeing this youth's persistence in a male identity as stable and positive, this professional labeled it as "rigid."[90] I have never had the opportunity to meet Jennifer, but I certainly wondered whether Jennifer was simply fighting for his life. Could it be that every time the therapist made misinterpretations, Jennifer's survival skills came to the fore and he put up a protective shield against the therapist's misunderstanding and attacks on *his* true gender self, that could be seen by the therapist only as *her* gender self. Wouldn't it have been nice if Jennifer could have come to the therapist and told his own life story in his own words, rather than having it defined by someone else as atypical and false? Wouldn't it be nice if therapists had the opportunity to examine their own gender biases that may cause children to take to the hills or clam up lest their true gender selves be trampled by these professionals' missteps? This will only happen when gender is truly relearned and when we mental health professionals receive intensive training that will allow us to facilitate and promote rather than control or pathologize children's gender destiny.

GENDER ACTION

As I write the final paragraphs of this book, I am also carving out time to attend the steering committee meetings of a partnership of community groups and a local university medical center that have come together to build a child and adolescent gender clinic without walls in Northern California. We have named our project the Child and Adolescent Gender Center (CAGC). We are an interdisciplinary team, comprising endocrinologists, pediatricians, nurses, allied health providers, social workers, psychiatrists, psychologists, family and marriage therapists, educators, lawyers, and community advocates and activists. The consortium of mental health professionals is already up and running, and we have named ourselves "Mind the Gap" (a name derived during the days when the center was provisionally called "BayGap," short for Bay Area Youth Gender Acceptance Project). We envision a village of sorts where families can seek all the services they need to foster their child's gender authenticity, with subsidies or provisions for families who would otherwise lack the financial resources for such services. We hope to provide informational consults; mental health consultations, psychotherapy and psychiatric and psychological evaluations; medical and health services, including provision of hormone blockers and cross-sex hormones; educational forums for professionals, families, and community; ongoing support groups for parents, for children, for siblings, for extended family; trainings for schools and community groups; advocacy for individual children in schools and the community; legal services; research; and I'm sure other services we haven't yet envisioned. It's a big undertaking but also a drop in the bucket, and it will only become a sea change when gender clinics without walls start popping up all over the map, not just in a few major metropolitan areas, the way Planned Parenthood has managed to do.

Another thing happened as I bring this book to a close. In October 2010, Dan Savage and his partner, Terry Miller, began an online project called "It Gets Better." Through videos, their hope was to send gay teens who might be feeling discouraged or suicidal a life-affirming message about how great it can be to be an openly gay adult, encouraging disheartened teens to remember that "living well is the best revenge." It has turned into a phenomenal success. Some have criticized the videos for not solving all the problems facing the youth, particularly bullying. The project has also been blasted for its privileged perspective and shortsightedness—"It gets better" is a great message from and for future upper-middle-class white men with financial means and social status, but what about all the people who don't have the same resources to make it better? Dan Savage has this response to the videos not being able to solve all the problems facing youth: "They don't. But we can't get all the stuff done by tomorrow. We can get these videos up today."[91] It would be better if they were also sensitive to class, race, geographic, and economic realities, yet as I held this caution in mind and switched my focus from gay youth to gender-nonconforming and transgender children and youth, I could only think of Pete Seeger singing to us that the only way to make a garden grow is inch by inch, row by row. Every video, every children's book about all the genders in our neighborhood, every school workshop about all those genders is one step closer to a world of gender freedom. We can't do it all but we can do our own part, as long as we know that there are so many other parts that also must come into play.

Very recently, I attended the wedding reception for the daughter of close friends. Many of her own friends were married or partnered, with young children. In walked a young woman and her three-year-old son, with another little baby in tow. The little boy walked in proudly in his plaid kilt, clasping a toy truck. His mother explained that at the last minute he announced that he really wanted to wear a white flowing dress like the bride wore at the wedding ceremony, which had occurred a few weeks earlier. But they didn't have one on hand. What they did have was a little kilt just like the one his father had worn at their wedding. That was the closest she could come to providing her son with a dress. The little boy stood by his mother's side, nodding his head adamantly as his mother told the partygoers around her how he really wanted to wear a white dress. The mom brought her story to a close, "I really wish we had one. What can I say? I'm a Berkeley parent." The little boy left his mom and trotted off to have a grand time, hopping around in his skirt and zoom-zooming his arsenal of trucks across the wood floor. The other children played happily around him and with him. For them, it appeared all as it should be. What a wonderful world it would be if his mother could be every parent, not just a Berkeley parent. What a wonderful world it will be when this little child is every child, freely exploring gender and weaving together a very special and unique gender web that affirms "all of me."

▪ NOTES ▪

INTRODUCTION

1. For a complete report on these findings, see C. Ryan, D. Huebner, R. M. Diaz, and J. Sanchez, "Family Rejection as a Predictor of Negative Health Outcomes in White and Latino Lesbian, Gay, and Bisexual Young Adults," *Pediatrics* 123 (2009): 346–52.

2. Will Roscoe, *Changing Ones: Third and Fourth Genders in Native North America* (New York: St. Martin's Griffin, 1998), 27.

3. Kenneth J. Zucker and Susan J. Bradley, *Gender Identity Disorder and Psychosexual Problems in Children and Adolescents* (New York: The Guilford Press, 1995), 76.

CHAPTER ONE

4. Jim Herron Zamora, "Newark Teen Beaten to Death," *San Francisco Chronicle,* October 18, 2002, A1, A24.

5. Kelly St. John and Henry K. Lee, "Slain Newark Teen Balanced Between Two Worlds," *San Francisco Chronicle,* October 19, 2002, A1, A7.

6. Stephanie Brill and Rachel Pepper, *The Transgender Child* (San Francisco: Cleis Press, 2008), xiv.

7. Ibid., 50.

8. As reported in Richard Green, *The "Sissy Boy Syndrome" and the Development of Homosexuality* (New Haven: Yale University Press, 1987), 116.

9. As reported by John Cloud, in "His Name Is Aurora," *Time,* September 25, 2000, 90.

10. For a discussion of gender identity disorder as a consequence of early traumas or attachment disruptions, in which the three-year-old boy whose mother died is presented as a case in point, see S. Coates, R. C. Friedman,

and S. Wolfe, "The Etiology of Boyhood Gender Identity Disorder: A Model for Integrating Temperament, Development, and Psychodynamics," *Psychoanalytic Dialogues* 1 (1991): 481–523.

11. For a discussion of the genetic roots of homosexuality, see S. LeVay and D. Hamer, "Evidence for a Biological Influence in Male Homosexuality. Biology and Homosexuality: A Debate," *Scientific American*, May 1994, 44–49.

12. For a full discussion of this, see P. T. Cohen-Kettenis and F. Pfäfflin, *Transgenderism and Intersexuality in Childhood and Adolescence* (Thousand Oaks, CA: Sage Publications, 2003).

CHAPTER TWO

13. As reported in Alix Spiegel, *Children's Health: Q and A: Therapists on Gender Identity Issues in Kids*, SearchNPR.org, May 7, 2008.

14. Robert J. Stoller, *Presentations of Gender* (New Haven: Yale University Press, 1985), 25.

15. Zucker and Bradley, *Gender Identity Disorder*, 90.

16. Ibid., 90.

17. Ibid., 226.

18. Edgardo Menvielle, "Parents Struggling with Their Child's Gender Issues," *Brown University Child and Adolescent Behavior Letter*, July 2004, 3.

19. Nancy Crawford, "Understanding Children's Atypical Gender Behavior,"*Monitor on Psychology* (2003): 40.

20. John Cloud, "His Name Is Aurora," *Time*, September 25, 2000, 90.

21 Alix Spiegel, "Two Families Grapple with Sons' Gender Preferences," National Public Radio *All Things Considered,* May 7, 2008.

22. Hanna Rosin, "A Boy's Life," *The Atlantic Online*, November 2008, 6, www.theatlantic.com/doc/print/200811/transgender-children.

23. At the writing of this book, a task force is at work constructing a new diagnosis to replace *gender identity disorder* in the forthcoming DSM-5, most likely with the diagnosis *gender incongruence*. But in the meantime, *gender identity disorder* remains on the books as the diagnosis applied to children who do not conform to the gender norms of the culture and/or identify as other than the gender stated on their birth certificate.

24. Susanna Moore, "Diagnosis for a Straight Planet: A Critique of Gender Identity Disorder for Children and Adolescents in the DSM IV," PhD diss., The Wright Institute, Berkeley, CA, 2002, 129.

25. See Alan P. Bell, Martin. S. Weinberg, and Susan Kiefer Hammersmith, *Sexual Preference: Its Development in Men and Women*

(Bloomington: Indiana University Press, 1981) for an excellent discussion of this feedback loop, particularly as it pertains to sexual and gender development.

26. See PFLAG, *Our Trans Children* (Washington, D.C.: Parents, Families and Friends of Lesbians and Gays, 2007), for an excellent discussion of parents' experiences with a transgender child.

27. Marilyn Shyer and Christopher Shyer, *Not Like Other Boys* (New York: Authors Guild Backinprint.com, 2001), 61, 75, 230.

28. See Irene Fast's work [*Gender Identity: A Differentiation Model* (Hillsdale, NJ: The Analytic Press, 1984) and "Aspects of Core Gender Identity," *Psychoanalytic Dialogues* 9 (1999): 633–61] for an excellent discussion of the parents' role in communicating to their child both their child's gender and the meaning of being that gender.

29. We might entertain a time in the future when "gender boxing" (i.e., checking off one box or another for a person's gender) will be eliminated as a category of identification, but until such time, parents will continue to have the task of communicating to their child a gender label, whatever traditional or innovate nomenclature they might choose in that endeavor.

30. For a poignant discussion of this scapegoating dynamic in adolescence, see Margaret Waddell, "The Scapegoat," in *Facing It Out*, ed., Robin Anderson and Anna Dartington (London: Duckworth, 1998), 127–41.

31. Rosin, "A Boy's Life," 6.

32. Brill and Pepper, *The Transgender Child*, 107.

CHAPTER THREE

33. Lauren Renée Hotchkiss, "The Girl Behind the Glass," in *True Selves*, by Mildred L. Brown and Chloe A. Rounsley (San Francisco: Jossey-Bass, 1996), 228.

34. As quoted in D. W. Winnicott, *Playing and Reality* (London: Tavistock, 1970), 71.

35. Wendell Glenn, "'For Colored Girls Only': Reflection of an Emerging Male-to-Female Transgender and Gender Variant Consciousness," in *Social Work Practice with Transgender and Gender Variant Youth*, ed. Gerald P. Mallon (London: Routledge, 2009), 109.

36. Brown and Rounsley, *True Selves*, 36.

37. This excerpt of a therapy session was provided by Domenico Di Ceglie in Di Ceglie, "Engaging Young People with Atypical Gender Identity Development in Therapeutic Work: A Developmental Approach," *Journal of Child Psychotherapy* 351 (2009): 3–12. Direct quotes were from page 6 of the article.

38. Dr. Phil, www.drphil.com/articles/article/258, January 21, 2009.

39. As quoted at the Bay Area Youth Centers conference "The Experiences and Needs of LGBTQ Youth in Out-of-Home Care," Oakland, CA, September 16, 2009.

40. Brown and Rounsley, *True Selves,* 43.

41. Ibid., 30.

42. J. Hoffman, "Can a Boy Wear a Skirt to School?" *New York Times,* November 8, 2009, Sunday Styles, 1, 10.

43. Brown and Rounsley, *True Selves,* 47.

44. As reported in *Social Work Practice with Transgender and Gender Variant Youth,* ed. Gerald P. Mallon (London: Routledge, 2009), chap. 2.

45. Brown and Brownsley, *True Selves,* 35.

46. Ibid., 37.

47. American Psychiatric Association, *Diagnostic Criteria from DSM-IV,* Washington, D.C.: American Psychiatric Association, 1994.

CHAPTER FOUR

48. Spiegel, 1.

49. Ibid., 9.

50. See S. Fraiberg, E. Adelson, and V. Shapiro, "Ghosts in the Nursery: A Psychoanalytic Approach to the Problem of Impaired Infant-Mother Relationships," *Journal of the American Academy of Child Psychiatry,* 14 (1975): 387–421, for a discussion of the remnants of our early experiences that remain embedded in our present relations and often obstruct the way we consciously are trying to be with others.

CHAPTER FIVE

51. See Diane Ehrensaft, *Parenting Together* (New York: The Free Press, 1987): 232–33.

52. L. Smiley, "Girl/Boy Interrupted," www.sfweekly.com, July 11, 2007.

53. See Brill and Pepper, *The Transgender Child,* which represents the proponents' point of view regarding the use of hormone blockers and cross-sex hormones to facilitate the healthy development of transgender children.

54. Zucker and Bradley's 1995 book, *Gender Identity Disorder and Psychosexual Problems in Children and Adolescents,* strongly represents this point of view regarding the harm of introducing medical treatments to youth who are too young to know for themselves and who would benefit first from therapeutic intervention with the goal of accepting their assigned gender,

rather than attempting to change it with drugs and hormones. However, Ken Zucker will support the use of hormones once a child fully enters adolescence and is fully insistent that he or she is transgender, because by then it is "too late" for therapy aimed at getting a child to accept his or her assigned gender.

55. L. Smiley, "Girl/Boy Interrupted."

56. See C. Adams, "Born in a Bind: Treating Transgender Children," *Gay Lesbian Times,* no. 1034, October 2007, www.gaylesbiantimes. com/?id=10795, and Brill and Pepper, *The Transgender Child,* for further discussion of the administration and costs of hormone blockers.

57. Regrettably, it is not only affordable but also accessible without medical prescription. Many youths buy T (testosterone) or E (estrogen) on the street, and self-prescribe, sometimes at dangerously high doses, with no medical monitoring, putting them at risk for serious medical complications.

58. It should be noted that the estrogen transgender females take is at doses two to three times higher than the amount recommended for postmenopausal women taking hormone replacement therapy. This is of particular concern given the potential health risks that have already been flagged for women taking the much lower levels of estrogen used in HRT.

59. For further discussion of the side effects of hormone treatments for transgender individuals, see E. Moore, A. Wisniewski, and A. Dobs, "Endocrine Treatment of Transsexual People: A Review of Treatment Regimen, Outcomes, and Adverse Effects," *Journal of Clinical Endocrinology and Metabolism* 888, no. 8 (2003), 3467–73.

60 D. W. Winnicott, *Playing and Reality* (London: Tavistock, 1960), 148.

61 C. Adams, "Born in a Bind: Treating Transgender Children," *Gay Lesbian Times,* no. 1034, October 2007, www.gaylesbiantimes .com/?id=10795.

62. Alix Spiegel, "Parents Consider Treatment to Delay Son's Puberty," transcript of National Public Radio *All Things Considered* interview, May 8, 2008.

63. Stephanie Booth, "Their True Selves," *Teen People,* June/July 2003.

CHAPTER SIX

64. Rosin, "A Boy's Life," 5.

65. Michele Angello offered this analogy as leader of a workshop on siblings at the Gender Spectrum Family Conference in September 2009.

66. These quotes are excerpted from Rosin, "A Boy's Life."

67. George Hagen, "Guys and Dolls," *Parents,* September 2002, 174.

68. Child Welfare League of America and Lambda Legal, "Faith-Based Providers Working with LGBTQ Youth," data.lambdalegal.org/publications/.../gdtb_faith-based-providers.pdf (2010): 1.

CHAPTER SEVEN

69. Winnicott, *Playing and Reality,* 57.

70. Mother of a transgender teen, as quoted in *Mom, I Need to Be a Girl,* by Just Evelyn (Longmont, CO: Just Evelyn, 2007), 79.

71. Zucker and Bradley, *Gender Identity Disorder,* 57.

72. As reported in N. Crawford, "Understanding Children's Atypical Gender Behavior," 40.

73 C. Heredia, "Transgender Teen's Slaying Shakes Nation," *San Francisco Chronicle,* October 23, 2002, A3.

74. Ellen Perrin, Edgardo Menvielle, and Catherine Tuerk, "The Beat of a Different Drummer: Children Who Do Not Follow Gender-Typical Expectations," *Contemporary Pediatrics* (February 2005): 38–46; also available as "To the Beat of a Different Drummer: The Gender-Variant Child, *Contemporary Pediatrics,* www.imatyfa.org/...files/to-the-beat-of-a-different-drummer-6-2007.pdf , 3.

75. *Cisgender* is a term that translates to "not transgender," which means a gender identity or performance in a gender role in which the assigned and affirmed genders match.

76. The World Professional Association of Transgender Health Standards of Care for Gender Identity Disorders, 6th version, 2001, 3.

77. See Peggy Cohen-Kettenis and Freidemann Pfäfflin, *Transgenderism and Intersexuality in Childhood and Adolescence* (Thousand Oaks, CA: Sage Publications, 2003), for a discussion of the protocols.

78. It should be noted at the same time that gender specialists have been observing a higher incidence of transgender or gender-nonconforming expression among children and youth with neurodevelopmental differences, with a working hypothesis that there may be a correlation between the two.

79. Di Ceglie, "Engaging Young People," 3–12.

80. Charlotte Zolotow, *William's Doll* (New York: HarperCollins, 1972).

81. D. Ehrensaft, "'A Child Is Being Eaten': Failure, Fear, Fantasy, and Repair in the Lives of Foster Children," *Journal of Infant, Child, and Adolescent Psychotherapy,* 7 (2008), 88–99.

82. I have removed identifying information, such as last name or dates from the letter, to preserve confidentiality. Note also that first names in this case have been changed for the same purpose of preserving confidentiality.

83. Colette Chiland, *Transsexualism* (Middletown, CT: Wesleyan University Press, 2003), 152.

84. Although I am adamantly opposed to the diagnosis "gender identity disorder—childhood," I find myself having to grit my teeth and use it to either obtain insurance benefits for a child who is in treatment with me, especially if I am not on that family's insurance plan and have been added as a single case [gender] provider, which will necessitate a gender diagnosis, or if the diagnosis is required to receive the services of a pediatric endocrinologist.

CHAPTER EIGHT

85. Chiland, *Transsexualism,* 157.

86. Jenny Nordberg, "Where Boys Are Prized, Girls Live the Part," *New York Times,* September 21, 2010, A1, A10–A11.

87. Dar Williams, "When I Was a Boy," Razor and Tie Records, 1993.

88. Phyllis Rothblatt's song and order information for the book *All I Want to Be Is Me* (2008) can be found at *www.alllwanttobeisme.com.*

89. D. B. Hill, E. Menvielle, K. M. Sica, and A. Johnson, "An Affirmative Intervention for Families with Gender Variant Children: Parental Ratings of Child Mental Health and Gender," *Journal of Sex and Marital Therapy,* 36 (2010): 20–21.

90. D. Di Ceglie, "Gender Identity Disorder in Young People," *Advances in Psychiatric Treatment* 6 (2000): 458–66, http://Apt/recpsych.org/cgi/content/full/6/6/458.

91. Peter Hartlaub, "Lifeline for Gay Teens a YouTube Sensation," *San Francisco Chronicle,* October 8, 2010, A10.

▪ REFERENCES ▪

Adams, C. 2007. Born in a bind: Treating transgender children. *Gay Lesbian Times* no. 1034 (October), www.gaylesbiantimes.com/?id=10795.

American Psychiatric Association. 1994. *Diagnostic criteria from DSM-IV.* Washington, D.C.: American Psychiatric Association.

Brill, S., and R. Pepper. 2008. *The transgender child.* San Francisco: Cleis Press.

Chiland, C. 2003. *Transsexualism.* Middletown, CT: Wesleyan University Press.

Cloud, J. 2000. His name is Aurora, *Time* (September 25): 90–91.

Coates, S., R. C. Friedman, and S. Wolfe. 1991. The etiology of boyhood gender identity disorder: A model for integrating temperament, development, and psychodynamics. *Psychoanalytic Dialogues* 1:481–523.

Cohen-Kettenis, P. T., and F. Pfäfflin. 2003. *Transgenderism and intersexuality in childhood and adolescence.* Thousand Oaks, CA: Sage Publications.

Crawford, N. 2003. Understanding children's atypical gender behavior. *Monitor on Psychology* 34:40–42.

Dennis, W. 2009. When girls want to be boys and boys want to be girls. *Toronto Life* (August): 54–61.

Di Ceglie, D. 2000. Gender identity disorder in young people. *Advances in Psychiatric Treatment* 6:458–66, http://Apt/recpsych.org/cgi/content/full/6/6/458.

_____. 2009. Engaging young people with atypical gender identity development in therapeutic work: a developmental approach. *Journal of Child Psychotherapy* 35:3–12.

Fast, I. 1984. *Gender identity: A differentiation model.* Hillsdale, NJ: The Analytic Press.

_____. 1999. Aspects of core gender identity. *Psychoanalytic Dialogues* 9:633–61.

Glenn, W. 2009. "For colored girls only": Reflection of an emerging male-to-female transgender and gender variant consciousness. In *Social Work Practice with Transgender and Gender Variant Youth*, ed. Gerald. P. Mallon, 104–14. New York: Routledge.

Green, R. 1987. *The "sissy boy syndrome" and the development of homosexuality.* New Haven: Yale University Press.

Hagen, G. 2002. Guys and dolls. *Parents* (September): 173–74.

Hartlaub, P. 2010. Lifeline for gay teens a YouTube sensation. *San Francisco Chronicle* (October 8): A1, A10.

Heredia, C. 2002. Transgender teen's slaying shakes nation. *San Francisco Chronicle* (October 23): A3.

Hill, D. B., D. Menvielle, K. M. Sica, and A. Johnson. 2010. An affirmative intervention for families with gender variant children: Parental ratings of child mental health and gender. *Journal of Sex & Marital Therapy* 36:6–23.

Hoffman, J. 2009. Can a boy wear a skirt to school? *New York Times,* Sunday Styles (November 8): 1, 10.

Hotchkiss, L. R. 1996. The girl beyond the glass. In *True Selves: Understanding Transsexualism,* by Mildred L. Brown and Chloe A. Rounsley, 228. San Francisco: Jossey-Bass.

Just Evelyn. 2007. *Mom, I need to be a girl.* Longmont, CO: Just Evelyn.

Lev, A. 2004. *Transgender Emergence.* New York: Haworth Clinical Practice Press.

LeVay, S. and D. Hamer. 1994. Evidence for a biological influence in male homosexuality. Biology and homosexuality: A debate. *Scientific American* (May): 44–49.

Mallon, G. P., ed. 2009. *Social work practice with transgender and gender variant youth.* New York: Routledge.

Menvielle, E. 2004. Parents struggling with their child's gender issues. *Brown University Child and Adolescent Behavior Letter* (July): 3.

Menvielle, E., E. Perrin, and C. Tuerk. 2005. The beat of a different drummer: Children who do not follow gender-typical expectations. *Contemporary Pediatrics* (February): 38–46.

Moore, S. 2002. Diagnosis for a straight planet: A critique of gender identity disorder for children and adolescents in the DSM-IV. PhD diss., The Wright Institute, Berkeley, CA.

Moore, E., A. Wisniewski, and A. Dobs. 2003. Endocrine treatment of transsexual people: A review of treatment regimen, outcomes, and adverse effects. *Journal of Clinical Endocrinology and Metabolism* 888 (8): 3467–73.

Nordberg, J. 2010. Where boys are prized, girls live the part. *New York Times* (September 21): A1, A10–A11.

PFLAG. 2007. *Our trans children.* Washington, D.C.: Parents, Families and Friends of Lesbians and Gays.

Roscoe, W. 1993. *Changing ones: Third and fourth genders in Native North America.* New York: St. Martin's Griffin.

Rosin, H. 2008. A boy's life. *Atlantic Online* (November), www.thealtlantic .com/doc/print/200811/transgender-children.

Rothblatt, P. 2008. *All I want to be is me.* www.alliwanttobeisme.com.

St. John, K., and H. K. Lee. 2002. Slain Newark teen balanced between two worlds. *San Francisco Chronicle* (October 19): A1, A7.

Shyer, M. F., and C. Shyer. 2001. *Not like other boys.* New York: Authors Guild Backinprint.com.

Smiley, L. 2007. Girl/boy interrupted. *San Francisco Chronicle,* www.sfweekly .com (July 11).

Spiegel, A. 2008. Two families grapple with sons' gender preferences. National Public Radio *All Things Considered* (May 7).

Stoller, R. J. 1985. *Presentations of gender.* New Haven: Yale University Press.

The World Professional Association of Transgender Health Standards of Care for Gender Identity Disorders, 6th version, 2001.

Winnicott, D. W. 1970. *Playing and Reality.* London: Tavistock.

Zamora, J. H. 2002. Newark teen beaten to death. *San Francisco Chronicle* (October 18): A1, A24.

Zolotow, C. 1972. *William's doll.* New York: HarperCollins.

Zucker, K. J., and S. J. Bradley. 1995. *Gender identity disorder and psychosexual problems in children and adolescents.* New York: The Guilford Press.

■ ACKNOWLEDGMENTS ■

The people who did the most to make *Gender Born, Gender Made* possible are the very ones who must remain nameless—the children and families who over these past three decades have opened their minds and hearts to me in their journeys to affirm the children's true gender selves. You are a remarkable group of people and I thank you deeply.

Now I would like to go back to the beginning. A deep thanks to my parents, Morris and Edith Ehrensaft, who brought me into the world and passed on to me their conviction that if you see the need for an important change you should do your best to make it happen. To my brothers, Philip and Rick Ehrensaft, I would like to express my gratitude for respectively allowing me to be a tomboy and a midget mother.

Leaping ahead to my graduate school years, I would like to acknowledge the pivotal role played by my graduate dissertation advisors, Drs. Joseph Veroff and Sheila Feld, in sharing their wisdom and supporting my first efforts to make sense of children's gender.

Fast-forward to 2008, when one day I received a call from someone named Matthew Lore. He had heard me speak on NPR's series about gender-nonconforming children and wondered if I would consider writing a book. Three years later, we now see the birth of that book through Matthew's publishing house, The Experiment, none of which would have happened without his wisdom and deep commitment to this project from beginning to end. I would also like to express thanks to Iris Bass for her excellent editorial work, and to Karen Giangreco, Managing Editor at The Experiment, for so expertly shepherding *Gender Born, Gender Made* through to completion. A special thanks to Edgardo Menvielle for being a pioneer in promoting the acceptance of gender-nonconforming children and for his generosity and wisdom in getting *Gender Born, Gender Made* off to a wonderful start with his luminous foreword.

To Barbara Waterman, my friend, colleague, and reader, I send my deepest gratitude for her careful attention to every word and for holding my feet to the fire to make those words the best they could be. To Eileen Keller, Stephen Walrod, and Bonnie Rottier, my partners in our child consultation group, there is no way I can express the extent of my appreciation for all the ways you have helped me understand and think about the children and parents who come my way. The same goes for Gloria Lawrence, my close friend, colleague, and suitemate, who shares her own gender work and listens to mine as we try to understand what makes gender tick.

To Catherine Tuerk, I will always cherish our yearly dinners together and how much I have learned from you as the person who broke ground in bringing services to gender-nonconforming children. To Stephanie Brill and Joel Baum, I extend my heartfelt thanks for building Gender Spectrum and then inviting me to be a part of it. To Caitlin Ryan, a new friend and colleague, my great appreciation for her playful spark and generosity both in sharing her work at the Family Acceptance Project and in letting me share mine. To Herb Schreier, dear friend and colleague, many thanks for our intellectual exchanges over years and years and for being the first to light the fire that we needed a gender clinic in the Bay Area. And I'd like to thank all the members of the Child and Adolescent Gender Center steering committee, who arrived on the scene when the book was nearly written and energized me to get it launched with their enthusiasm and dedication to gender-creative children: Joel Baum (again), Michael Baxter, Jamison Green, Dan Karasic, Stephen Rosenthal, Shane Snowdon, Ilana Sherer, and Dafna Wu. Thanks also to all the participants in the Mind the Gap group, for their commitment and for donating their time to provide gender-sensitive mental-health services to the children and families in our community.

Last of all, I send my deepest appreciation to my husband, Jim Hawley, who lovingly broke down the gender barriers of parenting with me and has been the most avid supporter anyone could ever ask for—of both my work and my occasional mania about it—over the past forty-plus years. To my children, Rebecca Hawley and Jesse Ehrensaft-Hawley, thank you both for teaching me that practical princesses are never as good as frilly ones and that trucks are best given away if no one wants to play with them. And to my granddaughter, Satya Hawley, I don't know if you will ever, ever wear a dress, but whatever you do, you have shown us in every creative way that you will always feel free to be you. From the bottom of my heart, I thank you for that.

▪ INDEX ▪

NOTE: Page numbers followed by "n" refer to endnotes.

DIANE EHRENSAFT, PHD, is a developmental and clinical psychologist who for over twenty-five years has worked with gender-nonconforming children and their families. Dr. Ehrensaft is the author of numerous books and articles on child development, gender, and parenting, published both nationally and internationally. Her previous books include *Parenting Together*; *Spoiling Childhood*; *Mommies, Daddies, Donors, Surrogates*; and *Building a Home Within* (with Toni Vaughn Heineman). She speaks in the United States and abroad on the subject of gender-nonconforming children at both community and professional conferences and is cited frequently in the media. She has appeared in the *New York Times* and many other media outlets and was featured in National Public Radio's landmark 2008 two-part series on gender-nonconforming children. She is a founding member of the Child and Adolescent Gender Center, a new university and community partnership developed to offer comprehensive health, mental health, educational, legal, and advocacy services to gender-nonconforming children and their families; organizer of the mental-health component of the Child and Adolescent Gender Center (a. k. a. Mind the Gap); and a board member of Gender Spectrum, a national organization that promotes gender acceptance through education, training, advocacy, and support to families and communities. She is a mother, grandmother, and a proud member of PFLAG. Dr. Ehrensaft lives and practices in Oakland, California.

WWW.DIANEEHRENSAFT.COM
WWW.GENDERBORNGENDERMADE.COM